PRAISE FOR 10 SECRETS OF MARKETING SUCCESS

"...a rare collection of powerful ideas that you will wish you'd thought of first. Reading this book gives you the distinct feeling of stepping into a mental gymnasium where you are challenged to do things differently than you may have ever done them before. The 'Secrets' are out."
— Stephen M. Riddell, author, *Selling Geni*... *, Achieving Extraordinary Sales Results with Or*...*ary People*

"...a gold mine of hands-on too[...] marketing minds in action today. I re[...]
— Joe Batten, author, *Toug*... *The Master Motivator*

"[This book gives you] advice from 24 experts, rather than just one—with each one offering loads of valuable and practical advice... crisp writing style...excellent use of graphic devices that make the text easy on the eyes and easier to digest...handy summaries—'10 Action Secrets' — at the end of each chapter."
— Jack Gillespie, editor, *Communication Briefings*

"...state-of-the art techniques. The text is lively and practical, focusing on examples to follow for marketing success. The disk filled with easy-to-use forms is a bonus. A real winner on all points!"
— Professor Ronald E. Goldsmith
co-author, *Consumer Psychology for Marketing*

"The best new ideas from every discipline of marketing packed into a brightly written book..."
— Edmund Lawler, author, *Underdog Marketing*

"...tremendous achievers share their tremendous marketing wisdom. The subject is old but their ideas are fresh and stimulating. I enjoyed every chapter."
— Charlie Jones
Life Management Services, Executive Books

"*10 Secrets of Marketing Success*...provides practical, hands-on advice. The ideas presented are both usable and implementable immediately. This book is *excellent* for any company that...needs to sell/market more powerfully and effectively.
— Mary and Mike Molloy, authors, *The Buck Starts Easy: Profit-Based Sales* and *Marketing Made Easy*

10 SECRETS of MARKETING SUCCESS

How To Jump-Start Your Marketing

Featuring chapters from marketing experts—

Peter Belanger • Rick Crandall • Stephanie Davis • Cynthia DeForge
Chip Eichelberger • Linda Fracassi • Mim Goldberg • Rick Goldberg
Linda Hanson • David Klaybor • Christine Lenick • Dedie Leahy
Ray Leone • Jeffrey Locker • Robert McKim • Sally Mizerak
John Mora • Patricia Obermeier • James Ray • Jim Rhode
Wajed Salam • Margie Seyfer • Scott Sindelar • Lynn Thomas

EDITED BY RICK CRANDALL

INSTITUTE FOR
EFFECTIVE MARKETING

Select Press
Corte Madera, CA

The Institute for Effective Marketing
The goal of the Institute is to provide information to help companies and individuals more effectively market their products and services by better serving the needs of their customers.

Select Press
PO Box 37
Corte Madera, CA 94976-0037
(415) 924-1612

10 Secrets of Marketing Success: How to Jump-Start Your Marketing/ Rick Crandall (editor)

ISBN 0-9644294-4-6

Printed in the United States of America
10 9 8 7 6 5 4 3 2 1

Contents

PREFACE

Are There Marketing Secrets In This Book?

Yes and no. There are many secrets in this book, "ideas that are concealed from general knowledge." But there is no one idea—or 10—that will mysteriously improve your marketing without effort on your part.

Each author in this book is a proven expert on some aspect of marketing. As speakers, consultants, and trainers, they have helped many people dramatically improve their marketing.

Marketing is anything you do to get OR keep customers. One area where many chapters in this book are strong is in their emphasis on *keeping customers*. That's one huge secret, because repeat business is far more profitable than new business.

The Secret Is In Taking Action!

Too many people put off marketing, or trying new ideas. Perhaps the simplest "secret" in marketing is that you have to take action to get results. Einstein said that the definition of insanity is doing the same thing over and over and expecting a new result. If you want new results, you must try new actions.

Each chapter ends with 10 "Action Secrets." You can "jump-start" your marketing if you'll apply them.

Good luck. You made your first commitment to action in buying this book. Please let any of us know about your successes.

—Rick Crandall, PhD, Editor

Part One

THE FIRST SECRETS

Target Marketing For Success
Rick Goldberg

Quality Qualifying For Winning Sales
Peter Belanger

Rejecting The Fear Of Rejection
Scott Sindelar

Chapter 1

TARGET MARKETING FOR SUCCESS

Rick Goldberg

Rick Goldberg is recognized as a leader, educator, entrepreneur, and motivator within the business world. His seventeen-year history in the professional beauty industry has afforded him an opportunity to experience all facets of the business, and to develop his expertise in the areas of consultative sales and salon marketing. He is an accomplished public speaker, having appeared both internationally and nationally.

Mr. Goldberg's success led to the development of Sigma 6, Inc., which applies the expertise learned in the beauty industry to businesses in general. Sigma 6 provides unique business programs, systems, and solutions to a variety of organizations throughout the world. This is accomplished through personal appearances by Mr. Goldberg, video- and audiotape series, and customized marketing programs based on "Client Direct Mail Retention."

Mr. Goldberg is a great believer in Sigma 6's motto: "Change is good. Change is growth."

Rick Goldberg, Sigma 6, 6811 Flying Cloud Drive, Eden Prairie, MN 55344; phone (612) 946-1992; fax (612) 946-1941; e-mail prbeauty@ix.netcom.com.

Chapter 1

TARGET MARKETING FOR SUCCESS

Rick Goldberg

"Good targeting is a creative process, split into two separate and very different issues: who the campaign is aimed at, and how to find them and gain access to them."
— M. Stone, D. Davies, and A. Bond, *Direct Hit: Direct Marketing With a Winning Edge*

In marketing, one size does not fit all.

I have worked with many businesses, both large and small, and have learned that, as far as marketing is concerned, "one size fits one." My company's (Sigma 6 Business Services) success with marketing programs has come from the fact that they are geared to meet the needs and desires of our customers, one person at a time.

Marketing has historically been based on the "Four Ps"—product, price, place, and promotion. We take a different approach when we sit down with potential customers and discuss their business.

As we enter the 21st century, we leave behind the concept of "mass marketing" in favor of the concepts of "one-to-one marketing" and "target marketing."

KNOW THY CUSTOMER

What kind of customers do you have and what kind of customer do you *want*?

It's important to closely analyze your customer base. Customers usually fall into one of three distinct types:

- transactional
- consultative
- partnering

Each type has their own unique characteristics and each must be dealt with in their own way.

Transactional Customers

The Transactional Customer is happy to purchase your product or service, but is not interested in developing a deeper relationship with you.

Whether they are new customers, or simply desire to interact one product or service at a time, with these customers you are basically an order taker. They have little loyalty and, if a "better deal" comes their way, you are likely to be the loser.

Consultative Customers

The Consultative Customer has begun to develop a relationship with you that will help to grow both your businesses. In addition to your product or service, these customers want your counsel as part of their purchases.

"We're going to need six more workstations. How do you think we should proceed?"

They may need your help in determining their (or their customers') needs, or perhaps some help in devising a promotional plan. As this relationship develops, customer loyalty increases. Your customers begin to look at you not as a vendor, but as a friend and a counselor who is available to assist them when they have a need.

Partnering Customers

Your Partnering Customers would not think of completing a major business transaction without first discussing it with you. You are no longer an order taker—you are a business partner upon whom these customers call for assistance 100% of the time.

Market By Customer Type

Once you have identified your customers by the three categories listed above, you need to determine how you can best market your product or service to each customer type—and decide whether you want all three types of customers!

HOW TO BUILD A BUSINESS

We have found that our customers' challenges are "Four Rs," categories that we call *"The Big Four."* No matter how large or small the business, we all seem to face problems of **Recruiting**; **Retaining**; **Revenue**; and **Rallying staff**.

Coming to this realization is the easy part. The challenge in your mind should be, "How will this help make my business a success?" and "Where do we begin?"

If you are going to be completely successful in your business, you will need to address your challenges in each of these areas.

RECRUITING

I have found that at least 20% of the customer base is departing a business at any particular time. This can occur for a variety of reasons—customers can die or move away, they can become disappointed in you and take their business elsewhere, or they can be stolen by a competitor's offering.

"A 5% increase in customer retention... can swing profits from 25 to 100%—overwhelming a 5% improvement in costs."

—Valerie Brown, Bain & Company, Inc.

It is important that you have a recruitment strategy planned to replace lost customers. Many businesses don't have large "recruiting" budgets, but you don't need a big budget. Here are five cost-effective "guerrilla" marketing programs that have proven successful for Sigma 6 Business Services' customers.

Referral Programs

Your best source of new business is your current customer base. Have you ever asked your current customers to recommend you to their friends, business associates, and family members? If you haven't, you are missing a very cost-effective, high return on investment (ROI) program that should be part of your recruiting strategy.

How you ask for business will depend on your field. One simple program is based on rewarding all those involved in referring business to you—the customer who refers new customers to you, the new customer who is referred, and the employee who encouraged the referral.

> ### Reward Referrals
>
> Rewarding customers for referrals may not seem appropriate for all businesses. But be creative. One accountant in the Napa Valley wine region in California owns a very small, exclusive winery. The only way you can get a bottle of his special wines is to give him a referral customer!

To implement a referral reward program you must:

- Determine the rewards to be offered each group.
- Design a form to serve as a vehicle for tracking referrals [Note: We use three perforated cards on a 8½" x 11" "Referral Program Sheet"—see next page).

The language should be simple but carefully worded to market both the referral program and your business image to the customer. Consider having the piece professionally designed so it stands out and convinces customers to "take action."

Finally, train your people to use the form. Carefully explain both the program and the rewards involved for actively pursuing referrals.

This program, if run properly and sparingly, can ensure that you recoup the lost 20%, plus increase your base for first time customers by another 5–15%.

(Also see chapter 12 for more ideas on referrals.)

Door Hanger Program

You've all been in a hotel at some point and utilized the "door hanger" for either maid service, privacy, or to order an early morning breakfast. With this program, you place door hangers on residences or businesses.

This great little program works to promote retail businesses to potential clients within a defined area. It's inexpensive and provides a measurable, high ROI for your business.

First, determine your offer—a product, service, or special discount. Next, design a hanger that will attract enough interest to minimize the chances of its being ignored or thrown away. Remember, an attractive, professionally-designed piece will speak volumes about the quality of your product or service.

You'll need to determine the geographic areas you want to cover in your campaign, determine the number of doors you will "hang," and prepare for either the phone calls or visits that you will receive.

Friends, family, or employees can be enlisted for the delivery of the hangers. Or you could involve a civic organization to do the "leg work" for a donation to their program.

If you make an attractive offer on the hanger, this program works like a charm in generating first-time business.

Capabilities Statements

New and prospective customers have a need for information to reduce their uncertainty and give them a reason to choose you over competitors. Current customers may also be unaware of the full range of your capabilities, creating an opportunity for cross-selling.

A general "backgrounder" and a listing of your products and services creates a reservoir of information that can flow into a variety of marketing pieces, from handouts and mailers to full-blown brochures. Strategically worded and professionally designed, these pieces can differentiate you from your competitors, and enhance your image.

Newsletter Program

As with many of the programs that are described here, the newsletter program is one that works for all of *"The Big Four"* challenge areas.

Newsletters can help you inform prospective clients and stay in touch with your regulars. They also contribute to image enhancement, market communication, and referral network development.

A newsletter is a marketing piece that takes dedication and a fair amount of time if it is to be a successful part of your business' marketing program. An investment in professional design of the newsletter format will pay big dividends.

Business Cards

Most of us look upon a business card as an identification piece that is a necessary part of doing business in today's world.

Have you ever thought about a business card as being "the world's smallest billboard?" Besides the normal information that you find on a business card, include information that will attract the attention of the person who receives your card. Also, don't forget about the back of a card. It provides you with excellent space to place a specialty message about your business.

Mary Arlington, CPA
We improve your profitability.

9999 Hill Road
Anywhere, US 00000   (555) 555-2345

Here again, the importance of professional design is important. This piece carries with it the first impression for your business to the person who receives your "personal billboard."

RETAINING CUSTOMERS

Keeping a current customer costs far less then finding a new one. Retention of current customers is the most cost-effective way to increase sales and build your business.

Do you know what the "value" of each of your customers is to your business based on a "lifetime" of loyalty to you? Have you taken the time to collect information on customer retention? If your customer retention is not in the area of 80%, you need to immediately begin a tested, proven retention program.

Collect Customer Information

Target marketing and one-to-one marketing are not necessarily the same thing. Most target marketing programs segment your audience into groups. One-to-one marketing focuses on a segment of one.

—Don Peppers & Martha Rogers, The One to One Future: Building Relationships One Customer at a Time

Having a system to monitor your customers is imperative to the success of any one-to-one or targeted marketing program. How can you give people personal treatment if you don't know anything about their history with you?

For example, if you do not know how many times a customer returns to your business for specific products or services, you are missing a prime opportunity to increase your sales to that individual. If you haven't created a tracking system (manual or automated), then you should consider doing so immediately. This will provide you with a wealth of information that will support ongoing business growth.

Over the years, Sigma 6 Business Services has developed and tested a variety of programs in the retention area. The following represent a sampling of ideas that are cost effective and offer an excellent ROI.

Client Direct Mail Retention Program

This system provides an excellent manual method to collect data on your customers. Basically, you track and store personal information along with what products and services each customer purchases from you.

If you determine what your goal is for a customer's buying cycle, you can then prepare targeted mailings to encourage additional visits to your operation. For example, you may target a group of customers who average seven visits per year to your business (you've identified these customers through your tracking system). You set a goal of getting each of these customers to purchase from you once a month.

Now, what can you do to reach your goal? Create a method of collecting every new customer's information for your system. Send out a note or card of thanks after each new customer's first visit.

"Trace" each customer's card for 30 days. Every time a customer purchases services or products, the purchase is indicated, and the card is retraced for another thirty days. When a predetermined number of days have past (30, 60, etc.) and that customer has not returned, send out a card with a special promotion that requires the customer to bring the card into your facility in order to receive a "special discount" or a "free gift." You will find a high rate of return with the customer purchasing more than you are giving away.

In the process of collecting the personal data on your customer, you have discovered the customer's birthday. Now design a birthday postcard mailer that includes the offer to return to your business with the card and receive a "gift" (product or service) in honor of their "special day." This further increases traffic and income for your business.

> *Birthday Greetings*
> *and*
> *A Gift for You*
> From your friends at Valerie's Hair Care

MARIO'S PIZZA				
For our valued customers—buy 10 pizzas and the 11th is on us!				
O	☾	O	4	5
6	7	8	9	10

Frequent Buyer Programs

Take a page from the airlines' marketing programs. No matter what you sell, you can create a frequent buyers reward program that increases the amount or the number of purchases your customers make.

Think about the retail businesses you personally patronize. Many have some program of this type. Purchase twelve cups of coffee and get your thirteenth free. For every sandwich you purchase, get a token or stamp. Complete twenty purchases and receive a free "whirligig" of your choice. Or, get eight haircuts and receive a free travel kit of product.

Take a look in your wallet. How many of these types of programs are your currently participating in? So, why doesn't your business have one? The end result is that you have just increased the number of visits made to your business by your customers, and the amount of dollars per visit.

Customer Appreciation Programs

Never forget that it's our customers who pay our salaries and wages. So, it is important that your business success includes the celebration of the customer. These types of programs can be simple (a gift of appreciation when a customer visits the business) to elaborate (incentive trips to exotic locations).

You might consider staging an appreciation event once a year where you provide food, beverages, entertainment, and gifts to those of your customers whom you feel are the "very best." The loyalty that these programs build with customers far outweighs any cost involved. In addition, these programs tend to increase sales since customers want to be part of the next "celebration."

REVENUE GROWTH

Raising prices can sometimes improve your revenues without hurting volume. Fortunately, there are also ways to increase sales without raising prices. Here are several programs that have been successful in a variety of markets.

Passport Program

This unique program takes the concept of government passports and transforms it to fit your business.

First determine what products or services you want your customers to purchase more of, and then create a "passport." Present this passport to each of your customers on their next visit. Explain to them that when they have a "stamp" on each page, they will be able to receive a predetermined product or service at no charge.

Each page of the passport requires the customer to complete an activity, or a purchase of a service or product. As each page is completed, it is stamped. The end result is more sales from each customer because they want to complete their passports and receive their rewards.

Gift Certificate Program

Design a gift certificate that carries the image of your business and promote it during the various holiday seasons. There are always individuals who are stuck for a gift idea. Whether you

> $50 $50
> *Gift Certificate*
> Cara's Meals to Go
>
> *To Mary, From Bill*

sell services or products, you can utilize this type of a program. Invariably the holder of the certificate will spend more than the value of the gift certificate, thereby increasing your sales even further.

RALLYING STAFF

Staff motivation takes a variety of forms. In its simplest form, it means that the "boss" takes the time to recognize in words and action the value of each team member. It might be a simple "Great job!" comment to a member of the team who has performed particularly well. Or, it might be in the form of a written "Applause Gram" from the team leader to a team member for their efforts on behalf of a customer.

Whatever its form, a business needs motivational programs that help keep the team focused on what's important—customer satisfaction. A brief list of programs is included here as a "jumping off" point for your consideration:

- special training for staff
- company parties and picnics
- incentive programs (product awards or trips)
- recognition awards programs
- community involvement programs
- tuition support programs for advanced learning opportunities
- attendance at manufacturer/vendor programs for company personnel from all levels of the team

CUSTOMER FOCUS

If you look closely at "The Big Four" (recruiting, retaining, revenue, and rallying staff), you can see that each of the areas is based on customer service. What you want to achieve is service that is "legendary" in its delivery.

None of the programs and systems that have been described here will be successful if your business doesn't provide the customer service that your clients want. There have been thousands of pages written on the topic of legendary customer service over the years. However, there still doesn't seem to be enough of it in practice.

Here are several of the customer service concepts that are directly related to the success you'll have with the marketing "Big Four."

> ### Legendary Service
>
> Legendary service describes service so good your customers want to brag about it....The most important part of creating legendary service is story generation. If your customers are telling positive stories about you and your service, you could not ask for better publicity. One of the best sources for service stories is all-out recovery. Recovery means if you make a mistake with a customer, you do *whatever* is needed to fix the problem and create or win back a devoted customer.
>
> —Ken Blanchard

Managing "Moments Of Truth"

The "Moments of Truth" concept was originally introduced by Jan Carlzon, former CEO of Scandinavian Airlines. A moment of truth is any event in which a customer comes into contact (directly or indirectly) with any part of your company. The customer forms an impression at each of these moments.

Each moment of truth provides you with an opportunity to manage your customers' perceptions. If your customers always have positive encounters with your business, you will build relationships with them that, in turn, build your business.

If you let these moments of truth happen in any manner that chance allows, you risk the creation of negative perceptions in the customers' minds.

Every business or department, no matter how large or small, has thousands of "moments of truth." In looking at your company's "moments of truth," you should observe:

- how your team handles a product defect
- what happens after a sale has been completed
- how service promises are handled
- how promptly customers are helped or served
- how your team works together

Through leadership and careful management, you can ensure that your customers will have "moments of truth" that exceed their expectations.

More Moments Of Truth

- when your team members smile and are pleasant
- how the phones are answered
- how fast the phones are answered
- what the general appearance of your team members is
- how clean the restrooms are
- what the dates on the magazines in your reception area are
- how clear your building's signage is
- what the decor and general appearance of your business facility is
- how quickly your team responds to complaints
- how your team handles routine customer questions

THE "COFFEE STAIN" PRINCIPLE

Carlzon also introduced the coffee stain principle. He realized that if their planes were dirty, customers would assume that the airline wasn't careful with their engine maintenance!

Customers often notice details about a company that are not seen by the company's employees because they are too close to them. How your accounting department impresses customers is impacted by the coffee stain on the chair in the reception area.

The perception that is created in the customer's mind from stains suggests that maybe the accounting group is "sloppy" in their handling of the accounts.

That's why the "Coffee Stain" test is so important. From the president to the counter service person, the responsibility belongs to every person on the team to ensure that there are no "stains" that reflect poorly on your business.

Customers Aren't Paid To Be Reasonable

Customers do make illogical leaps of judgment and come to unreasonable conclusions. But it doesn't make sense to argue with their opinions. The truth is, most customers form opinions about you before you ever get a chance to deliver the service or product that you sell. It's best to "clean up the coffee stains" and take care of the details that "irrationally" influence customer opinions about service.

Think of what happens in your mind when you drive past a restaurant whose sign is missing a letter.

What goes through your mind when you notice sticky rings on the flip-down trays of an airplane? What is your response to a fancy restaurant that has dirty restrooms? What do you think of the resort hotel you have just arrived at when you notice that the lobby floor is littered with scraps of paper and candy wrappers, and the ash trays are overflowing and dirty?

We've all been there, and we've all had about the same reaction: "Do I want to continue to do business with this type of an operation if they can't remove the 'coffee stains'?" Remember, the first impression is the longest lasting one.

The success or failure of your business will be determined by your success in satisfying your customers' needs. By ensuring that your programs, systems, and solutions are legendary in their service to your customers, you are ensuring your business success.

SYNCHRONIZING YOUR PROGRAMS WITH AN OVERALL MARKETING PLAN

We've discussed a variety of simple and cost-effective marketing "tools" that can be very effective. Now, it's time to caution you about the dangers of haphazardly throwing programs at your market without careful coordination of your efforts.

Few companies have money to waste. No company benefits from marketing efforts that pull in opposite directions and confuse their customers. A well-planned marketing program will return a profit many times greater than a haphazard one.

In helping our clients develop their marketing plans, we've found that the best first step for them to take is to find some quality "quiet time" and think strategically. Here are some basic questions to answer:

- What is your vision of the future?
- Where do you want your company to be five years down the road?
- What is the overall image you wish to have with your customers, your competitors and the marketplace as a whole?

A good exercise to focus your thoughts is to write down a clear and concise mission statement that covers the purpose of your company and its ultimate objective. It always helps to know where you're headed before you begin your journey.

STRATEGY AND PLANNING

Strategic thinking determines your company's long-term marketing direction, telling it *where it should go*. Your marketing plan directs your company's short-term (usually one year) marketing steps, telling *how to get there*. It usually consists of five parts:
- a situational analysis
- marketing objectives
- the overall strategy that will help you achieve the objectives
- an action plan of marketing programs
- a way to monitor and evaluate the marketing program as it works its magic

Situational Analysis

The first step in developing a marketing plan is to prepare an assessment of your company and its market. It should include who you are, what you do, where you've been, where you are now, and (to some extent) where you're going.

Put It On Paper

Putting your insights down on paper helps to give context to your marketing thoughts. Many other questions need to be looked at.
- Who are your customers?
- On what basis do they make their buying decisions?
- Who are your competitors and what are they up to?
- What are your strengths and weaknesses?
- What are the threats and opportunities facing you?
- What are your competitive advantages?

Marketing Objectives

Given your situation, what are reasonable marketing objectives? You should come up with three major objectives *at most*. Whatever the objectives—sales, awareness, customer attitude, etc.—make them measurable and as specific as possible so you can track your progress and evaluate your efforts.

Strategy

Given your situation analysis, what strategy or strategies are you going to use to reach your overall marketing objective(s)? Essentially, you are answering three questions here:

- What is the consistent image and message that I wish to convey?
- To whom do I want to convey it?
- How can I best do this?

Action Plan

Which of the many marketing programs available best suit your situation, objectives, and overall strategy? A real understanding of yourself, your competitors, and your customers is vital here. The final configuration of programs you decide on should be well-balanced, convey the same consistent message or image, and reinforce each other.

Monitoring And Evaluating

Today's marketplace is in a constant state of change. Consumer attitudes and perceptions change, competitors and their offerings change, and you must change.

Marketing plans are built on the shifting sands of the market-place. They need regular monitoring and adjustment to remain effective. Programs that work best today may not be optimal next quarter. Remember, change may be frustrating and a bit scary, but it also makes life interesting and offers valuable opportunities to those who remain on top of things.

PARTING THOUGHTS

As you begin your venture into target marketing, it is important to understand the six key factors that underlie the change in focus from mass marketing to target marketing.

Viewed separately, they probably are not surprising to you. Viewed as a group, however, they represent a startling change of direction in the field of business that will continue to affect the way we look at our customers for years to come. As a target marketer, you need to remember that the following factors will continue to affect your marketplace no matter what product or service you are involved in selling:

1. Changing Consumer Demographics And Lifestyles. When was the last time you came in contact with the "traditional American family" of the breadwinner father, housewife mother, and two and one-half children?

2. The Changing Demands On Personal Time. We are a society that has become "time poor." We have difficulty finding leisure time to do any relaxing. We have found that we are constantly "booked" in our daily organizers for working, exercising, commuting, shopping, entertaining, computing, and finding quality time for friends and family. How will your business reach these people, and keep them coming back for more?

3. The Weakening Hold Of Mass Marketing. One size fits everyone is no longer accepted by our customers. We expect to be treated as individuals by our vendors. Are you actively working on programs for the "one size fits one" concept?

4. The Decline (And Possible Demise) Of Brand Loyalty. In a world of continuous discounting and overnight product and service "knock-offs," it is almost impossible to find any brand loyalty. Where will you fit in this process?

5. The Ever-Increasing Amount Of Advertising Clutter, Overkill, And Waste. Businesses and consumers are bombarded by thousands of advertisements, brochures, and direct mail pieces a day. How will you reach your current and potential customers in an efficient, effective, and economical way? What will make you believably better than your competitors?

6. Too Many Products, Services, And Businesses. There is not much to say about overcrowding in the marketplace. All you need to do is take some time to observe the "new" products and businesses that are introduced to the market on a daily basis to understand this point.

How Will You Adapt?

Where do you and your business fit into this avalanche of offerings and information? How will your customers know that you are still out there providing excellent products and services?

Target marketing is the answer to these challenges. Target marketers are professionals at the cutting edge of marketing and communications. They are committed to their goals and to their customers. They know that marketing doesn't work overnight. They understand that by setting goals, following a plan, and focusing on their customers one customer at a time, their chances of success are immeasurably improved.

By investing in target marketing programs, systems, and

solutions, you will be investing in the profits of your company.

You will find out who your customers are and what they want from your business. Eventually, you'll find yourself thinking not like a supplier but like your customers, building a relationship that consistently meets and exceeds customer expectations. The result—customer loyalty will grow, and so will your business!

TEN ACTION SECRETS

FULL SPEED AHEAD

1 Classify your current customers into transactional, consultative, and partnering. Decide how you want to treat each group. Do something special for the partners regularly.

2 Develop a systematic referral program. Ask customers, friends, employees, or all three for referrals. Develop appropriate rewards for employees and customers who refer. Even professionals should cross-refer or officially thank colleagues for referrals.

3 Pick a "guerrilla" marketing activity such as door hangers in local neighborhoods.

4 Develop a "capabilities statement" to share with prospects and customers.

5 Consider the costs and benefits of a regular newsletter program.

6 Decide how you could make your business card a more effective "billboard" for your business. Consider giving all of your employees their own cards.

7 Develop a program to increase your customer retention rate. Remember that a 5% increase in retention can mean as much as a 90% increase in profits.

8 Develop a program to remind good customers to come in more regularly for specials, etc.

9 Involve your staff in your marketing. To encourage them, let them define the rewards they want.

10 Analyze the "moments of truth" in your business when customers form impressions of you.

Bonus Tip: Develop a coherent, integrated marketing mission statement, plan, and strategy.

Chapter 2

QUALITY QUALIFYING FOR WINNING SALES

Peter Belanger

Peter Belanger
is one of the best telesales trainers in the country, A veteran of 16 successful years as a top telesalesperson making over 300,000 telemarketing sales calls, Mr. Belanger has developed relationships from scratch, and sold millions of dollars of sophisticated products and services to over 100 *Fortune* 1000 companies.

His company, Outbound Resources, has started and managed dozens of successful telemarketing programs both here and overseas. Outbound Resources helps companies establish or improve their business-to-business telemarketing/ telesales programs. One of Mr. Belanger's most important functions is assessing telesales talent, and providing advanced relationship-based telesales training.

Mr. Belanger's "Ten Commandments of Telemarketing" are an industry classic, and he publishes feature articles and a monthly column for *Teleprofessional* magazine. He also lectures regularly on telesales at UCLA.

Outbound Resources' clients include MCA Universal Studios; Wells Fargo Bank; TRW Information Systems; CareerTrack; Allergan Pharmaceutical; McGraw Hill; the Bureau of Alcohol, Tobacco and Firearms; and many high-technology companies such as Microsoft, Hewlett-Packard, and Sun Microsystems.

Peter Belanger, Outbound Resources, 15000 Ventura Blvd. #375, Sherman Oaks, CA 91403; phone (818) 379-8444, (800) 788-8822; fax (818) 379-8448.

Chapter 2

QUALITY QUALIFYING FOR WINNING SALES

Peter Belanger

Qualify: Synonyms: Discriminate, compare, diagnose, sort, differentiate, separate, select, refine, appraise, give weight to (Roget's Thesaurus)

Qualifying is the heart of selling.

Without qualifying, wants and needs do not become opportunities and opportunities do not become sales. Qualifying is the key to a salesperson investing exactly the right amount of time on an account. Without good qualifying, the salesperson wastes the company's money, the buyer's time, and his or her own time.

HOW TO USE QUALIFYING

In this chapter, I will analyze the qualifying process from both the buyer's and seller's view. I will discuss the difference between decision makers and decision influencers, and provide *four useful qualifying tools* you can begin to use immediately.

My experience is largely with telesales professionals. The sales process is similar between field and phone, with the exception that the process is somewhat collapsed in telesales. The total amount of time spent with the prospect is severely reduced, and keen qualifying skills are at a premium.

The heart of this chapter is a simple *seven-point qualifying methodology* which can be used by most salespeople in most sales situations.

QUALIFYING BY BUYERS

Qualifying takes place on both sides of every sales call.

From the beginning of the call, the buyer is evaluating: whether this person is intelligent and well spoken, and whether the message is worth the time. If any of these qualities are missing, buyers will end the conversation, often brutally.

Courtesy requires that conscientious salespeople approach prospects respectfully and appropriately, but clumsy qualifying is thrust upon buyers daily.

Sales champions exhibit enormous patience, tact, and judgment. Awkward salespeople make the good salesperson's job harder, but they also make the good salesperson stand out.

A Quick Start

A salesperson's opening dialogue needs to be short yet thorough, of clear potential benefit to the buyer. Good salespeple either script their greetings or know them by heart. At its most

Your customers are tuned into radio station WII-FM (What's In It For Me)

basic, the greeting is the answer to the question, "Who are you and what do you do?"

Professional delivery is vital—clear and understated usually gets more high-level buyer respect than over enthusiastic. Greetings and headlines (reasons for the call) should be brief, compelling, and nonthreatening.

You need to get the prospect's attention quickly and professionally. Tell them—or imply—what's in it for them, wilthout stating your case—before they think of asking.

UNDERSTANDING THE PROSPECT

Once the salesperson has identified him or herself and been given permission to speak further, qualifying the prospect begins in earnest.

While the prospect is judging the salesperson, the astute salesperson is also measuring the prospect's responses for intelligence and "temperature."

Buyer (and seller) intelligence is measured on many levels—technical skill, phrasing, vocabulary, humor and wit, speed of dialogue, speed of understanding, etc.

Temperature is a complicated assessment based on a lifetime of human interaction—warmth versus hostility, pointedness of questions and responses, outright challenges, etc. Woe to the salesperson who is a poor judge in any of these areas.

A Series Of Questions

Logic demands that we qualify by branching out from preliminary questions. Good analytical skills are required to determine which questions will be acceptable yet most revealing. The best salespeople gauge dozens of variables—the response itself, the tone of the buyer, how much was revealed by the response, etc.

The salesperson must be acutely aware of when to push and when to quit probing and leave the buyer alone. One must also be able to distinguish when "Call me back in three months" means exactly that or instead means "Never call again!"

It is conceivable that, in a business-to-business call, a sale might be consummated in one call, but this is the exception.

COMMON QUALIFYING MISTAKES

Too Much, Too Soon

A serious mistake is asking for too much too soon. Trust takes time. Asking for personal or private company information before trust has been established is akin to taking liberties on a first date.

Obvious examples of asking too much or asking too soon might include:

"Hi, Jeannine, it's Carl Sandman with Bubblehead Dolls. **How are you today?**" *(The classic bonehead beginning—this pseudo-intimacy is obviously insincere—get to the point!)*

"June, my name is Bud Abbott with Thinknot Software. We produce curriculum software for schools. **Would you be interested in information** about our new curriculum software?" *(Asking too soon; buyer can easily dismiss the sales attempt without knowing any potential benefits—non-threatening probing is required before this type of literature close.)*

"Joseph, my name is Cal Puttnam from Album Collections. **I'd like to ask you a few questions** to see if you might be interested in our new Bazooka Joe comics collection album...". *(Asking too much—one needs to establish the identity of the buyer and identify the seller more completely before asking for a nondefined period of interrogation.)*

After the greeting and one or two preliminary questions:

"Jordan, **what are you spending per minute** with AZ&Z for your long-distance service?" *(Asking too much too soon; private or privileged information requires a closer relationship to be established.)*

Delicacy should be employed at the start of any relationship. Direct, pointed questions threaten the prospect almost as badly as the insincere back-slap of the plaid-jacketed salesman.

Build A Base First

For long-term, customer-for-life relationships to bloom, start with nonthreatening, general knowledge questions. Later in the sales cycle, get more specific. (Of course, if the call is going well, you can accelerate the pace.)

Nonthreatening, indirect questions might include:

"John, are you the one responsible for bringing in new e-mail technology?"

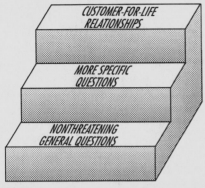

"Would you be the person I send information to regarding our new bolster repairing machines?"

"Are you still at 123 Walnut Cove?"

"Does Jill Stamford still work out of your New York division?"

"When's the best time to try to reach you in the office— early morning, lunchtime, late afternoon?"

"I just wanted to make sure you've got our up-to-date catalog or get one to you if you didn't...". *(This is a statement which is actually a question but is framed to avoid double-entendre [see below].)*

Depending on the industry and your level of company knowledge, you might even be charmingly aggressive:

"Justin, what hoops do I need to jump through to compete for some of your business?"

More Advanced Questions

Later, when Justin's trust has been won, it may be acceptable to ask more personal and private questions such as:

"Do you know exactly what they spent on copiers and service last year or will be spending this year?"

"Have you been looking at Abacus or Korngold Software as an alternative to what we have?"

"Are there any political situations going on I might need to know about?"

THE DOUBLE-ENTENDRE

Salespeople are often blind or deaf to the threat and entrapment of their questions. Buyers are fiercely protective of their time and will flinch at poorly phrased probing attempts.

Buyers See Traps

Perhaps the most obvious example of the double-entendre (French for "hearing twice") is this standard recommended question for many closing-oriented sales systems:

> "John, if I could show you a way to double your widget output while at the same time slashing your production costs by a third, you'd be interested in that, wouldn't you?"

This patronizing attempt to qualify can back-fire even further if asked inappropriately early in the sales cycle or before complete trust has been established.

The buyer hears an entirely different question being asked:

> "John, are you so naive that you've never been 'sold at' before so you'll give me the next ten to thirty minutes of your life to clumsily try to convince you of something that your experience tells you can't be done?"

Not only does the buyer hear a different question altogether, this question is phrased to give the buyer no out. If he answers no, he is an impolite dummy. If he answers yes, he is giving permission to be pitched at for Heaven knows how long.

Buyers not only flinch when they hear such obvious manipulation—they find a way to permanently get rid of salespeople who show such amateurishness.

Amateur Pressure

There are many common variations of the double-entendre. The forced choice close, for example, has been used so many times that it is hard for me to keep from laughing when I hear it.

Sometimes the forced choice close is accept-able (see "suggested answers" on page 33), except

that the buyer often hears manipulation coming a mile away:
> "We'll be in your area next week. Will Tuesday morning or
> Wednesday afternoon be better for you?"

The best way to avoid double-entendres is to make sure questions come across as fresh and unscripted. Carefully scrutinize your Call Outline, or tape a few sales conversations and prepare the associated transcripts. Have your best sales professionals look these over and edit them.

Most sales professionals are able to avoid the double-entendre, but even some of the best fail the next test.

WATCH OUT FOR THE THREE BRAIN-DEAD QUESTIONS

Here's a mistake nearly all salespeople make. The initial cold call has gone well and the buyer is primed to see the new literature. Fulfillment has sent a beautiful five dollar mailing piece, and the salesperson follows up with these three classic questions:
> "Did you get the literature?"

> "Did you have a chance to read it?"

Then (pick one):
> "Any questions?" –or– "Does that look like something that might prove useful?"

Ouch! Of course, by the time they hear the second question, any buyer with an IQ over 70 is anticipating question number three and has already come up with 14 polite, or other, ways of saying "No."

This process may continue for YEARS. The salesperson asks dull questions and the buyer fends them off easily. The sales manager never knows that nothing is happening on this account because the salesperson isn't finding out what the real situation is. It's criminal, and it happens everywhere. I even catch myself doing it occasionally!

The Easy Brush-off

Most buyers do not see their IN boxes as an opportunity to find out the latest and greatest products! They see every mail piece as another project, forcing them to refocus their attention. The smartest buyers sort literature over the wastebasket.

If it's been a week or two (or longer) since you've called the buyer, he may have gotten to your package. But chances are, you're going to have to remind him of what it was you sent. And he won't be expecting your call because he's got a project or three of his own to worry about.

When you call and ask if he got it, read it, and has any questions, his first reaction will be to fend you off politely, which may well mean that he won't be completely honest with you:

Your prospect will be busy with projects of his own. You may have to remind him about what you sent.

> Q: "Do you have any questions regarding our Band-o-Magic models?"

> A: "Not really, no. I think we're pretty fine for now—why don't I get back to you if and when we might have a use for those?"

This is the standard brush-off. Chances are good that when the buyer said those words he had a pretty limited knowledge of the benefits of the Band-o-Magic line. Because he was not engaged in the conversation, he dismissed the opportunity.

Get Visual And "Zero In"

One of the best solutions is to *use visual and directed activity.*

By getting visual, the salesperson is taking into account that the typical buyer has a foot-high stack of literature in his IN basket.

Since the salesperson has to fight for the buyer's attention, drawing attention to the visual elements of the package helps, as does focusing the buyer on only one element of the package. Since our attention spans are getting shorter and shorter, making bite-sized demands on the buyer's time usually works best:

> "John, **you'll be getting a gray brochure with a four color 3-D image** of our latest Band-o-Magic model on the cover. **Just take a look at one item—on the back left of the brochure is our current pricing which lists our specials for June**—and I'll check back with you on Tuesday at 8:00 a.m. after you've had a chance to see that."

And, of course, when John looks at the price sheet, he won't be able to help himself from glancing at a couple of other items in your literature packet.

FOUR QUALIFYING TOOLS

Provide Suggested Answers

Salespeople have been taught that asking open-ended questions is the key to getting a buyer to open up. But it is often impossible for a busy buyer to redirect himself easily to answer a salesperson's questions fully, or even accurately.

Sharp salespeople often provide suggested answers to their open-ended questions which the buyer can pick and choose from or bounce away from.

This is actually just a variation of the forced-choice close. If carefully scripted and delivered, it will usually reveal more than a simple open-ended question:

"Jane, where are you getting your graphic supplies from— Fastech, Integral or ABC?"

"How many students are attending now—1000, 1500?"

"How often are you getting supplies delivered now—once a week, twice a week?"

"Who have you been sending people to for the seminars Lockhart & Briggs, or Anacapa Motivation?"

Use Indirect Questions

Indirect questions require forethought, strategy, and subtlety. By asking indirect questions, salespeople can glean important information without sounding like interrogators.

For example, if the salesperson knows that the three big distributors are all in the buyer's home state and he can offer sales-tax free interstate supplies, he might ask:

"Jane, we might or might not be able to save you some significant dollars on those graphic supplies. What's the tax rate in your state right now—8.25%?" *(To reveal possible interstate competition)*

– or –

"Josh, who were the big groups when you were in high school? Were Emerson, Lake and Palmer still big or had they died out by then?" *(To tactfully uncover someone's age)*

– or –

"Jody, have they been shifting priorities lately or talking about
expanding in any particular area such as facilities or new
people?" *(To find out the budget)*

Indirect questions gain more and more importance as buyers
get more savvy to traditional sales questions. A little time spent
carefully crafting indirect questions will pay off handsomely.

Use Contact Managers

Contact managers are the big brothers of PIMs (personal
information managers) and the little brothers of mainframe databases. A good contact manager can make qualifying almost a
paint-by-numbers exercise. And it can provide a salesperson with
a boiler-plate template for cover letters and proposals.

Contact managers are wonderful for keeping all the details of an
account in an organized and tidy package (pharmaceutical companies even call sales calls "detailing").

Contact managers can get very specific. Harvey Mackay, of
Swim With the Sharks fame, is noted for his "Mackay 66," a series
of 66 questions detailing prospects' lives. Mackay also provides a
methodology for getting intimate details about prospects.

You may not need to collect 66 items, but most people collect
too little information about prospects. The more you know about
their interests, the more ways you have to build relationships with
them.

Besides the basic contact information (name, address, phone, fax,
e-mail, etc.), the typical contact manager provides user-defined fields. For
a company offering sales training, some of these fields might be designated as:

Lead Source_____   Number of salespeople_____
Avg.$/year/salesperson_____   Coaching days req'd._____
Final prep_____   Formal prep_____
Post train_____   Total trg. days_____
Follow up_____   Total investment_____
Payments_____   Increase $ per rep/yr._____
ROI_____   Total increase $/co._____

These field entries can also drop directly into a boiler-plated proposal.

Prices for PC-based contact managers start at under $200 for single user versions with a lot of power. For more flexibility, expect to pay more. But be aware that sophisticated packages which promise the moon often result in data processing running the sales department.

Build Trust By Admiting Faults

Paradoxically, showing your weaker side can be interpreted by the buyer as great strength. Most salespeople hide their own or their product's flaws and wind up missing golden opportunities for trust generation.

Most sales calls do not end up as sales because the buyer perceives one or more areas of conflict with the seller—price, timing, service, etc.

Bringing up these conflicts first can reduce sales pressure. This allows you to frame the drawback in the best possible terms, and establish rapport with the buyer as she sees she is dealing with a human being, not a vendor presenting a false front.

"The mark of good salespeople is that customers don't regard them as salespeople at all, but as trusted and indispensable advisors, auxiliary employees who, fortunately, are on someone else's payroll."
—Harvey Mackay

Some examples:
"Actually, Judy, we're not very good at the technical side of radial tire construction—you might be better off trying Yokohama for that. We tried it a couple of years ago and we couldn't develop the volume. Yokohama has a custom radial specialty shop in Nara. You can reach Mr. Ichi Tasoro through their Los Angeles office, their number is 818-555-1212. Where we shine is in the area of tire distribution—how are you handling that currently?"

"You know, Jeannette, I might be able to help you integrate your system but it's not my greatest strength. You might contact Novell directly and ask them for one of their Platinum resellers. When you get to the part where you want to customize your scanning and fax-broadcasting, that's when I can be of some real service to you..."

These admissions of weakness get prospects' attention by their frankness. They make you more believable when you say something good about yourself. They build trust in general. They even act as qualifying questions clarifying their needs. (And many times you're admitting a weakness in an area that you know they don't need now!)

A WINNING 7-POINT PROBING METHODOLOGY (AND SIMPLE TOO!)

To achieve success, I have always tried to make things simple and repeatable. I believe that the qualifying process can be simple and repeatable as well.

Let us assume that we now have run into a suitably intelligent person who is warm enough to let us know that we may continue our conversation. The seven-point methodology shown below should work for most salespeople in most qualifying situations.

This method is designed to be easy to use and yet get all the information necessary for closing business. In its most truncated and simplest form, these seven points can actually be put on the salesperson's wall or computer as a "cheat sheet."

This is not intended as a complete list, however, a sales professional with street smarts and an abbreviated style can quickly analyze the quality of a prospect from a few notes along these lines.

Many firms assess these items and develop prospect scores—highest scores being best prospects, etc. But there is a catch to this approach.

Make sure your salespeople avoid the trap of focusing exclusively on the highest valued accounts. Sales often come from entirely unexpected places. And the expected purchase order from your big customer is often **not** in the mail. Steady, smart prospecting should be a well-developed habit.

7-Point Probing Methodology

1. Determine RESPONSIBILITY
2. Analyze the PAIN/PROBLEM
3. Assess the PROBLEM IMPACT
4. Get the BUDGET
5. Clarify URGENCY/TIME FRAME
6. Know the COMPETITION
7. Learn their BUYING PROCESS

1 **Assess responsibility.** How many billions of hours have

How To Identify The Four Types Of Buyers And Decision Influencers

The **economic influencer** signs the checks. He or she makes the final decision and is a crucial part of the process, but will often need the advice of the following three people.

The **technical influencer** makes the technical evaluation of the product or service.

The **user influencer** is the person who actually makes use of the product or service.

The **political influencer** has no direct evaluation function except that he or she has the ear of one of the other decision makers or influencers.

been spent by salespeople selling to non-qualified people?

Not ferreting out all important players in the decision-making process can paralyze the sales process.

Questions used to determine all the players might include:

"John, my name is XXX with ABC Widgets and we make the widgets with the hole in them for aerospace sprockets. I wanted to make sure you have an up-to-date catalog from us **but I'm not sure if you are the person I should be sending this to—am I barking up the right tree or do you know who I should be dealing with?**"

"So I know what tech sheets should be included and where I should send them, **are there any other people you confer with who would be involved in deciding on this software?**"

2 **Determine the problem.** No one is going to look at your solution unless they have a problem which needs to be fixed. Your job is to determine what that problem is.

It is crucial when selling high-ticket, or even low-ticket, items to determine problems, patterns and wish lists. Some suitable questions might be:

"John, **what is the beta group trying to achieve with the new** equipment—are they trying to increase production, reduce downtime? What's the primary focus?"

"Judy, if you took off for a four-week vacation in Bermuda, what do you think would start falling apart first?"

3 **Determine problem impact.** Just as important as knowing what the problem is, is determining how that problem affects the people involved

and the overall performance of the company. Here's how one salesperson detailed the impact of some network downtime:

> Q: "So last year the sales group was down about 20 work days due to computer network problems? Besides hurting your sales, what was the impact on salesperson morale?"
>
> A: "Just terrible. Turnover went from under 20% last year to 35% this year, and I think a lot of that was salespeople just getting fed up."
>
> Q: "Based on your sales levels, that must have cost around $5,000,000 in lost revenue—were there other repercussions from losing the system in morale or in fulfillment?"
>
> A: "Oh, sure. We wound up pushing back our literature drop dates by four weeks and that cut into our Christmas sales something fierce."
>
> Q: "And then your boss wonders why your motivation tools aren't working."
>
> A: "It made me crazy but least we're finally going to do something about this year."
>
> Q: "What exactly are they doing; increasing budget, improving the technology?"
>
> A: "Both, and I think that's where you come in..."

4 **Get the budget.** Even where no set budget has been approved, buyers always have in mind some approximate value judgment on the products or services being offered. When selling customized products or services, it is invaluable to pinpoint what the upper limits of the buyer's budget might be.

By not finding out about the budget early on, one or both parties is likely to be hurt. Buyers may be shocked at what they feel is a vendor's high price or, conversely, puzzled by what they see as too low a price for quality work. The vendor may wind up overbidding without a fallback position, or may underbid and lose credibility or money.

Finding out budget details is a delicate process. Sellers know you may use the information against them. Strong trust must be established. Indirect questioning works best. (See the disk for a detailed example.)

5 **Nail down urgency/time frame.** Since you can't eat what you haven't got or won't get for a while, the time frame is a crucial factor.

Time frame questions tend to be relatively straight-forward:

"John, when are you planning on getting started with this?"

"How soon did they want to have this up-and-running?"

"Is this on your wish list for the current quarter?"

If the object is to suggest that time is of the essence, gentle reminders of the cost of the passage of time may be employed:

"Jane, you mentioned that the software problem is slowing your bike production down by a couple of days per month. From what you told me in our last conversation, that sounds like it's costing about $4000 per day in downtime. We can solve the problem and have you up-to-speed within a week -- is there anything I can do to grease the skids here?"

If you have the luxury of enough business, you can goose activity by suggesting they may lose out by delaying:

"John, we're actually doing okay on time frame now but we get really busy in September. Is there any way to get this going by late August before we get booked up?"

6 Know the competition. Obtaining competitive information is one of the most delicate areas of qualifying. The prospect has spent considerable time getting competitive information and knows that giving this information to you can influence your bid.

By asking the prospect how they have tried to solve the problem in the past or asking indirect questions (see above), you may be able to get the prospect to reveal the information:

"Jane, what other things have you done to try to solve the problem?"

"John, I know you're near some of the

schools that might provide these people for you—haven't you been able to get what you needed from them?"

"Are there internal resources at the company like HR that have tried to help you?"

You can also damn with faint praise:

"John, I must say that ABC company is really good in the area of widgets, but from what you're saying, that's only part of the solution, isn't it?"

7 **Learn their buying process.** Sizable companies tend to operate bureaucratically. Buying includes a lengthy paperwork and hierarchical process. The government is particularly notorious for red tape and making things more difficult than necessary.

Though this area of qualifying can be the most straightforward, politics can also come into play. It is imperative that you determine what procedure you must follow.

Sample questions might include:

RED TAPE

"Jane, I want to make sure that I follow all the rules here. Who do I need to talk to or what process do I need to follow to get the purchase order on this?"

"John, do you have a purchasing department or can I just use your name on this?"

BIGGER SALE, MORE INFORMATION

When the dollars are big, the sales cycle long, or the product is technical or sophisticated, it is important to get as much information as possible. Sales consultant Jeff Baker suggests to his high-technology reseller clients that they develop such information as:

- interests, needs, hot buttons for each decision influencer (expect to deal with several influencers)

- concerns, points of resistance, objections for each decision influencer
- a complete organizational chart of the prospect's company

Naturally, each of the areas you want information in can result in dozens of subquestions and probing areas. All of the information gathered can be compartmentalized easily with a flexible contact manager with user-defined fields (see the disk for 16 examples).

Using quality questions as a jumping off point, even multi-million dollar products with years-long sales cycles can be effectively qualified and eventually sold—sometimes completely via phone!

CONCLUSION

Qualifying is crucial to selling—indeed, it is the essence of determining whether the product or service will be of any use to the buyer. Without an easy qualifying methodology, many salespeople fumble sloppily through the probing process, wasting both their and the buyers' time.

The qualifying methodology presented here can be a guide to getting effective information crucial to judging how much time and resources to spend on a prospect account.

Placing the checklist within easy view or committing it to memory will ensure a thorough qualifying effort. This will result in more opportunities discovered, more sales pitches listened to with interest, more demonstrations, more appointments, and—of course—more sales and dollars in your pocket!

FULL SPEED AHEAD

TEN ACTION SECRETS

1 Qualify prospects as much as they qualify you. Stop dealing with people who aren't ready for you.

2 Develop a set of nonthreatening probing questions to find out about prospects' situations.

3 When you send material to prospects, make sure at least one element will stand out on their desk, such as the color of the paper.

4 Either use a contact manager or keep very good written records on each prospect and your interactions with them.

5 If you work with telephone and field salespeople together, get agreement on how to process a lead and who's responsible for each part. Then share commissions.

6 Develop a list of companies you can refer prospects to for their related needs to build your credibility as an expert consultant with their best interests at heart.

7 Be sure to track different contributors to the prospects' decision making, such as the user, technical expert, political influencer, and final decison maker.

8 Define your benefits in terms of dollars and time value to prospects.

9 Know your competition better than your prospect does.

10 Understand prospects' buying processes and get them to help you deal with their processes.

Chapter 3

REJECTING THE FEAR OF REJECTION

Scott Sindelar

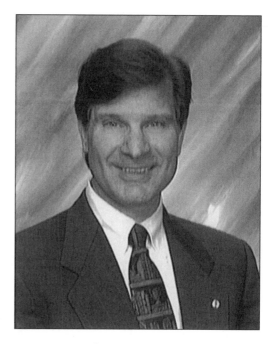

Scott Sindelar, PhD, BCFE is a business psychologist with a mission: *to tackle the tough people problems* in businesses and organizations. He teaches organizations how to get and keep people performing at their best. He believes that, with the right programs, any company can become a magnet, attracting the best employees and best customers.

From cities throughout the United States to Singapore to Saudi Arabia, Dr. Sindelar presents and consults on: Conflict Resolution, Secrets of Effective Communication, and Down-Stressing.

As the editor and publisher of *Advanced Business Psychology*, he provides practical tools to help organizations transform costly workplace problems such as the fear of rejection, anger, drug abuse, and violence into passionate productivity.

Trained as a psychologist and neuropsychologist, Dr. Sindelar has over twenty years of hands-on experience.

Scott Sindelar, PhD, BCFE, Institute for Advanced Business Psychology, 4839 East Greenway Road, Suite 369, Scottsdale, AZ 85254; phone (800) 636-3371, (602) 481-3400, fax (602) 867-0368; e-mail Dr.Sindelar@asu.edu Web page: http://www.speaking.com/sindelar.html

Chapter 3

REJECTING THE FEAR OF REJECTION

Scott Sindelar

"Our doubts are traitors, and make us lose the good we oft might win by fearing to attempt."
—William Shakespeare, *Measure for Measure*: (I, iv)

Fear of rejection is an enemy of marketing success. Fear is an instinctive survival emotion.

The primary goal of fear is to get us out of the perceived dangerous situation to one of safety. But your prospects are not your enemies. Fear will not mobilize effective problem solving. Instead, fear clouds judgment and smothers creativity.

Imagine what you could do if you did not have a fear of rejection. How would your life be different? By learning to reject rejection you:

- will perform your job better than you do now
- will be more fun when you get home from work
- will unleash the real you that has been hidden away behind the walls of fear and defenses

My overall goal for you is dramatic performance improvement! Overcoming your fears and learning to handle rejections are the building blocks to freedom and success.

To succeed in marketing, as in sales, you must be relatively fearless, tolerant of ambiguity, and able to adapt to rapid change, fierce competition, and ambiguous circumstances.

This chapter will give you powerful tools to reject the fear of rejection.

AN EXAMPLE OF REJECTION AS A GOAL

How bad is rejection really?

A man I know was born without any of the attributes our society considers to be attractive. He was relatively poor, short, skinny, had bad skin, and, for him, every day was a bad hair day. He was sickly with kidney and pancreatic problems. He had minimal athletic ability. His voice was thin and reedy. He was, however, blessed with the determination of a pit bull, a wry sense of humor, and a good brain.

He wanted a date, some female companionship, but women were not knocking at his door. Rather than giving in to his fear of rejection, he was determined to discover just how many rejections it would take before he got a date. Each day he would go to the park and attempt to "market" himself by starting a conversation with every potentially eligible woman who passed by him.

As expected, he was rejected over and over again. He was rejected ten, twenty, thirty times, and more. At the end of the week, he had approached nearly a hundred women. He was successful three times. One of the three women, however, was a professional escort, so he eliminated her from the list. He dated the other two.

When these did not work out, he repeated the process again in a different setting. His success rate was about the same: two out of one hundred women showed an interest.

He now knew something valuable. It would take about 50 rejections to get to someone who was interested in his "product." Instead of focusing on the fear of rejection, he focused on the goal of gaining interest.

Set A Rejection Goal

Tell yourself that this week you will prospect as many people as it takes to get 50 rejections. Your success ratio will be far better than the man in the park.

Refuse to stop until you have achieved fifty rejections. By the time you have all fifty you will likely have some very positive responses. Rejection is a big part of marketing success.

Take Control of Your Success

Many pop psychology books teach us to blame our parents, the neighborhood, the government, or successful businesses for our problems.

When we do this, we give up our own personal power. We give others the power to push our buttons. We are taught that they make us feel rejected instead of recognizing they are merely rejecting our product or message. They cannot reject us because they can never fully know us.

> "We need to teach the next generation of children from Day One that they are responsible for their lives. Mankind's greatest gift, also its greatest curse, is that we have free choice. We can make our choices built from love or from fear."
> —Dr. Elizabeth Kubler-Ross

REASONS PEOPLE WON'T BUY

There are at least five reasons people will reject your marketing message:
- no want
- no money
- no hurry
- no guts
- no trust

The last reason for rejection is the focus of this chapter. If you fear rejection, you are conveying a message of untrustworthiness.

Buyers can sense fear or a lack of confidence in marketing and sales efforts. If you do not confidently present your product and ask for the order, buyers may conclude you are selling an inferior product.

HIDDEN MOTIVES:
THE THREE As

If you know the enemy and know yourself, you need not fear the result of a hundred battles.

If you know yourself but not the enemy, for every victory gained you will also suffer a defeat.

If you know neither the enemy nor yourself, you will succumb in every battle.

—Sun Tzu (6th–5th century B.C.),
Chinese general, *The Art of War*

Dealing with rejection requires that we understand the differences among what I call the three As of personal psychology. Most buying situations involve the basic emotional and motivational psychology of the three As:

Attitude

Affect (Feelings)

Action

An understanding of buyers' thinking habits, styles, and patterns (the Attitude part of an emotion) and feelings (the Affect component of an emotion) can help uncover the hidden forces that motivate Action. These attitudes and affects motivate the actions of your buyers.

Understanding the hidden motives, the three As of your buyers, will help you design your marketing approach. This will reduce the chances of rejection. When buyers come into contact with your product, this is how the three As influence the result.

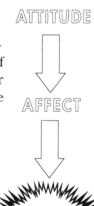

HOW ATTITUDES INFLUENCE RESULTS

Buyers bring a complex set of attitudes into the situation. Attitudes are primarily based on prior experiences. In some cases they are rigid and fixed, in other cases they are changeable. There are four main forms of attitudes. I use the BOAT acronym to clarify the concept of attitudes. Attitudes are comprised of:

Beliefs
Opinions
Automatic responses
Thoughts

Beliefs are the general ways we look at the world. They are convictions that develop out of regular experiences.

We may believe that people are generally good or bad. We may believe in our product or ourselves. This refers to confidence in our product or in our capabilities. Beliefs tend to be strong and enduring. We bring beliefs to and impose them on situations.

Opinions are judgments. Opinions are conclusions held with confidence but not substantiated by positive knowledge or proof. Opinions can be enduring, or they can be formed on the spot.

Automatic responses are the brain's shortcuts. With repeated experiences, we automatically respond in the same way or with the same feeling to an event. Hearing a police siren may automatically trigger anxiety. Seeing a brand name we like may automatically trigger a buying response.

Thoughts are the moment to moment mental evaluations and analyses of events. This is the self-talk we engage in when responding to the world. Thinking also examines issues in depth to make new associations or form new opinions. Insight and understanding come from deep thinking.

HOW AFFECT INFLUENCES RESULTS

Affect refers to feelings. Here is my simple formula to clarify feelings:

Feelings are always one word.

We often confuse ourselves when talking about feelings (affects) when we really mean attitudes. For example, "I feel like a failure," is not a feeling. It is an attitude, an opinion, belief, or a label.

That simple clarification changes the focus of your problem solving.

Trying to change "feeling like a failure" will get you nowhere. You may be feeling sad, hurt, angry, or fearful. Identifying your affect is crucial to making a change. Once you find the affect, you can look for the attitude that is causing it.

Attitudes ≠ Feelings

Here are some other examples of attitudes masquerading as affects:

"I just feel you don't like me"

"I just feel like I need more space"

"I feel like quitting my job"

"I don't feel like making another phone call"

Try changing feel or feel like, to *think or want to:*

"I *think* you don't like me" (or *I believe* or *It is my opinion*)

"I *think* I need more space" or "I *want* more space"

"I *want* to quit my job" or "I'm *thinking* about quitting my job"

Give Yourself A SWOT

If you were sure that your product or service was the best one in the market, you would be unlikely to take rejection personally. One way to strengthen your own beliefs and opinions about the value of what you sell is to do a formal analysis of how you stack up against the competition.

A SWOT analysis is a technique that can help determine your position in your market. Positive results from this tool can also be used to help overcome fear of rejection.

SWOT stands for
  S trengths
  W eaknesses
  O pportunities
  T hreats

It is important to be as objective as possible: What you might see as a strength may not be a strength from the buyers' point of view. Know where you are and where you want to go. Analyze yourself as you would analyze your marketing plan. Know where to focus your energies.

This is a powerful tool to use when dealing with rejection.

Instead of feeling rejected, now you can ask yourself: What is rejection?

Is Rejection an ACTION ?

Is it an AFFECT [or FEELING] ?

Or, is it an ATTITUDE ?

We cannot really *feel* rejected. We can only feel fear, anger, or sadness. Rejection is their attitude, opinion, or belief. When you are "rejected" by someone, ask yourself:

- What is their attitude? [What are they thinking?]
- What is their opinion? [What parts are they rejecting?]
- What is their affect? [What are they feeling? Is this affecting their thinking?]
- What is their action? [What are they doing? Are they acting based on incorrect or inappropriate attitudes or affects?]

Think About Your Buyers

Most of the time when you are fearful of rejection, you are spending too much time thinking about yourself.

To reduce your fear, focus the spotlight on your buyers rather than on yourself. Remove the spotlight from you and return the focus to where it belongs.

In face-to-face contacts with buyers, pay attention to their wardrobe accessories. For men, notice their ties, shirts, shoes, and haircuts. These all have a story. Ask about them and you will learn important information about your buyers. For women,

The Whites of Their Eyes

One way to remind yourself to pay attention to your buyers is to make a note of the color of their eyes. There is research that blue-eyed people set their own pace and dark-eyed people are more reactive. But the real purpose is to focus your attention on them. And you'll make better eye contact as a bonus!

focus on their position, jewelry, children, grandchildren, perfume, or shoes. You cannot be focused on your fear if you are focused on their face.

The only appropriate time to feel fear of rejection is when the person doing the rejecting is acting on murderous attitudes and affects (thoughts and feelings). Rarely do we have to fear that from our buyers!

HOW ACTION INFLUENCES RESULTS

Action Tool #1

The first action tool for rejecting the fear of rejection is forcing yourself to behave differently from the way that you feel or **Acting Against Your Feelings.**

Acting against my fear will overcome my fear. That's a keeper. Break the link between the attitude and affect by acting against the affect.

To help you make these attitudes more powerful, we next add an action component.

Make a fist with your dominant hand and put it into your other palm. Then repeat to yourself or, preferably say out loud, "Acting against my fear will overcome my fear." Do this at least three times right now.

Use this technique just before calling on prospects or to overcome procrastination or avoidance.

As a psychologist and seminar leader, I know that it takes at least six repetitions to learn new information. To learn how to reject the fear of rejection, you will have to review this chapter and repeat the main points to yourself at least six times. Then you will achieve success by put-

> "Most of our obstacles would melt away if, instead of cowering before them, we should make up our minds to walk boldly through them."
> —Orison Swett Marden

"Acting against my fear will overcome my fear."

My Goals

1. Bring in 3 new clients a month

2. Call one past client each day

3. At the end of each day, take 15 min. to organize thoughts & work for tomorrow

ting those points into action.

No Goal, No Go. To take action, you should have a written list of goals and how you will attain them. This is not new advice. The question is, have you ever done it? Have you ever developed a written goal list?

If not, you have come face to face with your hidden fear. You know that successful people make written goal lists. You know that most business consultants, gurus, writers, and speakers recommend written goals. Yet you have not taken this step. This means that fear is ruling your actions.

You may not feel the fear. You may be rationalizing, minimizing, or making excuses for your failure to take this step. You may blame it on procrastination. Those are all gentle covers for the true underlying problem: fear. Face your fear with goals and you will conquer any fear of failure or rejection.

Action Tool #2

The second way to reject fear of rejection is to harness and use your internal power source—your warp engines.

Harness **Y**our **I**nternal **P**ower, otherwise known by the initials Y-I-P-I-E. **YIPIE.** Here is a physical technique to draw on your power.

Touch your solar plexus and say **YIPIE!** Feel that power?

We can make that stronger and more useful for you today. Add a forceful **HUH** after the YIPIE.

Touch your solar plexus and, by pushing the words out powerfully, say **YIPIE! HUH!** Feel the power increase? Try it again. Say those words like a chant, over and over. This action will decrease fear and make you feel passionate and strong.

You will be able to harness and use that energy to make the kinds of changes you want to make in your life. You will be able to harness that energy to deflect rejection, negativity, criticism, pessimism, anger, and hatred.

[Just don't do this out loud in front of your clients!]

Action Tool #3

The third action tool for rejecting the fear of rejection is to talk back to your midbrain.

What is your midbrain?

It is the primitive part of your brain that is in the middle of your head. It is about the size of your fist.

It is the source of your drives and your feelings. But it is raw, undisciplined, unthinking power. It is a loose cannon. It is designed to react quickly without thinking.

If you step off a curb and you hear a loud horn, you do not want to be considering, "Is that a Ford or a Chevy?" You do not want to ponder, "Is that a friend honking at me or are they honking at someone else?"

NO, you want to be able to RUN, to REACT NOW, to STEP BACK.

Your midbrain immediately energizes your body for fight or flight. It is like a keg of gunpowder exploding. It is unconfined raw power.

The midbrain has a hair trigger, a short fuse.

Your Midbrain Doesn't Listen? The midbrain keeps generating the affect (feeling), hoping you are paying attention and receiving the message.

What Good Is Fear?

The purpose of fear is twofold:

Fear is designed to energize your body to do what? To RUN or FIGHT. Fear is designed to give the energy to RUN from or FIGHT a danger.

The second purpose of fear is to make sure your computer—the thinking part of your brain, (the cortex)—is awake and paying attention.

The big problem with fear is that the midbrain gets so excited, that it cannot listen very well. The connection is all in one direction.

Once it gets activated by a perception that there is something to be afraid of, the midbrain just keeps pumping out the fear chemicals. It knows how to turn on, but it is lousy at turning off.

The Big Turn Off. Fortunately, your cortex, the thinking part of your brain, has the **off** button.

When you find yourself afraid of something, such as rejection, your midbrain wants to alert you to the danger. The midbrain will do everything to get your attention. But remember, it is lousy at recognizing that you received the message.

Push your finger to your forehead to help your midbrain know to turn off. You can use this gesture to help your midbrain turn off the fear. This is how it works:

When afraid, talk back to the midbrain and let it know:

1. I heard the message;
2. I am taking it under advisement;
3. I will act on it.

We can talk back to the midbrain by saying: I've Got It, Shut DOWN.

Your cortex is like the warp containment field on a starship. It contains, controls, and directs the raw energy of the midbrain. We have to make sure the cortex is in charge.

Never believe your midbrain, unless there is a horn blowing, or you are falling. Your midbrain doesn't really know what is going on out there. Remember, it has a hair trigger. It shoots first and asks questions later.

UNDERSTANDING BUYERS' ATTITUDES, AFFECTS, AND ACTIONS

On one important attitude dimension, buyers are on a continuum ranging from an Open attitude to a Closed attitude. By understanding your buyers, you will reduce rejection.

Open buyers seek new, unusual, and surprising experiences. They prefer to explore and take risks. They feel most comfortable and excited in situations where this attitude style can be expressed.

- They like to touch, smell, and explore products visually and physically.

- They prefer many choices.
- They respond favorably to new and improved products.
- They prefer product literature that is exciting, unusual, and emotional.

Closed buyers seek safety, routine, and tradition. They want to know they are doing the right thing by purchasing a product.

- They prefer one choice or very few options.
- They resist changes to products.
- They often require repeated exposures to a product in order to develop a comfort that the product is solid and here to stay.
- They prefer product literature that is organized, structured, and detailed.

Customize Your Approach

Approaching a Closed buyer with Open-style marketing will typically result in a rejection. The Closed buyer will reject your product and keep rejecting it until a sense of tradition and consistency is established.

Similarly, Open buyers will not stay long in a Closed-style marketing situation. They will become bored, reject your product, and seek the exits.

For example, Cadillac represents a strong tradition of standardization, minimal change, and few options. Buyers know they are making the right decision. But when Cadillac introduced new sporty models, their traditional Closed buyers avoided and rejected these models.

On the other hand, Toyota started in this country by at-

Sink back and feel how comfortable the seats are.

tracting more Open buyers. Models and styles changed dramatically each year. An aura of excitement and exploration was promoted to these Open buyers.

Then as years passed, Toyota automobiles became known for their dependability and quality. They developed a tradition of reliability. Once that was in place they created a new line—Lexus. The Lexus line could capitalize on the legacy of reliability and appeal to the more Closed buyers. As the Open buyers matured, they began exchanging some of their Open values for more Closed, traditional values. Toyota had a place for them with their Lexus model.

"There are two levers for moving men—interest and fear."
—Napoleon Bonaparte

Approach-Avoidance Buyers' Attitudes

A second important dimension is the *Approach* and *Avoidance* continuum. This relates to the Open-Closed dimension.

When we have *approach* attitudes, we desire something unique. We focus on newness, freshness, and difference. When we have *avoidance* attitudes, we desire sameness and certainty. We focus on stability, durability, and safety.

Approach Attitudes lead to Approach *Feelings.* We feel eager, excited, and energized when thinking about, buying, or possessing the product.

If the marketing approach is congruent with these attitudes, we are more likely to feel interested in, and excited about, the product. If, however, the marketing program is perceived as incongruent with our attitude style, this will deflect an approaching buyer.

Approach attitudes and affects lead to approach actions, particularly if the environment is "approachable." Interest in the product can be enhanced by comparing and contrasting the approachable product to a product that can be perceived as one that the attitude style would typically avoid.

Approach attitudes seek pleasure or comfort.

Avoidance attitudes seek to avoid pain or discomfort. Avoidance reactions can also take the form of freezing (indecision, procrastination) or fleeing.

An Example Of Combined Open And Closed Styles

Home Depot has been successful because they use a balance of both Open and Closed styles.

For the Open-style buyer, they market new products, new learning opportunities, and a warehouse style of shopping that encourages exploration. Their marketing flyers highlight new products and specials. They create an atmosphere of possibilities for those buyers who are excited about making changes.

For the Closed-style buyers, Home Depot provides exceptional help. Employees are knowledgeable about the products and how to use them. The stores are well organized, providing a balance between options and standardization. They provide a sense of safety and security, instilling confidence in less adventurous buyers. Their marketing flyer comes out regularly, with a consistent style and standardization.

Although they are unlikely to reach a completely closed buyer, who probably would not try something new, they reduce the possibility of rejection by offering lines of traditional tried-and-true products. They have also done well on the stock market. That appeals to both buyers.

Home Depot understands the fear of rejection from the marketer's and from the buyer's perspectives. They have done well to overcome it.

Attitude
Begin each day as if it were your first.

Affect
Feel passion, enthusiasm and excitement for the possibilities.

Action
Live each day as if it were your last. (One day you'll be right.)

A PARTING SHOT

In summary, the way to overcome fear of rejection is to:

Deliberately do something uncomfortable in your business every day. Talk to strangers. Start or increase your networking. Practice cold calling. Do the things you are afraid to do. This prevents stagnation and promotes growth in your business.

Talk back to your fear instincts. Use the physical process of contact with your solar plexus and head to harness your internal power, not be controlled by it.

Most people take rejection as a wound. The Vikings believed that each time you were wounded, you came back stronger. My wish for you is that you be wounded a lot, and come back very, very strong.

FULL SPEED AHEAD

10 ACTION SECRETS

1 Remember that rejection is an action, not a feeling. Instead of choosing to feel hurt, think about what they are rejecting, and why.

2 Force yourself to behave differently than you feel about rejection. Then reward yourself.

3 Harness negative emotional reactions to rejection to energize new behaviors.

4 Talk back to your primitive brain. Tell it you're aware of the danger and will take care of it.

5 Develop some physical habits to take control of you primitive brain's fear messages. For instance, push the off button on your forehead.

6 Set a rejection goal. Count how many rejections it takes to get a yes. Consider thanking people who reject you because it is getting you closer to the next yes.

7 Analyze your position in the marketplace. Correct some factors that cause rejection.

8 Analyze your prospects and buyers. Which ones are motivated by newness and excitement? How do you approach them? Which are motivated by fear to avoid change? What can you offer them?

9 Don't let your fear of rejection stop you from asking for the order. When designing a product or service, develop ten benefits of what you offer.

10 Develop a series of facts that you can provide to prospects. Most sales take a half dozen contacts. You need to have new information so prospects can change their original defensiveness to Yes.

BONUS TIP: Don't beg people who aren't ready to buy. You'll never feel stronger than when you reject them. That confidence will show in your next sales call.

Part Two

FOCUS ON THE CUSTOMER

Chapter 4

3 WAYS TO SERVE YOUR CUSTOMERS <u>AND</u> SELL MORE

Linda F. Fracassi

Linda F. Fracassi
began her telephone sales career in 1979 as a line telephone sales representative. She has since educated over 15,000 people on how to use the telephone to its maximum sales and service potential.

She is president of her own firm, Learning Essentials, Inc. Clients include Sony; Duracell Battery; New England Telephone; Dupont Safety; Hewlett Packard; Providian Life Insurance; Bayer, Inc.; SKF USA; and Nobody Beats the Wiz.

Since 1988, Ms. Fracassi has been writing a regular column for the monthly newsletter *The Telephone Selling Report,* and is author of the cassette series, "How to Provide Excellent Customer Service." Ms. Fracassi is releasing audio and video versions of the program "Service: It's a Strategy, Not a Transaction" in 1997.

Ms. Fracassi started her career as an educator at Notre Dame High School. She received her Bachelor of Arts degree from Georgian Court College.

Linda Fracassi, Learning Essentials, Inc., P.O. Box 5141, Toms River, NJ 08754; phone (908) 341-7356; fax (908) 341-8145; e-mail leinc@aol.com.

Chapter 4

3 WAYS TO SERVE YOUR CUSTOMERS <u>AND</u> SELL MORE

Linda F. Fracassi

"When you don't take care of your customers, someone else does."

—Anonymous

What if you had to quit looking for *new* customers? What if you diverted the resources traditionally allotted to advertising, promotions, and direct mail to customer enhancement and retention?

It costs six times more to get one new customer than it does to keep an existing customer. Instead of investing your time, energy, and money devising strategies to bring in new customers, why not focus your attention on your existing customer base?

Marketing is a gamble. There is no way of knowing how effective any outreach marketing efforts will be until after the ad has appeared in the newspaper, the brochure has been delivered, the salesperson hired, and the commercial has aired.

We do everything we can do maximize our results. But the cold hard facts are we will not know how, or if, our marketing was successful until after the money or time has been spent.

OUTREACH IS NOT CUSTOMER SERVICE

Here is one example of how customer service was ignored by focusing on marketing outreach. I have a client whose marketing department ran a TV ad during a major sporting event. The sporting event was held on a Saturday. Calls were invited, even though the normal call center hours of operation were Monday through Friday, 8 am–6 pm. The marketing department had neglected to alert the inbound call center of this new ad!

The call center manager was watching the sporting event on a Saturday afternoon. She was shocked to see a commercial airing encouraging viewers to call her inbound department (that at the moment was unmanned!). Anyone who called in response to the ad did not receive an answer to their inquiry. Not only were all those marketing dollars wasted, but potential customers ended up angry and frustrated because there were no "operators standing by."

For more information, call
1-800-IGNORME

UPGRADE YOUR CUSTOMERS

Rather than recommend strategies for increasing the size of your customer base, I'll focus on ways to improve service, and get more from your current customers while making them happier.

I'll encourage you to use service as a strategy rather than a transaction. In that way, you can keep your customers immune from the overtures and price incentives of your competitors.

You could invest your money in beating the bushes for new customers. But why not invest that money in the service opportunities that present themselves with each customer? Why not encourage your existing customers to purchase more?

SERVICE TRANSLATES TO SALES

Your customers should perceive sales and service as one and the same. Customers shouldn't have that, "Uh oh, here comes the sales pitch" feeling in the pit of their stomachs.

We must balance our needs with our customers' needs. It's important to recognize that there are situations when we need to recommend that the customer not purchase from us at all, or not add on to the purchase. We make this recommendation because we know it is best for the customer.

It can be in our long-term interests to encourage the customer *not* to buy. We do this because we want our customers to trust us over the long haul, not the short haul.

We do this because we want our customers to refer other customers to us. Happy customers tend to multiply. Unhappy customers are prime targets for your competitors to raid.

There should not be a conflict between servicing and selling to your customers. When there is a doubt, it is better to recommend the customer not make the purchase or additional purchases. When sales are pushed more than service, your custom-

---

Santa Claus Marketing

"If you don't have something appropriate, send people to another source." Remember Kris Kringle in *Miracle on 34th Street*? People became more loyal Macy's customers when he sent them to other stores. "You build great credibility when you point out things you can't do... Good referrals to other sources show them that you really have their best interests at heart."

—Rick Crandall, *Marketing Your Services: For People Who HATE to Sell*

ers will lose trust in your company. First, satisfaction with service will fall. Then, sales will drop.

ADD-ON SALES

Whenever we make a purchase, it is easier to purchase more. We are already spending money. The inclination to spend *a little more* is an easy decision.

I have heard people who are redecorating a room of their home say that "We might as well" is a most expensive phrase. Once the big decision has been made—the decision to remodel the kitchen, or redo the bathroom—incremental decisions become easier. You already have the floorboards torn up or you've always wanted a bigger pantry. As long as you've got the whole kitchen torn up, you "might as well" keep on going.

We Might As Well...

I'll take this "might as well" approach and look at three companies to see how add-on sales contribute to their success. Then you can decide how you might incorporate their approaches to your existing market and customers.

The first two examples show how the companies approach the add-ons. The third company has taken add-ons to the point where, to the customer, there is no difference between the service and the sale. To the customer, it is perceived as additional service—added value.

1 **The McDonald's approach.** You step up to the counter and order your food. If you have not ordered fries to accompany your meal, you will be asked, "Do you want fries with that?"

It doesn't matter which meal you ordered. You could have ordered a salad or a pretzel. It does not matter if you think fries will complement your meal or not. You will be asked if you want fries to go with your meal.

It's a simple approach. It's an effective approach. Every customer is asked the same question regardless of what they have ordered.

2 **The Kmart approach.** You are shopping in your local Kmart. Maybe you have just run in for one item. Maybe you are there to get your children outfitted for school. You hear, "Attention Kmart shoppers. We have a flashing blue light special in aisle number 7." You are in the store already, so you "might as well" take a walk over to aisle number 7 and see if the special interests you. You may do it. You may not. Some people will. It's an effective approach. It's a simple approach. It works.

3 **The Nordstrom approach.** You enter Nordstrom intending to buy a pair of slacks to go with the new sweater you received as a birthday present. You don't have anything in your closet to match the sweater. The salesperson didn't just march you over to the slacks section and assist you. The salesperson asked you some questions— what you did for a living, etc. Small talk, you think. In selling parlance this is called, "probing for your needs."

You exited the store with the new slacks—plus a jacket, another sweater, and oh, by the way, a new pair of shoes. The sales person asked if you had a pair of shoes to match the new slacks. You didn't. You were sent happily to the shoe department with the name of a salesperson to assist you, and you purchased a pair of shoes to complement your new outfit.

The Nordstrom approach is a thorough, time-consuming approach to servicing customers. They attend to the customer's short-term (new slacks) and long-term (a complete new outfit) needs. It's a simple approach because you are thoroughly servicing your customer. It's a complex approach because you need a company culture that enables and encourages employees to invest time with each and every customer. You also need a culture that encourages collaboration among departments.

How can you make any or all of these three separate approaches work for you? Do you have to choose? No. Do you have to be a huge department store like Nordstrom to emulate their seamless sales and service? No. Start small. As results improve, expand the opportunities and training for your staff.

THE McDONALD'S APPROACH

"Do you want fries with that?" With this approach, there is a greater return on your investment because the individual sale size is increased. When the sales ticket goes up, profits go up. You're not investing much more to get a larger sale.

Segmenting The Experience

Waiters and waitresses know all about the value of a larger food bill. When the food bill is larger, their tip will be larger, as most patrons tip 15% of the total bill.

Here's how a skilled waiter will segment parts of the dining experience to increase the order.

When the waiter approaches the table, he asks if you want to start off with a cocktail. He doesn't know if you normally order one or not, but now he's got you thinking about one. If you say yes, he brings you one.

When he returns, he asks if you'd like to begin your meal with an appetizer. He doesn't know if you normally order one or not, but now you consider one. After he has cleared your table from the main course, he asks if you would like coffee or tea. First he brings out the beverages, then he moves to the desserts.

He knows your chances of ordering dessert are greater if he can present a dessert cart or tray. Why? Impulse buying. Gee, that looks good. "We might as well."

The waiter has segmented the dining experience at several

points to increase the dinner bill, and consequently increase his tip. This is the same principle that prompts grocery stores to line the checkouts with magazines and candy. It's the same principle that causes stores to have food demonstrations and give out samples.

Little Training Needed

We are not talking a whole lot of training with this "McDonald's approach." First clarify your opportunities. Can your sales be increased with a simple add-on like McDonald's? Or can sales opportunities be segmented and expanded along the way?

Instruct all of your employees to ask a similar question of all of your customers. There are many opportunities to increase the customer's average order. A few more examples follow.

Simple Add-ons

Every time I get my car washed, I am asked if I want the hot wax ("Yes"), and the air freshener ("No"). I have been going there for the past three years and I am always asked the same two questions regardless of who is handling the job.

When you order an ice cream cone, you are asked if you want sprinkles or jimmies on it.

Add-ons = Service + Good Business

Whenever I get a haircut, my hairdresser always schedules my next haircut appointment. He always schedules my haircuts five weeks away. There are two benefits. One is for me, and one is for him. I don't have to worry about scheduling a haircut and his appointment book is filled.

My hairdresser is providing a service and protecting his customer base. For me, it's one less appointment to worry about scheduling.

The purchase of my family's big screen TV is an example that illustrates the service perception to the customer and the add-on sale to the salesperson. When we bought our home theater system, the salesperson asked my husband who was going to do the installation.

My husband replied that he was, and the

salesperson recommended the proper cable to use for the installation.

> ## Alliances For Customers
>
> Another way to add things for your customers is through other businesses. Look for businesses that you can form partnerships with to add services or products that your customers need. You can benefit directly from cross-referrals or commissions, or indirectly from increased customer loyalty.

We left the home theater section and went over to where they sold the cables. My husband bought the cable. Why not? We were already in the store. It was a convenience to us to buy everything we needed at once and be done with it. It was a service to us—now we could go home, install the system and enjoy it. To us, this exchange was seamless service.

The salesperson increased his sale. But there is another side to this add-on. If the salesperson had *not* asked about the installation, we probably *would have assumed* no special cables were necessary. If we were to discover we needed a particular cable to complete the installation, we would have been annoyed at the salesperson.

More Add-Ons

Here are more examples of products with natural add-ons.

- You buy a new VCR and the salesperson asks you how many videotapes you want.

- You buy a new CD player and the salesperson asks you which CDs you'll be purchasing today, so you can go home, listen to your new CD, and enjoy your favorite artist in the new sound.

- You buy a smoke detector and the salesperson sells you the batteries for the smoke detector to work. You buy a battery-operated anything, and the salesperson sells you the batteries to go along with it.

Help Customers, Help Yourself

I have a client who markets computer education classes via direct mail. Their multiday classes are held in hotels nationwide. When customers call to register for seminars, the customers are asked, "What credit card will you be using today?"

Encouraging their customers to pay their registration with credit cards has benefits for the customers and the seminar company. Customers are offered a small discount with their cards. Customers are less likely to be "no shows" when they have already paid for a seminar. Additionally, the seminar company does not have to prepare an invoice or pay postage to mail the invoice.

When you go to pay for an item you've selected at a department store, you are asked how you will pay for it. If you choose an option other than the department store credit card, you will be asked if you have a department store credit card. If you answer "yes," you'll be asked if you'll be using it for today's purchase.

If you say you don't have a department store credit card, you are offered an incentive on the spot if you open a credit card and use the card for that purchase. It is usually a 10% discount.

Keep Asking

The gas station attendant asks to check your oil while you are having your gas tank filled. Some customers will have the attendant check their oil. When the attendant tells them they need oil, some customers will have the gas attendant put the oil in the car, despite the fact

---

? Good Questions

What questions can you ask your customers consistently every time they order? What else can they use that will complete, complement, or as in the case of the batteries and cables, enable the product to work?

Make sure your customers realize the scope of your product and service lines. Think of additional products. Think of additional services. Think of something that may benefit both you and your customer. Think of the items the customer would expect you to recommend to complete his or her selection.

that it costs more. Why? Because it's convenient and it will get done—one less thing to worry about.

Remember, we only need some of our customers to take advantage of our extra offers in order to make the program or the effort successful.

THE KMART APPROACH

"Attention Kmart shoppers." This greeting announces limited offer specials when we are in the store doing our shopping. If we returned to the store later the same day, chances are there would be a different product being featured.

When we go out to eat, the waitperson often apprises us of the specials of the day. The special could be an incentive to try an entrée at a more attractive price or a seasonal entrée.

When we order products by telephone, we are made aware of what other products are on special that day.

When we get sale flyers from department stores, we can be inspired to go to the department store. Something in the flyer has caught our eye. It prompts us to go to the store, where we may or may not buy the item that originally caught our eye.

Do you think the store cares if we buy the specific item featured or not? No. The department store has achieved its objective: The advertisement brought us into the store.

THE NORDSTROM APPROACH

You go into the store to purchase a pair of slacks to go with the new sweater you received as a gift. As mentioned earlier, you exit the store with not only the new slacks to go with your sweater, but also with a new jacket, another sweater, and a pair of shoes.

Customers Are Everything

"Now that actually tracking and managing individual customer patronage patterns and service relationships, one customer at a time, is a viable, realistically achievable task, it's easy to see that customer management is much closer to the genuine function of any firm."

—Don Peppers & Martha Rogers, *The One to One Future: Building Relationships One Customer at a Time*

Now you're probably thinking I'm going to rhapsodize about legendary Nordstrom service and how we should all follow their sterling example.

In the long term, I think we should. Nordstrom's approach is a very effective way to spoil your customers rotten, so that they begin to measure every service exchange by the standards they have set.

This should be your long-term goal. But there are many incremental steps you can take to get there.

GETTING TO NORDSTROM

The McDonald's, Kmart, and Nordstrom approaches that we've been discussing follow a natural sequence. Starting with McDonald's, you can progress to the Nordstrom style of spoiling customers on a one-to-one basis so that they don't want to go anywhere else.

Step One

"Do you want fries with that?" When a customer is ordering a product, what natural add-on products, services, and supplies can you mention? What natural add-ons will complete the customer's order? Toner, paper, tapes, cartridges, leader guides, etc.?

Think of what would make the order complete, to enable the customer to use the product or service immediately completely upon receipt. The benefit of this approach is its simplicity and consistency. Every customer is asked the same question or questions every time.

Step Two

"Attention Kmart shoppers." When your customers are buying, are there other products currently being featuring that they could purchase while they are ordering? This approach is successful because it is mentioned consistently to all customers. With all customers being told, somebody is bound to purchase.

There are ways to make this approach even more successful, more personal. Your success ratio improves when you can match your product specials with your customer's regular buying habits. Now you're not just making announcements. You're matching the incentives with the group of customers who regularly purchases the products already.

This approach involves more employee training. Your employees need to know who their customers are and their buying habits. They also need more product knowledge. Is there a sequence of product or service usage? If you buy one product, will you buy another?

Step Three

The Nordstrom approach. This approach works best when you are selling concepts and approaches versus trying to move product out the door. It also takes the most time, product knowledge, and selling skills. The benefit of this approach is bringing a level of service to your customers that makes them immune from the overtures of your competitors, and desensitizes them to pricing. In my opinion, this is the best approach.

Nordstrom has certainly done very well with

Caution: Do Not Sell Your Guarantees Or Warranties This Way

When guarantees and warranties are positioned the same way as french fries, it is very easy for the customer to say, "No, I don't." It can also look like you're trying to squeeze extra dollars from customers rather than serve them.

EXTENDED WARRANTY

this approach. They have grown from being a West Coast department store to a nationwide chain that has pummeled firmly-entrenched stores.

SERVICE CREATES REPEAT BUSINESS

Perhaps the most overlooked value of great service is repeat business. We can begin to take our customer base for granted and not do anything proactive with existing customers.

Here are some simple examples of how great service can lead to repeat business. You ordered Thanksgiving flowers one year, and the next year you receive a call asking if you wish to order again. You ordered flowers for your spouse's birthday last year, and a month before the date, you get a call asking if you wish to order again.

From the customer's point of view, it is a service to be reminded of a gift-giving occasion. From the company's point of view, the customer's business is "locked up." The company knows you won't be going anywhere else for your flowers. The company has put last year's business back on the books. They can do better projections so they won't run out of stock when their competitors do. This program also gives their employees tasks to do during the off season.

Here is the proactive approach our local oil company is currently taking. The company is contacting all of their customers to ask them if they want to be

Accentuate Value and Incentive

Use language that accentuates value and incentive; for example, "This week we are featuring...We are putting on special."

That language sounds better than discounts. Discounts take away from the value of the product. Every one knows it is a reduced cost because of the language.

Example: "This month we're featuring XYZ product. I can see from my notes this is one of the products you usually order. Now would be a good time to take advantage of this special because you would be saving 20%."

locked in to a 99 cents per gallon fuel cost for the '96-'97 heating season.

Last year we got two deliveries. Our October delivery was $1.04 per gallon; our February delivery was $1.11. Sounds like a good deal to me. Sounds like a service to me. "We might as well."

For the oil company, there are numerous benefits. They are locking in their old customers for the coming heating season. They can now invest in bringing in new customers. And their cash flow is more regular and predictable.

How can you encourage your customers to keep repeating?

INACTIVE CUSTOMERS

What about the customers you haven't seen for a while? Give them a call and ask them why. This is a soft, proactive approach. It shows concern and recognition. All customers want to be recognized. All customers want to be appreciated.

This approach can also alert you to problems, new competition, and situations of which you are not aware. Remember, most unhappy customers don't complain. Instead, they simply don't return.

CONCLUSION

To bring all of the points together, I'm going to close with an example from a jewelry store in our neighborhood. They have been in business for over 25 years. They are not Nordstrom. They are a single, family-owned-and-operated concern. They have used service as a strategy, not a transaction.

They have been busy while other stores in the area have floundered or even closed.

The last time I was there, I had them repair a clasp on a bracelet. I had not bought the bracelet there. I was also shopping for a gift. When the woman behind the counter rang up the gift, I asked her how much I owed her for the repair and cleaning. (She cleaned the bracelet even though I hadn't asked them to. That's their approach to repairing jewelry: They have it, so they "might as well" clean the item for you at no additional cost.) The woman just waved me off, saying, "You're in here enough. Don't worry about it."

Extras You Remember

This store is always doing little things like that. They'll clean jewelry and not charge their customers. They'll make minor repairs and not charge their customers.

I can tell you what receiving that level of service has accomplished with me: I don't even look at the brochures from other jewelry stores— I'd feel guilty. I don't know how price competitive they are, but I can tell you I trust them.

Their business does well, consistently. They have strategized their service. They have sacrificed the short term for the long term. They are successful. I can see they will continue their success.

They do very little marketing outside their store. From my vantage point, they do all they need to right in the store. They are marketing through their service.

Shouldn't you be doing the same thing?

FULL SPEED AHEAD

10 ACTION SECRETS

1 Pretend you had to stop taking new customers. How would you treat your existing customers differently? Start treating them that way.

2 Decide what you already offer that your customers might want along with what they normally buy.

3 Look for new products and services that you can add which fit your customers' needs.

4 Develop special offers that you can make to good customers at least once a quarter.

5 Create alliances with other businesses that will benefit your customers and bring you commissions or cross referrals.

6 Train your staff to add to a database on customers. Gather their birthdays, family names and buying habits.

7 If you were giving customers free extras, what would they most want? Which of these can you give away or sell them as an extra service?

8 Can you segment the purchase experience in a way that encourages customers to buy more?

9 Can you schedule customers automatically for service, deliveries, or repeat orders? Can these be automatically charged to their credit cards?

10 Develop an explicit program to add services that will bring you closer to customers. Try starting with simple add-ons and moving toward the seamless service of a Nordstrom.

Chapter 5

CUSTOMER LOYALTY: The Ongoing Secret

Linda Hanson

Linda L. Hanson founded LLH Enterprises in 1981 to provide businesses with the marketing and sales knowledge and skills to stimulate sales, productivity, and profitability. Her background, including marketing positions with Fortune 500 Companies such as Jones Intercable, Economics Laboratories, and Max Factor Canada, has provided Ms. Hanson with extensive marketing experience in all phases of marketing from planning to implementation and selling.

Since 1981, LLH Enterprises has built an extensive array of clients. Ms. Hanson's work in marketing, sales, and customer service has helped her clients identify problem areas, change the way they work, and grow stronger businesses. She has spoken to thousands of business owners, managers, and corporate executives about marketing and management issues.

Ms. Hanson lives with her husband, David, and their two Cavalier King Charles Spaniels in suburban Houston, Texas. Ms. Hanson is an active member of the business community. She is a member of the National Speakers Association, Chamber of Commerce, Toastmasters International, and several other community organizations. She is also a volunteer teaching Applied Economics at local high schools on behalf of Junior Achievement.

Linda Hanson; LLH Enterprises, 4510 Willow Pond Court, Sugar Land, TX 77479; phone (281) 265-9688; fax (281) 265-8736.

Chapter 5

CUSTOMER LOYALTY: The Ongoing Secret

Linda Hanson

"Gather as much information as you can about customers, then tailor the entire enterprise to customers' very personalized needs."
—Tom Peters

If you could have the ultimate competitive weapon against your competition would you want it?

Of course!

What if it meant changing some of your thinking? Would you still want it?

Use value-added programs built on long-term relationships with customers to gain a competitive advantage. This can turn a small customer into a million-dollar customer.

Since you are reading this chapter, you must be—and should be—interested in answering these questions:

1. **What exactly is customer loyalty?**
2. **How can marketing strengthen customer loyalty?**
3. **How do you keep customers loyal?**

1. WHAT IS CUSTOMER LOYALTY?

Customer loyalty doesn't just happen because you are a nice person or you care about people. It requires commitment, assessment, and ongoing work. Customer loyalty is not a one-shot deal.

Delighting Customers

Delivering a quality service or product (which customers expect), providing that service or product with support (which customers expect), and then finally adding value (which customers don't expect but are delighted to get) are the three components of customer service that will give you a competitive edge and build loyalty.

Many companies don't even deliver the service their customers expect. Companies ignore customers and continue to take the easy way out—reorganize, reposition, downsize, rightsize, and trim the fat instead of finding and fixing the problems that are driving customers away.

Satisfaction Down

According to the latest American Customer Satisfaction Index, customer satisfaction in the service industries hit a record low the first quarter of 1996. The index is compiled by the University of Michigan Business School and the American Society for Quality Control.

The question is whether even modest improvements in meeting expectations are good enough to create loyalty.

The answer has to be a resounding no. Otherwise companies would be doing better.

CUSTOMER SERVICE RATINGS DOWN

Satisfaction with the service at hospitals, hotels and motion pictures fell in the quarter to 71.2, from 74.2 on a scale of 0 to 100. That rating is 3.9% lower than the prior year's.

Customer satisfaction is not sufficient to create loyalty. It only means that customers get what they expect and pay for. That's not enough.

The Effects Of Corporate Culture On Customer Loyalty

Your employees control your customers' experience with your company. Employee attitudes impact your customers' experience, and hence your customers' loyalty to you.

If you listen to your employees, you are probably aware of the problems and challenges you face in helping your employees develop customer loyalty. It is painful to think about the cost of not having good customer service. With poor marks here, it will be impossible to develop customer loyalty.

Employee Attitudes

Think about the impact of employee dissatisfaction, loss of pride and morale, employee turnover, and the inability to find good new employees. The manager, business owner, or head of a company needs to be a strong role model. Managers must help employees share responsibility, be focused on their tasks and use their creative talents. Employees must be aligned with the needs of their customers.

The way to create loyal employees and customers is not the band-aid approach of downsizing. It's fixing the problems. It's coaching employees to their full potential.

Ask Yourself...

1. What are the attitudes and messages that my employees send to my customers?

2. What should I be doing to ensure that my employees meet customer expectations and company performance goals?

3. What are the implications of the level of empowerment of my employees at this time?

4. How does the corporate culture I created drive my employees' focus towards or away from the customer?

YOUR MANAGEMENT STYLE MAKES A DIFFERENCE

Managing in a participative style will empower your employees. They will be happier, more productive, and more interested in serving customers.

Since employees know the customer better than you do, true empowerment allows them to utilize their expertise fully.

The worst thing you can do is manage your employees in an autocratic style.

The major point to remember about empowerment is that you can't go to work one day and announce to employees, "Okay, as of today you are empowered. You can make your own decisions." You have to define the structure in which they will be working. That means helping them know the boundaries in which they can make their decisions.

ZAPP Employees

One of my clients recently read the book *ZAPP!, The Lightening of Empowerment* written by William C. Byham with Jeff Cox. It is a

Care About Those On The Front Lines

The front-line service providers-people—who tend to get beat up and abused and used—are the keys to success in any service organization.

What do you do to cultivate that relationship so they provide exceptional service? The...principle of reciprocity applies. You realize those people are in the crossfire between the demands of the customers and the operational policies of management. They are really in no-man's land, and they need to be understood and appreciated.

I've seen stewardesses on airplanes, for example, shed tears and share sad stories as they get treated poorly. Over time, some grow calloused....

In his book *My American Journey*, General Colin Powell writes disparagingly about a particular general's leadership style. "He was a tough overseer. The job got done, but by coercion, not motivation. Staff conferences turned into harangues. Inspections became inquisitions. The endless negative pressure exhausted the unit commanders and staff."

In sharp contrast, the leadership style of General Bernie Loeffke, a colleague and mentor of Colin Powell, created an esprit de corps that invigorated the troops. In Vietnam, Loeffke rewarded the top performers in his unit by allowing one man each night to sleep in his tent as he took his place on the front lines. Who would not fight for such a leader?

—Stephen Covey

© 1996 *Executive Excellence*

Ritz Carlton hotels have extraordinary customer service, in part because each employee has a fund of two thousand dollars a year to spend on extras to delight customers. For instance, if a bellboy overhears that a customer wants a soft drink that is not available in the hotel, the bellboy then has to money to run out to the store to buy a six-pack and deliver it to the customer's room.

wonderful book with all the steps to empowering your employees.

My client decided this was a model he wanted to implement. Unfortunately, he did not provide employees with the structure or boundaries within which to work.

The result was that some of his managers, because of their past experiences, were afraid to make decisions. Some made the wrong decisions because of inexperience and were penalized instead of being helped. Some managed to give the president what he wanted and got promoted, but by luck, not by design.

Empowering Your Employees

Empowering your employees is much easier than you think, but it does require a commitment. Here are some things you can do to set up a program:

- **Share your philosophy** and your values with your employees to ensure they understand how their performance impacts the customer.
- **Hire right**—hire employees who share your values.
- **Invest in strong orientation programs** so employees know exactly what is expected of them and have the skills to do it.
- **Involve others**—use managers or members of the team in the orientation process.

Empowerment will not succeed unless employees fully understand their roles and the limits on their rights to make decisions. Carefully and fully explain and obtain buy-in of these boundaries.

You must still maintain reporting controls so you know both the decisions that are being made and their effects.

Make the employees accountable. If your incentives and promotions ignore this, employees will get mixed signals and the plan will fail. Tie employee rewards to measures of customer loyalty like repeat business.

Adding Value for Customers

Providing extra value creates customer loyalty. Try to create an added-value program that makes another contribution to your customers' success or provides a lasting impact for the dollars they spend with you.

One of my clients told me one of his best ideas for adding value. It was to do something the customer couldn't do easily for himself but which saved the customer time and money. Because my client is in the commercial heating and air conditioning business and he has a great computer system, he decided to do a customer's scheduling for him. The customer was delighted.

The cost to my client was minor, but the benefit to the customer was great and unexpected.

Are Your Workers Empowered?

Which of the following could your employees do without prior approval from you?

✔ Guarantee a special delivery date to a good customer

✔ Order an item for a customer that you don't typically carry

✔ Grant a customer a special discount on a large order

✔ Decide what adjustment a customer gets on damaged goods

✔ Make a refund without a sales slip

✔ Offer free service if initial service was poorly delivered

✔ Stop the assembly line

✔ Make a refund to an unhappy customer

✔ Deviate from standard procedures to improve quality

✔ Work paid overtime to resolve a customer problem

If you checked seven or more, there is a high probability that your employees feel empowered.

Source: Gerald Graham, Wichita State University.

Providing extra value to clients ensures their desire to continue doing business with you in the future.

Build a strong relationship with your customer and your customer will:

1. Do business with you, not your competitor
2. Continue to do business with you in the future
3. Call you for assistance
4. Communicate problems and opportunities

2. HOW CAN MARKETING STRENGTHEN CUSTOMER LOYALTY?

Your marketing plan must address customer loyalty. Planning doesn't deal with future decisions; it deals with the future of today's decisions. How does your plan create loyal customers?

Companies tell customers everyday that they are customer-oriented. Yet customer satisfaction is declining in some industries and barely getting better in others.

If you've ever been promised a particular type of service from a service provider, and your expectations weren't met, you'll understand the critical nature of integrating your marketing plan and messages with your service delivery.

HOW MARKETING AFFECTS CUSTOMERS

Marketing has always been concerned with company efforts to bring in new customers and retain old customers. It also impacts how and when you deliver your message to your customers.

Today, marketing professionals, through the advent of Total Quality Management, are confirming a lesson some of us learned years ago. You have to satisfy your internal customers as well as your external customers if you want everything to work well.

In the past, customer service tended to be a separate department set up for the purpose of dealing with customer complaints. Today, companies are integrating customer

Marketing Plan

1. Ask customers
2. Create loyalty
3. Benchmark

CUSTOMER LOYALTY TOOLS

Some marketing tools you can use to help increase customer loyalty are:

Internal Marketing Tools

- New employee orientations
- Employee newsletters
- Videos
- Training programs
- Internal mentoring or coaching
- Employee surveys
- Employee personal interviews
- Involve employee teams
- Visits with employees
- Show employees appreciation
- Respond to employee feedback
- Walk the talk
- Listen to your employees
- Keep communications simple and clear

External Marketing Tools

- Develop a plan
- New customer orientations
- Videos
- Customer newsletters
- User training programs
- Respond to customer feedback
- Customize products and services
- Give referrals to customers
- Live up to marketing messages
- Surveys; focus groups
- Customer visits
- Customer appreciation
- Speeches and articles
- Customer-oriented sales programs

service with marketing as a way of finding problems and stopping future complaints. If we use marketing to integrate sales, advertising, public relations, customer service, and operations, we build a stronger base for growth because we are all working towards the same goal.

Customers are your most valuable ally for quality. You have to listen to your customers (especially) if they are complaining!), fix any problems, and continually work to improve to be the best you can be.

WHO ARE THE PEOPLE YOU HAVE TO PLEASE?

The most important person in the company is not you, nor the person with the biggest title. It is the customer. The customer is

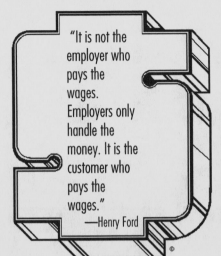

"It is not the employer who pays the wages. Employers only handle the money. It is the customer who pays the wages."

—Henry Ford

ultimately the person who signs your paycheck.

Without the customer, there would be no company and no job for you. So, the development of a good customer-oriented sales program is critical. This means looking at how you sell, how often to contact customers and prospects, what other marketing tools can back up your sales efforts, and how you will build long-term, solid relationships.

I always tell clients that you need a plan for each of the three categories of customers:

1 **Potential customers or prospects**. These are the most expensive customers to gain. Businesses need new customers to grow and to replace customers who are no longer doing business with us. This may be because customers no longer need our service or product, have relocated to another area, or are unhappy with us and chose to do business with someone else.

2 **Those who are doing business with us on an ongoing basis**. These customers cost the least to retain but are often ignored. All businesses need a stable ongoing customer base to survive. It is this group that we focus our immediate attention on. They provide the sales and generate the profits to sustain our businesses. They are our lifeline and, without them, we would have no business.

3 **Past customers**. They are fertile ground for investment. They have not come back because they do not know they have a need. Or have finished working with us because their immediate need is over. Usually, this group would do business with us if they had, or recognized, a specific need.

DON'T TAKE CUSTOMERS FOR GRANTED

There is often a false sense of security with the second and third groups of customers.

We think customers will be with us over a long period of

Never, never, never provide a customer with an opportunity to do business with someone else. Keep your customers close to you as though they are the only customer you have. **Be Active, Not Passive!**

time or that they are **our** customers. Or, we think that past or dormant customers have no immediate need and will come back to us when they need us. This, of course, is passive thinking. It drives us away from, and out of the minds of, our customers.

You lose control of your destiny if you take a passive approach and assume your current customers are yours for life. Tend to all your gardens, not just the "greener" ones across the fence.

Listen to Customers or Lose Them

The most important people to listen to are your customers!

In the pursuit of aligning your company more closely to your customers, you have many opportunities to listen to them. Marketing can help you listen through ongoing research and focus groups, newsletters, sales materials, direct mail, advertising, press releases, and sales activities.

Listening means uncovering needs, problems, and requirements. You can understanding how your customers work and why, identify other sales opportunities and set up an atmosphere for a good relationship.

Listening and hearing are two distinctly different things. A person can hear but not listen. A lot of roadblocks interfere with listening:

- Unclear communication
- Communicating infrequently
- Listening defensively

- Not changing or following up
- Listening to the same small group of people

8 Marketing/Listening Tools

Make an investment in the eight marketing tools below. These tools are designed for listening. If you don't invest in listening, the customer won't see the reason for investing in you!

1 **Observe your clients, competitors, and peers** to gain insight into the kind of improvements and value-added services you can provide. Going to customers' and competitors' facilities to establish interpersonal relationships, and to watch how they communicate and operate, is paramount to your learning about the environment in which you must survive.

2 **Establish internal teams to visit your customers** to work with them on projects or to help build their businesses. Also use your teams to brainstorm ideas to help your business run more effectively.

3 **Use surveys with customers as well as employees** to uncover your customers' needs, wants, problems and corporate cultures. The more information you have, the better you can develop your plan to bring yourself closer to your customers.

4 **Set up a hotline or toll-free line for customers** to call when they have questions, problems, or critical issues so

---

Listening to Customers

Listening to customers can educate you on such things as:

- The expertise you need now and in the future
- The products and services you need to offer
- The service and added value you need to back up your products and services to build customer loyalty
- How to go about regaining lost or dormant customers
- The organizational structure and behaviors you need to work best with customers

that you can keep *their* businesses running smoothly.

5 **Establish an open-door policy** so your internal and external customers can discuss complaints and suggestions. Ensure you are available when they need you.

6 **Arrange for focus groups** to discuss your ideas, and test products and services before launching them with your customers.

7 **Schedule periodic meetings with your customers** to review and discuss your progress, discuss concerns, new ideas, problems, and where they are headed.

8 Above all, **set up a communication system** to tell customers about changes. Strive to keep ahead of your customers' expectations.

Listening to your customers requires a commitment to them, a commitment to your employees and, a commitment to the systems you put into place to ensure that you listen.

3. HOW DO YOU KEEP CUSTOMERS LOYAL?

You make the transition from customer service to customer loyalty by keeping ahead of customer expectations. Listening to customer input from your marketing program is your best tool.

The hope is that you delighted them yesterday, and you are delighting them today. The only way you can delight them tomorrow is to know what they will need in the future and ensure that you give it to them better than anyone else.

Four ways to create ongoing customer loyalty are:
- conduct customer service audits
- relate audit results to strategic tactical and operational issues

"Business is built on the loyal customer, one who comes back and brings a friend."
—W. Edwards Deming

- practice benchmarking
- keep customers involved

Conducting A Customer Service Audit (Another Form Of Listening!)

A customer service audit is like a financial audit. It ensures that you are following procedures and meeting your service goals. There are costs to your company for not having excellent customer service. The benefits, of course, translate into customer loyalty.

Compare the costs of poor service with the benefits of great customer service (see page 96). Try to attach actual dollars to the costs for your business. You might be surprised how much more expensive it is to give poor customer service than it is to give great customer service.

Customer Surveys

Customers whose expectations are not met likely will leave you and search for another service provider.

To better understand the expectations of today's consumers, we must better understand them. Knowing how your service and company are perceived can help you develop strategically positioned marketing programs. Customer satisfaction surveys help identify what you are doing well and what needs improving. Surveys are the first step in your audit.

This Is The Easy Part Of The Audit

Surveys are easy for me, because I provide customer satisfaction surveys for my clients in a wide variety of industries, in small and large companies. Below are some basic considerations to be aware of before you develop your survey.

Surveys are not complicated, but a lot of thought and planning need to go into them to get the desired results. Surveys are research, and research is a marketing tool that almost every company needs to find out how it is doing.

Recipe for a Successful Customer Satisfaction Survey

Preparation. Define what you want the survey to accomplish. Clearly state your objectives and outline the types of questions you

Customer Service Affects the Bottom Line

COSTS OF POOR CUSTOMER SERVICE	BENEFITS OF GOOD CUSTOMER SERVICE
– Lost customers—losing customers means lower sales and increased marketing costs.	+ Retain existing customers—sales costs decrease because these customers cost less to keep (but don't ignore them!)
– Low customer confidence—costs to repair your image and increased sales costs	+ High customer confidence—a good image means lowers sales costs.
– Fewer referrals and less good word-of-mouth	+ Referral business—your satisfied customers have become your best (and lowest cost) salespeople!
– Errors—costs to rework and address complaints	+ Better quality products and services—because you listened to your employees and customers, you have designed and produced better products and services and eliminated rework costs.
– Low employee morale—higher turnover and training costs for new employees, more costs to attract new employees	+ Higher employee morale—again, you listened to your employees' suggestions, they are listening to the customer and everyone is having more fun and being more productive at the same time! Turnover is down and everyone is applying for jobs at your company.
– Competitors gain market share—your costs to attract their "loyal" customers go up!	+ You gain market share—you have a customer loyalty plan in effect and its working. Congratulations!

want to ask. Decide whether the information you wish to obtain would be best gathered via focus groups, mail, telephone, or by personal interviews. Whatever type of survey you decide to use, be sympathetic to the customer's time and make the encounter short.

Focus groups. Focus groups are often done before it is determined whether more extensive information must be gathered through mail or telephone surveys. Some companies use focus groups on a regular basis. They bring in customers (usually six to 12 people) to give them a chance to talk about the service they have been receiving.

Like other methods of gathering information, focus groups must be scripted for consistency of information and to avoid interview bias. Even so, they are a more free-form discussion. Focus groups usually last about an hour and a half and participants are usually paid for their time.

Mail surveys. Collecting data through a mailed survey involves preparing a carefully-worded questionnaire in the correct sequence, mailing it to customers, and having them complete it and send it back. A well written introductory letter must explain the reason for requesting this information.

Telephone surveys. Telephone interviews can be relatively low cost if you do not have to call long distance. The information can be gathered faster than by mail and, if done properly, can provide more detailed information.

Certain types of questions like rating or ranking are difficult to do over the telephone. Rating involves verbally giving the respondent a list of items to rate on a scale of one through ten or one through five. Ranking involves verbally giving the respondent a list which he or she must put in order of preference.

Personal interviews. Personal interviews are time consuming but are a more thorough

---

Return Rates May Be Low In Mail Surveys

Be advised that the rate of return can be low in mail surveys.

We quite often include an inducement such as a pen to help increase return rates. We have had as high as a 66% response with an association member survey.

Customer and employee surveys usually have a higher rate of return than general mailings. One national employee survey using candy to induce response got a return of 18%, while a pen was enclosed in a survey of a neighborhood surrounding a bank and got a 10% response.

means of collecting information. Interviews can get more respondents, clear up any confusion about an answer to a question, note reactions, and gather more in-depth and accurate information. In personal interviews, the interviewer must be careful not only in avoiding bias in questions or leading the interviewee but also of facial and body expression.

How Customers See You Vs. Competitors

Most managers know that the success of the business depends on how they adapt to a changing business environment. So it makes sense that the second step in a customer service audit is to evaluate your company based on what your customers and potential customers want from you and your competitors.

You and your competitors are the business environment. You not only need to understand what your competitors are doing but also how they are rated compared to you.

You need to know which customers, if any, you have gained and lost during the year. You need to know why you have gained or lost them.

Your original assumptions about what your customers want may not be correct any more. You need to listen on a regular basis to see if those assumptions have changed.

Another part of the audit covers the basic areas of your business: operations, finance, marketing, and management.

Personal Interviews Uncover Needed Changes

A client of mine in the irrigation industry asked me to conduct some personal interviews with both his customers and employees when his company was going through a period of rapid growth. Because he was so customer-service oriented, he feared that he was losing touch with both groups. The results showed him where to make changes by pointing out training needs for his managers and the need to realign his pricing and promotional support. Implementing these changes made him a leader in his market area.

An Open Office

One of my healthcare clients took a bold step when he built a new facility six years ago. Not only was the glass window in their reception area removed, but the whole wall was removed and the reception area set up like a normal business (which it is).

The glass window had always been a barrier which shielded the medical practitioners from the patients

My client wanted to be more accessible and allow the patients to have a total experience that would make them relax and feel good about their visits. This client was innovative about quite a number of operational functions that were turned into marketing opportunities and led to loyalty from referring physicians as well as patients.

Walk around your company and see the physical structure through fresh eyes. Ask yourself if you are customer-service oriented. Have you built artificial barriers? Are you set up to serve yourself or to serve your customers? Are customers accessible to you, and you to them? If you aren't providing your customers with ongoing satisfaction, you won't be able to attain customer loyalty. Get rid of that "glass window."

Measure Your Environment

A very important part of the audit is done through personal observation of the environment with employees, customers, and competitors. In addition to direct observation, read business publications, review systems, and review complaints.

Trends, forces, and phenomena inside and outside your company have an impact on your ability to establish customer loyalty. Because you can't track every piece of paper and each bit of information you are exposed to, it is best to look at what in your environment has the greatest impact on customer loyalty.

The intellectual part of this exercise, thinking about your environment, should stimulate some creative thinking about how you can increase your value in your customer's and prospect's eyes.

Using Audit Results

The most important part of the audit is being able to look objectively at your operation. The second most important part is to take what you have learned from your customers, prospects, competitors, the industry, and your own operations and make the necessary changes. Relate audit results to strategic tactical and operational issues to reach your overall customer loyalty goals.

This simply is the feedback on what your customers want and how to attract new customers to your organization. Ask the questions, get the information, assess the strengths and weaknesses of the information, and make the necessary changes. Take a bold step, be innovative, and delight your customers.

Benchmarking

Benchmarking is measuring your performance on various quantifiable indicators against your past performance and the industry. You have to determine the key indicators of success. Some measures you could use are:

- Customer longevity (How long do you keep your customers?)
- Customer turnover (What percent do you lose over a period of time?)
- Cost of attracting new customers (Marketing costs for new customers divided by the number of new customers)
- Cost of rework (Cost to fix breakdowns or remedy customer complaints)
- Average order per customer (And lifetime value)
- Costs to service your existing customers (Are you investing in your best asset?)

Where You Are Vs. Marketing Goals

Benchmarking often paves the way for change by measuring where you are now compared to where you want to be. The audit is the best way to measure where you are at this point in time.

Benchmarking not only identifies where you

Why Companies Neglect Customers

Companies face many ongoing "fires" that distract them from listening to customers. These include:

- pressures from government regarding employment, health and safety
- whistle-blowing and class action suits
- consumerism, environmentalism, industrial reorganization, inflation and a workforce with growing demands

are but also gets you where you want to be by measuring you against certain marks along the path. You can benchmark your customer service improvements against yourself and how you are doing against the competition. Use your audit to determine the beginning mark on the path and then benchmark yourself every six months to measure what changes have taken place.

Do the same benchmarking against the best service providers among your competition. Also look at other industries to see who are the best service providers. When you identify companies with clearly higher marks, go talk to them. Find out how they did it. And don't be afraid to adapt successful techniques.

KEEP CUSTOMERS INVOLVED, PROVIDE ONGOING FEEDBACK

If you are keeping your customers involved, if you are providing ongoing feedback by making changes, if you are doing more than your customers expect by delighting them with value-added service, you have conquered the mystery of keeping customers loyal.

SUMMARY

You may be reading this and thinking you have bigger fish to fry than taking the time to visit with employees and customers. That trap can cause you to deviate from your sole reason for being in business: To build customer loyalty and the value of your business. Despite other urgent distractions, you must be a fanatic about customer service if:

- you want to be here in ten years,
- you want to sell your company,
- you want to reach all of your goals both personal and business.

Customer loyalty means a commitment from customers to you. It's not surprising that to earn it requires a commitment, on-going planning, and assessment from you! This is not a one shot deal but a lifelong commitment.

Customer loyalty makes good sense—dollars and cents, and common sense. It's never really been a secret.

With all the new business jargon and buzz words, people tend to forget the simplest thing of all: Focus on the customer! That's the secret of customer loyalty. And it's alive and well.

10 ACTION SECRETS

1 Call ten customers you've lost and find out why they left.

2 Develop a marketing plan with specific steps to thrill customers. (You can use some of these points.)

3 Decide what unexpected value you can offer customers.

4 Survey your employees about how to improve customer service (or form a team).

5 Survey your customers about what they like and dislike.

6 Develop a special reward for employees who deliver great service.

7 Empower employees to take new steps to thrill customers.

8 Check your marketing claims to see if you're living up to them.

9 Set up a focus group or customer advisory panel now.

10 Observe service at a competitor by visiting or calling them now. (Also find someone outside your industry with great service to benchmark against.)

Bonus Tip: Send a newsletter to customers as a bonus.

Chapter 6

MANAGING YOUR GREATEST ASSET: CUSTOMER RELATIONSHIPS

Christine Lenick & Patricia Obermaier

Christine Lenick (right) and **Patricia Obermaier** (left) are co-founders of The Alleris Group, Inc., formerly Alliance Enterprises, a leading national customer relationship management firm. Working with *Fortune* 500 clients, The Alleris Group has established a reputation for their expertise in the "art" and "science" of managing business-to-business customer relationships.

Ms. Lenick and Ms. Obermaier have over 20 years of strategic marketing experience in industries including telecommunications, health care, high technology, insurance, manufacturing, and information services. They frequently publish on customer relationship management and present at industry conferences and corporate training events. They also serve as executive editors of The Alleris Group *Advantage* newsletter, a specialty publication on customer-relationship management.

Ms. Lenick earned her JD from Northeastern University School of Law and her BA from Bucknell University. Ms. Obermaier earned her MBA from the University of Virginia and her BS from the Massachusetts Institute of Technology. Ms. Obermaier is a member of the board for the MIT Enterprise Forum of Washington/Baltimore.

Christine Lenick and Patricia Obermaier, The Alleris Group, Inc., 11490 Commerce Park Drive, Suite 360, Reston, VA 20191; phone (703) 758-8500; fax (703) 758-8503; e-mail: Alleris@aol.com.

Chapter 6

MANAGING YOUR GREATEST ASSET: CUSTOMER RELATIONSHIPS

Christine Lenick & Patricia Obermaier

"There is only one boss: the customer. *And he can fire everybody in the company, from the chairman on down, simply by spending his money somewhere else."*

—Sam Walton, founder, Wal-Mart

A COMPETITIVE ADVANTAGE

Customer relationships are your company's single greatest asset.

Well-managed customer relationships provide a competitive advantage and the basis for profitable growth. In most companies, the value of customer relationships is overlooked. As a result, the management of those relationships is often neglected. By understanding your high-value customers, you can determine the path to future profitability and growth for your company.

FOCUS ON YOUR BEST CUSTOMERS

Customer-relationship management is not about how fast a company responds to customer complaints, how often the company surveys customer satisfaction, or whether sales reps are taking customers to sporting events. It is a systematic approach to creating a business system that holds as its supreme value the retention of its BEST customers. It is a customer-centered business system that is designed to attract, meet, and exceed the needs and expectations of the *right* customers.

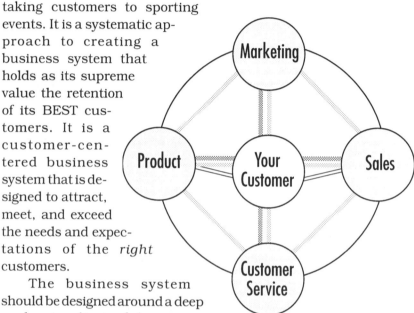

The business system should be designed around a deep understanding of how your company's BEST customers build relationships. Customer-relationship management must become part of your company's culture—integrated into every aspect of your business.

In our work with *Fortune* 500 and high-growth companies, we find that companies are shifting their strategies to focus on maximizing the value of their customer relationships. To do so, they are looking for guideposts and tools to determine the best approaches for their companies.

FROM CONQUEST TO RETENTION

Why do so many companies leave untapped the potential of their customer relationships? Many

Customer Relationship Management Quiz

- Do you know which customers you serve most profitably?
- Are referrals a growing source of new business?
- Are you seeing significant repeat purchases?
- Do your marketing programs achieve higher than average results?

If you answered yes to these questions, you are managing your relationships with your "best" customers,. If not, you are probably leaving a lot of business potential untapped.

of today's senior marketers were educated in, and gained their formative work experience in, the era of "conquest" marketing. The traditional business model focused on acquiring rather than retaining customers.

The postwar economic environment, characterized by robust growth, capital markets favoring short-term earnings, and limited national and international competition, allowed companies to focus on market share as a means of increasing growth. The guiding belief for most companies was that increased volume resulted in increased profitability. It worked *then*.

From Past To Future

Since the mid- to late-1970s, the economics of the marketplace have changed at an increasing rate.

Experience and research show that increased volume does not necessarily mean increased profitability. We have entered a period when the leaders will be those companies that understand how to succeed by gaining "share of customer" rather than "market share."

Today's share of customer environment favors those companies that:

- practice customer selectivity
- build relationships with the "right" customers for their business
- recognize the value of increasing retention of the right customers
- understand that building a relationship with their BEST customers has everything to do with the customer

- build a business system focused on developing key relationships

Throughout this chapter we will explore these components of customer-relationship management. But first, to understand why any of this matters and what matters about it, we need to understand what a customer is.

CUSTOMERS' COMMITMENT TO YOU

To understand customer-relationship management and its value, you must realize that a customer is someone who makes both a *financial* and *psychological* commitment to your company. An individual or business is not a true customer of your organization until they have passed a threshold level for both commitments.

Financial commitment. Anyone who buys from you is making some financial commitment. But that's only a start. You'll want to discriminate among buyers by their spending *and* their potential spending.

Psychological commitment. The psychological commitment—the "personal investment" a customer makes in doing business with you—is a key concept that is often overlooked.

The personal investment reflects the confi-

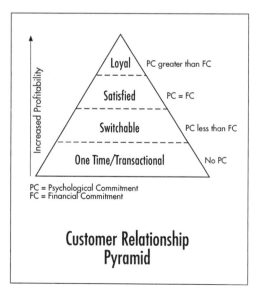

Customer Relationship Pyramid

dence level customers have in you as a result of their experiences. The commitment is driven by the degree to which your customers' needs and values are met through their experience with your business. This commitment then acts as the catalyst for increasing the customers' financial commitment.

MULTIPLE PRODUCTS, MULTIPLE CUSTOMER GROUPS

For a company with a line of products—therefore multiple "best" customer groups—the company's business system needs to be flexible enough to service various best customer groups.

Marriott Hotel has a line of hotel products—including Ritz-Carlton Hotels, Marriott Courtyards, and Residence Inns. All meet guests' needs for lodging services. But the business system for each hotel, and the best customers they serve, differ significantly. At the Courtyard hotels, room service is not available. In contrast, at the Ritz-Carlton, room service is customized to the preferences of each guest.

Selectivity Pays Off

The Ritz-Carlton hotel chain, winner of the 1992 Malcolm Baldrige Award for customer-driven quality, determined that their BEST customers made up only 1% to 5% of the traveling public. The whole Ritz-Carlton system—from the types of employees they hire, the training programs, strategic plans, facilities, computer systems, pricing, marketing, and growth strategies—are geared to serving only their best customers.

THE VALUE OF CUSTOMER SELECTIVITY

The key to understanding the value of customer selectivity is recognizing that some of your customers are of greater value to you than others. Seventy-five to 80% of a company's profitability is frequently generated by 20% to 30% of its customers.

Companies committed to a strategic approach based on

customer-relationship management create their whole business system around the customers who fit the profile of the top 20% to 30% of their customer base.

Three Types Of Customers

In working with our clients, we typically find that businesses have three types of customers:

Loyalists. These are a company's best customers. These are the customers the organization can serve most profitably over time to position the company for growth.

For Lexus, the luxury car manufacturer, loyalists are customers who have the means to purchase luxury automobiles and whose purchasing decisions are influenced more by value, reliability, and impeccable service than image. When determining which automobile owners to target at launch, Lexus targeted former Mercedes and Cadillac customers, known to be the most loyal customers in the industry. By "selecting" them, Lexus targeted a solid, loyal customer base that can, if well managed, sustain and accelerate in growth for many years.

Providers. These are the customers you can serve profitably, but at some additional cost. For Lexus, providers are the purchasers who place image or having the newest and latest type of automobile over value and service. While these customers may perceive the Lexus as the "hot" car one year, they

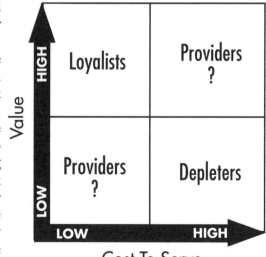

will move to another brand when that perception changes.

Depleters. These are the customers who cost the organization money to serve. For Lexus, these are price shoppers.

The diagram on the opposite page shows a quadrant analysis of these three customer groups. For Provider customers, you should determine if you can move them into the Loyalists quadrant by decreasing your cost to serve them *or* by increasing their volume with your company (a "share of customer" approach).

The Benefits Of Selecting Your Customers

Companies that effectively practice customer selectivity and customer management tend to have higher rates of both employee loyalty and customer loyalty.

Customer selectivity is valuable because a company's business system is more effective and efficient when aligned with their best customers. These customers have a better "fit" with your company's business system. For instance, the Lexus "Provider" customers are more likely to switch than the Lexus "Loyalist" customers when the next, latest "hot" car is released. The Lexus "Loyalist" customers are more valuable because their loyalty generates increased profitability.

When customers value the products, services, and approach of a company, the employees experience the positive reinforcement of feeling valued as well. It is a self-fulfilling prophecy. As employees feel valued, they are more highly motivated, and continuously strive to improve their products and service.

The Value Of Selectivity

The value of customer selectivity and loyalty is demonstrated quite clearly by two studies. First, a Bain consulting firm study of various industries, including software, credit cards, publishing, and banking, shows that by increasing retention *only* 5%, a company can increase profits per customer by 35% to 95%!

Companies that retain a greater number of their best customers create a situation where new best customers increase the company's profitability at a much faster rate. Instead of replacing lost best customers, the new customers are adding to the overall profitability.

In addition, mature customers are more profitable to a business because they are less costly to serve. They purchase more and more often. They are often less price sensitive, and also provide more referrals. Therefore, the loss of one mature customer often requires the addition of more than one new customer to compensate.

Best customers experiencing a well-designed business system have a greater likelihood of being "highly satisfied" by their experience with the company. In the second study, Xerox has demonstrated that a highly satisfied customer is six times more likely to be a repeat purchaser in the next 18 months than a "satisfied" customer.

If companies do not practice customer selectivity and customer-relationship management, the challenge of moving customers from the "satisfied" to "highly satisfied" level is much greater. In those companies, the business system is not designed to serve any one group in particular, so it is likely to fail to serve all groups.

CUSTOMER SELECTION

With a new business or product, customer selection can determine success. It should be one element of product development.

Like Lexus, you can select more profitable customers by identifying those who have demonstrated higher loyalty factors. It is a matter of understanding what the loyalty drivers of your product or service will be and which customers will respond to those loyalty drivers.

Lexus understood that a critical loyalty factor for Mercedes and Cadillac owners was service. By

Lifetime Value Analysis

The basis for customer selectivity is lifetime value analysis. This is an economic model applied to a company's customer base to determine the customer group with the greatest profitability based on future cash flow. For the purpose of this chapter, we will only introduce the determinants of customer selection necessary for lifetime value analysis.

understanding that element of their customer profile, Lexus was able to design a business system to exploit it.

Customer Lifetime Value

Lifetime value analysis is determining where customers are in the life cycle and estimating future revenue growth from them. It takes into account the benefits and costs of doing business with customer groups over their life cycles. Lifetime value analysis considers:

- acquisition costs
- base profit
- average length of customer life cycle
- defection rates
- discounted future revenue
- service costs
- referral value

In most cases, this information is not readily available. However, if you dig, you can create a portrait of the estimated values of your customer groups. You will also have invaluable tools to focus your resources, measure your results, and link your strategy to the economics of your business.

Once you know the true value of a customer, you can project how much an increase in loyalty of differing percentage levels is worth. To do so, you need to overlay the analysis of your customers' profit pattern with retention analysis. With this information, you can determine what levels of additional investment are warranted for your various customer groups at increasing retention levels.

UNDERSTANDING YOUR CUSTOMERS

Your company will derive limited benefit from customer selectivity unless you understand *how* your best customers build relationships.

In our experience, most companies believe that sales is "responsible" for relationship building. Many create elaborate launch events and training programs to provide their sales forces with the motivation and enhanced personal skills to build relationships rather than close transactions.

What most companies do not understand is that relationship

building is a company-wide responsibility. And it must be designed from the customer's perspective, not the company's.

Working with numerous *Fortune* 500 and emerging high-growth companies to design and execute relationship-building programs, our research has revealed that members of customer groups have similar relationship-building styles and profiles. By understanding the shared characteristics of their customers, companies can develop and build relationships with targeted customer groups. Without this understanding, the relationship-building process is "catch-as-catch-can," with limited potential bottom-line impact.

To develop a profile of your best customers' relationship-building styles, you must create a picture of these customers in four areas: product, perspective, process, and perceptions.

Product

Determine what values your best customers seek to derive from your product or service. Look at the profit drivers of the product and business, pricing strategy, distribution, packaging, and industry environment issues in the context of the needs and wants of your best customers. If the value you provide does not meet or exceed their needs and desires, your best efforts will be useless.

Perspective

With an understanding of your best customers' product needs and desires, you must now delve into their relationship value systems. While every group of

The 4 Ps Of Customer Profiling

Using The Alleris Group's proprietary *Customer Relationship Insight System*[SM], we apply a systematic approach to determine a customer's relationship profile and answer two critical questions:

- **What** does your customer want from your company?
- **How** do they build a relationship?

To answer these questions about your best customers you must address the four Ps of customer profiling:

- Product
- Perspective
- Process
- Perceptions

Two Hotels, Two Sets Of Values

The power of knowing your customers' relationship values can be seen by looking at the relationship value systems of companies providing the same service. For instance, both the Ritz-Carlton and Motel 6 hotels provide lodging for their customers. But the relationship value systems of the best customers for these two companies are very different.

For the Ritz-Carlton's best customers, achievement and intimacy are so high on the customers' relationship value hierarchies that they will pay a premium for the same basic lodging services. In contrast, however, it seems apparent that the Motel 6's best customers are satisfied if their security needs are adequately met.

customers has its own unique relationship-building characteristics, there are common threads in all business relationships.

To build a relationship with your best customers, you must understand what their core relationship values are, how those customers feel about those core values, and the importance they place on each one.

Process

Process is the way in which your customers assimilate and act upon information. Groups of individuals share universal "processing" characteristics depending upon their personality profiles. Most individuals can be typed across a range of personality types, with one or two that are dominant. "Adventurous," "serious," "leisurely," and "dramatic" are a few.

By understanding your best customers' processing characteristics, you can design your business system to speak to them in a way that validates and connects with those customers.

Perceptions

To complete the picture of your best customers' relationship profile, you must understand their perceptions of your brand, your company, and the nature and quality of the relationship they have with you.

In working with our clients, we find that, at the completion of our work identifying their best customers, we can create a customer profile that answers four questions:

- Who are their best customers?
- How does that customer group build a relationship?
- What does that customer group expect from their company?
- How should their company relate to that customer group?

With the answers to these questions, you will be ready to take the first step towards increased profitability by creating a customer-relationship management plan.

CUSTOMER-RELATIONSHIP MANAGEMENT PLANNING

> ### A Mismatch
>
> We worked with a major national health insurance company to evaluate why its five regional customer events for employee benefit managers were not attracting customers. We discovered that their customers were "process-oriented" rather than "issues-oriented."
>
> Since the company had shaped their conferences as "calls-to-action" around infant mortality, their customers found the topic compelling, but not relevant to their jobs. By repositioning the topic to focus on "how to" manage the cost of prenatal care to connect with the process orientation of the customers, the company had an 8- to 10-fold increase in the number of customers attending per market.

The goal of customer-relationship management is to create a business system that intentionally and actively enhances your best customers' experiences with your company.

Your best customers should experience a refreshing and validating satisfaction after every encounter with your company. This is a sense that they feel fortunate to be doing business with you and want to tell their colleagues to do the same.

To manage your customers' experiences with your company, you need to systematically speak to *the right customer, the right way* [SM]. Every point of contact your customers have with your company becomes a marketing event—a moment of truth that either positively or negatively affects your customers' relationships with your company.

Moments Of Truth

Here are examples of marketing leaders that have created seminal moments of truth:

- Nordstrom, the retail chain renowned for customer service, has floor clerks walk around the counter to hand customers their bags at the conclusion of the sale. At that moment, the customers' relationships with the clerks are personalized and the customers are shown respect.

- Saturn, the innovative division of General Motors, has transformed the purchasing experience by establishing a nonnegotiable pricing strategy. This approach discourages price shoppers, who are the least loyal customers. It also allows the sales representatives to establish positive and long-term relationships with the customers.

Create A Business System

Moments of truth are the results of a well-planned and managed business system. The business system can be compared to a software interface. Just as the interface is what the user experiences in trying to use software, the business system is what the customer experiences in trying to do business with the company. Interfaces that (a) meet the users' needs, (b) are easy to use, and (c) create few demands for learning new behaviors create loyalty, as do business systems that create similar experiences.

Business systems created without a true understanding of the customers create a vulnerability, and provide competitors with the opportunity to build a relationship with those dissatisfied customers. All too often, business systems are developed based on a company's assumptions about its customers, and are designed to suit the needs of the company. Retail establishments, for instance, create difficult return policies to save money. Banks and medical practices set hours of operation to meet their needs and styles.

To create a business system that enhances your best customers' experiences with your company, you need to understand what the customers' experiences are now. To do so, you need to identify and delve into your customers' experiences with your business system.

Plan For Success

Now you are ready to develop a plan for how you will manage your best customers' experiences with your business system. The customer-relationship management plan should address the following:

- describe the key points of customer contact in each functional area
- outline the customers' expectations for their experience in each area
- identify the key elements in the relationship profile that need to be addressed in each area
- outline a comprehensive plan for how the customers' experiences will be managed by identifying specific elements
- identify how the impact of each area on the development of the customers' relationship will be measured

Tom's Of Maine: An Example

Tom's of Maine, an environmentally-sensitive personal-care products company, provides a fascinating example of customer-relationship management in the context of commodity products not traditionally thought of in terms of relationship building.

Tom's of Maine oral- and body-care products include toothpaste, soap, shampoo, dental floss, and mouthwash. In the broadest sense, Tom's of Maine's customers are all people who use

Tom Chappell On Developing A Mission Statement

"We tried to integrate everybody's thinking into one common point of view that says, 'Here's what we believe.' Everybody has been involved in drafting it, so it's not just my values. It's open enough so that both conservatives and liberals can be motivated by it, whether it's about the environment, the community, or just respecting your fellow workers and customers as human beings. I think it helps motivate people and shows them we're all on the same side, working for the same things. Having a shared sense of purpose can turn a company into a community in which daily work takes on a deeper meaning and satisfaction."

—Tom Chappell (interview in *Executive Edge* newsletter)

personal care products. But, in reality, Tom's of Maine's best customers are individuals who care about what is in the products they use and who care whether the products are good for their health. After profiling these customers further, we discover that Tom's of Maine's best customers can be characterized as follows:

- passionate about ingredients
- informed about health
- care about the environment
- believe in "living their values"
- make educated choices
- want to positively impact the world around them
- value intimacy and respect

With this profile, Tom's of Maine developed a business system around the mission statements shown in the box below.

Tom's Of Maine Mission Statement

- To Serve our customers by providing safe, effective, innovative, natural products of high quality.

- To Build a relationship with our customers that extends beyond product usage to include full and honest dialogue, responsiveness to feedback, and the exchange of information about products and issues.

- To Respect, value, and service not only our customers, but also our co-workers, owners, agents, suppliers, and our community; to be concerned about and contribute to their well-being, and to operate with integrity so as to be deserving of their trust.

- To Provide meaningful work, fair compensation, and a safe, healthy work environment that encourages openness, creativity, self-discipline, and growth.

- To Acknowledge the value of each person's contribution to our goals, and to foster teamwork in our tasks.

- To Be Distinctive in products and policies which honor and sustain our natural world.

- To Address community concerns, in Maine and around the globe, by devoting a portion of our time, talents, and resources to the environment, human needs, the arts, and education.

- To Work Together to contribute to the long-term value and sustainability of our company.

- To Be a Profitable and Successful Company, while acting in a socially responsible manner.

Tom's of Maine's mission statement captures and honors the values of Tom's of Maine's best customers. With this mission, a schematic of Tom's of Maine's customer-relationship management plan looks something like this:

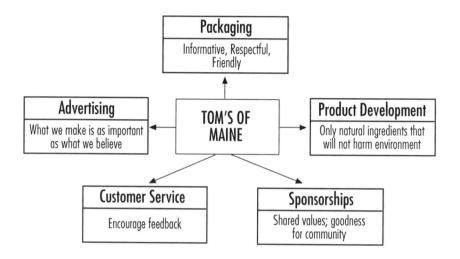

ALIGNING YOUR ORGANIZATION

Aligning your organization to effectively implement a customer-relationship management plan will require that the whole organization be prepared to do what is necessary and right from the customers' perspectives.

Every department and every staff member is responsible for the company's success in building and enhancing their relationships with their customers. "Fiefdoms" and "political" sensitivities tend to fight this process. You need to challenge

Managing Customer Relationships Brings Success

Tom's of Maine demonstrated some impressive results that hint at the breadth of potential impact from customer relationship management. Three years after implementing the mission statement, sales increased by 31% during a recession, and profits by 40%. The previous five-year annual growth of sales and profits was 25%. Because Tom's of Maine knew their best customer's needs so well, they were able to expand to 14 products even when standard industry research said there was no opportunity in certain ar-

employees to develop new perspectives and skills. The realignment must be driven from the top.

No two organizations will be aligned the same way, even for companies ostensibly in the same business. With different best customers, even organizations providing the same type of service will set up their business systems differently to serve their best customers.

CONCLUSION: MEASURING THE RESULTS

While this process is a challenging and continuous one, you will find immediate, measurable results. You will discover new, more effective marketing tools that will allow you to interact with your best customers more effectively and efficiently.

The key to measuring results is making sure that the mechanisms you choose are meaningful, given the profit drivers of your business, and that they are objective. To do so, the business needs to take a disciplined approach.

Each business area will need to establish success measurements that are relevant to their operation. The most telling overall measurements, however, will be increased customer retention, decreased employee defection, and increased profitability. It isn't easy to adopt a systematic program, where before there has only been guesswork. However, for those who persist, the rewards will be great.

FULL SPEED AHEAD

10 ACTION SECRETS

1 Educate your management teams on the value of managing customer relationships.

2 Analyze your product lines to determine if they serve the same customer groups.

3 Focus your efforts on retaining your best customers and expanding your share of customers.

4 Use lifetime value analysis to determine who your high-value customers are for each product line.

5 Determine which customer groups are costing you money to serve and begin disengaging from them.

6 Talk to your best customer groups to profile their relationship styles, needs, and experiences.

7 With your new focus and understanding about your customers, analyze your business system.

8 Develop a plan to increase retention of your best customers by 5%.

9 Build company-wide buy-in and motivate fellow employees to execute the plan.

10 Develop new products or services for specific high-value customer groups.

Chapter 7

CONNECTING WITH YOUR CUSTOMERS

Sally Mizerak

Sally Mizerak
consults, trains and speaks in
those areas that enhance customer-driven effectiveness for
organizations and individuals. She is particularly effective in working with service
organizations who must market an intangible product, and those in consulting
and professional service fields where the individual is also the product.

Ms. Mizerak draws from over 25 years of marketing experience, having
been in the trenches in developing and implementing marketing campaigns, and
at the marketing director level where she focused on strategic marketing
approaches for clients. She also launched and led an innovative marketing firm
for nonprofit and government clients, most of whom were not used to thinking in
customer and marketing terms.

As a partner in the consulting firm of Mizerak Towers, headquartered in
Pittsburgh, Ms. Mizerak now consults and conducts marketing workshops for
small business, independent professionals, governmental agencies, and nonprofit organizations.

Sally Mizerak, Mizerak Towers and Associates, Inc., 118 Marlin Drive West,
Pittsburgh, PA 15216-1408; phone (412) 343-7460; fax (412) 343-7465; e-mail
MTpgh@aol.com.

Chapter 7

CONNECTING WITH YOUR CUSTOMERS

Sally Mizerak

"There is intrinsic security that comes from service, from helping other people in a meaningful way."
—Stephen Covey

Marketing people talk about the "four Ps"—product, price, place, and promotion. These factors influence the decision to buy.

There is a fifth "P" that probably has as much influence on the decision to purchase as any of the preceding elements. That "P" is the person—often a salesperson—who links the customer with the buying experience. A sale can be lost, even when the product is exactly what the customer wants if the customer doesn't connect with the salesperson.

RELATIONSHIPS COUNT

Think about a significant purchase you made recently where you felt comfortable with the person you bought from. The purchase might have been a car, a house, or a major insurance policy.

What made you comfortable with this person? What words would you use to describe him or her? Helpful? Interested? Knowledgeable? Trustworthy? How important was this person to your decision to buy? Do you feel that you can go back to this person if there is a problem with your purchase?

Selling Depends On Connections

Any business which requires personal contact at some point in the customer process needs to be concerned about the people who provide that contact.

In the case of a service business, such as consulting, accounting or legal services, the person IS the product. The ability of that person to connect with the customer and establish a positive relationship determines whether there will be a sale.

Selling is very much an interactive process, particularly when it involves helping customers solve problems.

If we are selling ourselves in some way, we need to establish rapport. We need to enter into a partnership where the customer is willing to trust us enough to share what may be very sensitive information *and* to respect the solutions we offer. Without openness and rapport, accurate diagnosis cannot happen and solutions will not be accepted.

For many years, I patronized a local pharmacy because of their personal service. I knew their prices were a little bit higher than the chains but the pharma-

Service Keeps Customers

Consider some meticulous research done by the Forum Corp. Fifteen percent of those who switched to a competitor did so because they "found a better product"—by a technical measure of quality. Another 15% changed suppliers because they found a "cheaper product" elsewhere. Twenty percent hightailed it because of the "lack of contact and individual attention" from the prior supplier; and 49% left because "contact from the old supplier's personnel was poor in quality." It seems fair to combine the last two categories, after which we could say 70% defected because they didn't like the human side of doing business with the previous product or service provider.

—Tom Peters

cist knew me, seemed glad to see me when I came in, and helped solve lots of little problems when my children were young. Saving a few cents on a prescription wasn't worth losing that.

When that pharmacist retired, he was replaced by another, younger pharmacist with no sense of what it meant to connect with customers. She would talk on the phone while she waited on us, frown at us when we asked for advice, and talk loudly to other associates in the store as though there were no customers standing at the counter.

Now price mattered because the service I had prized was not there. It didn't take long for me to find another pharmacy.

DON'T THINK INSIDE-OUT

A customer-driven company thinks from the outside-in. It is concerned about how to improve the relationship—the involvement experience—for the customer. And it lets the customer decide what constitutes improvement.

My local bank is guilty of inside-out thinking in the guise of customer responsiveness.

They have recently introduced a package of banking products, including the ability to access one's account online, which I have eagerly awaited. However, they have bundled that option, which I find useful, with other options such as bill-paying-by-phone and on-line stock quotes that I don't find useful.

Those who opt for online banking also have to agree not to use tellers for any services or deposits, but to transact all business through an ATM. Failure to observe this rule will increase the monthly account charge by 350%.

All I wanted to do was access my account to check on activity, the same way I can now access my American Express account on-line. American Express listened to what its customers wanted and made the service available. My bank's own agenda took precedence over service!

CREATING CUSTOMER VALUE

Author Karl Albrecht notes the difficulty that companies have in focusing their attention on customers. Albrecht cites the words companies use to avoid calling people customers, words such as policyholders, patients, rate payers, and passengers—a practice which he says depersonalizes customers and creates a perception of them as powerless objects.

So What Is Customer Value?

Value is the importance a customer attaches to the combination of product and experience, tangible and intangible, involved in dealing with you. Take the example of gasoline. Gasoline is the product. But the experience of obtaining that product counts for more than the features of the product, as long as the product is somewhat competitively priced. This combination of product and experience equals value in my mind. And that's where it counts.

Value is a perception. It lives in the mind of the customer. Often it lives in comparison to other options. It doesn't have to be true.

> "The loss of this focus on the customer as a human being is probably the single most important fact about the state of service... today."
> —Karl Albrecht, *The Only Thing That Matters: Bringing the Power of the Customer into the Center of Your Business*

Customer Research

In *A Complaint is a Gift* by Janelle Barlow and Claus Møller, the authors encourage everyone in business to seek feedback from both external *and* internal customers.

Dissatisfied external customers can go somewhere else to do business. Disgruntled internal customers (employees) can either slow progress or take their talents to a competitor. Wouldn't you rather fix the problem before either happens?

Too often we ask for validation of what we are doing right. "Was everything satisfactory?" is a leading question that often prompts a perfunctory "Fine." That answer really isn't useful.

Complain: Verb, from Latin *plangere*, to hit!

"Complaining has never had a positive meaning...It is time for all organizations to think of complaint handling as a strategic tool—an opportunity to learn something about our products and services we did not already know—and as a marketing asset, rather than as a nuisance or cost."

—Janelle Barlow and Claus Møller, *A Complaint Is a Gift*

A complaint is much more useful because it gives you something to work on.

Research shows that a customer who complains, and then has the problem fixed, is far more loyal than a customer who never had a problem. Smart companies have a policy of making their recovery from a problem a chance to shine with customers. There is even discussion of a software company that *deliberately* left a problem in their software so that when customers called to complain, the company could be prepared to thrill them with how well they handled it!

ARE YOU COMPLETING TRANSACTIONS OR DELIVERING CUSTOMER VALUE?

"Efficiency is doing things right. Effectiveness is doing the right thing."
—Peter Drucker

What do you measure to determine your success? If you measure transactions completed—no matter what you call them, you are in the transaction business. If you were in the customer business, you would be measuring the things that matter to your customers. Not the things you THINK matter, but the things they tell you matter.

Many salespeople and companies get very good at doing the wrong things.

The hotel industry is a case in point. Hotel chains have gotten very good at outdoing each other in amenities such as phones in the bathroom or extra choices in the mini-bar. But business travelers have indicated that what they really want are quiet, smoke-free rooms with good reading lights, comfortable chairs, and desks where computers can be connected to phone jacks. Women want skirt hangers in the closet, not just suit hangers. Gradually hotels are making these amenities available but the slow pace of change indicates how hard it was for them to really listen to their customers.

The Purpose Of Any Organization Is To Serve Customers

When structure or process interferes with delivering customer value, it should be changed. According to Richard Whiteley and Diane Hessan, authors of *Customer Centered Growth*, customer needs should be at the center of the organization's being.

These needs should be communicated throughout the organization. Every employee should evaluate every process, every task, and every decision by asking one vital question: How will this add value for our customers? The answer determines how something gets done or *if* it gets done.

In customer-centered companies, no one has to be reminded that the customer is the center of everything.

COMPETING ON RELATIONSHIPS, NOT PRICE OR PRODUCT

If you compete on price or product, you are setting yourself up for duplication and therefore competition. If you compete on value, including the experience of dealing with you, then you can differentiate yourself in a way that is hard to copy.

Think of your favorite restaurant. No doubt the food (the product) is good, but is that the only reason it is your favorite? Or is there personal treatment of you as a customer that makes you feel special?

There are lots of restaurants with good food in a similar price range. The one you find yourself returning to is often the one where the staff knows your name, remembers your favorite wine, and provides little services that make you feel special when you entertain guests. And if something goes wrong, they are sufficiently appalled

Serving up the best in service

Customer Satisfaction Is Not Enough

The Ritz Carlton hotel chain has become synonymous with extraordinary service. When you arrive at a Ritz Carlton property, you have the feeling that people are really glad you've joined them.

The appointments in the rooms seem to anticipate your needs. And if something was overlooked, a phone call immediately fixes the oversight. If you need a special service—as I did when staying at the Ritz Carlton in Philadelphia—staff members go out of their way to find someone to help, even if it's after hours and on a weekend.

Contrast that with my recent stay at another hotel near JFK airport in New York. The prevailing attitude seemed to be one of annoyance that I was there and indifference to what I might need.

The desk clerk was surly, answers to questions were abrupt, and no information was volunteered. In the dining room, I watched a customer being reprimanded for not understanding the buffet line procedure while a young woman traveling with two children struggled to keep them quiet while the waiter arranged new place settings at an empty table instead of waiting on her.

The Ritz Carlton pampers its customers. The New York hotel was filled with people putting in time doing tasks.

to make it right immediately or remove the cost so you won't be distressed.

A recent example of this occurred in one of Pittsburgh's leading restaurants, The Carlton. My husband and I are fairly regular customers, but not in the celebrity category. When we pointed out that entrees were not up to standard, we were impressed with the response.

First the assistant manager came over to find out exactly what was wrong and to apologize profusely. Then the manager came to apologize and to offer us another choice (time did not permit) or at least dessert and an after-dinner drink on the house. When it came time to pay the bill, there was no bill. Everything, including the wine and the à la carte appetizers, had been taken care of!

THINK LIKE A CUSTOMER

According to Karl Albrecht, the most important thing any salesperson or employee can do is learn to think like a customer. Ask questions such as:

- "If I were the customer, how would I feel about this?"
- "Would this explanation satisfy my needs?"
- "Does this procedure

make sense to me?"

- "Do I understand what's going to happen to me?"

Albrecht describes "Moments of Truth" as any episode in which the customer comes into contact with the organization and gets an impression of its service. In many cases, these Moments of Truth are not positive. If all employees would think in terms of creating positive experiences *from the customer's viewpoint,* the customer's experience would improve and the company's relationship with that customer would grow with every contact.

Find Moments Of Truth

To trace the cycle of Moments of Truth experienced by your customers, start with any series of contacts and events leading to a result. Note each place where that customer has an experience that would produce an impression of your company or service. Look at the printed material that caused that customer to call you. Examine the phone interaction including your voice mail message and the way phone contacts are handled. Walk through every step to the end result.

- Were there forms to complete?
- Was information requested?
- Was the person required to:
  - visit a certain site?
  - wait?
  - return a second time?
  - answer the same questions several times?
- What was the experience like?
- How did people interact with the customer at each step?

Eagles Of The Moment

"I don't particularly believe in having an employee of the month. I believe in employee of the *moment.* What this means is that any time anybody exceeds a customer's expectations, whether it's an internal or external customer, it is a time for celebration.

"Anyone can nominate another employee for this award and several eagle trophies constantly rotate throughout our organization. When someone is selected, a group surprises them with a presentation and they take a photo, which is then permanently displayed in our lobby."

—Ken Blanchard

TLC = TLC

It's a happy coincidence that TLC stands for both "Tender Loving Care" and "Think Like a Customer." If you think like a customer, you will be in a great position to deliver tender loving care!

At each step, keep Thinking Like a Customer (TLC)—"If I were the customer, how would I feel about this?"

When you know that each Moment of Truth is positive *from your customer's viewpoint*, you have begun to create value for your customer and connect in a way that will produce customer loyalty.

DEVELOPING RAPPORT WITH YOUR CUSTOMERS

Thinking Like a Customer is a major step toward connecting with your customers. It enables you to remove barriers to a positive customer experience. Once you have ensured that each customer will have a positive experience with your company, you are ready to ensure that each customer has a positive experience with you personally. You are ready to begin developing rapport.

There are a number of factors that contribute to rapport:

- trust
- verbal communication style
- nonverbal communication style
- behavior
- personality and interest match

Of these, trust is probably the most important. If I don't trust you or feel comfortable with you, I'm not likely to be open with you or accepting of your advice.

According to Stephen Covey, author of *The Seven Habits of Highly Effective People,* you must be trustworthy before you can expect others to trust you. Covey defines trustworthiness as a balance between Character and Competence— between knowing that you *can* do what you say and that you *will* do what you say.

"I believe that if you cultivate the habit of always keeping the promises you make, you build bridges of trust that span the gaps of understanding...."
—Stephen Covey

Effective Listening Increases Rapport

If you want to develop a positive relationship with any customer, you need to encourage them to talk. You can encourage them to talk by asking questions and demonstrate your caring by listening, attentively and effectively.

Asking questions effectively is like peeling an onion. Each layer drops away to reveal another layer until you get to the heart of the onion—the true problem or concern.

Once your customer begins to talk, gently encourage the conversation with probes such as:

- *Could you help me understand*
  _____?
- Would you tell me a little more about that?
- How did that work?
- Could you give me an example of
  _____?

> "People don't care how much you know, until they know how much you care."
>
> —Abraham Lincoln

Ask About Feelings

Feelings are often as important as facts in understanding a situation but they also represent the most sensitive areas of the discussion. In a nonjudgmental tone, ask questions such as:

- How do you feel about this?
- What concerns you about
  _____?

Do not interrupt the flow of conversation until your customer signals that it is coming to an end. Then summarize and feed back key points to check out what you heard and to ensure that you are interpreting it correctly.

You still have offered no solution at this point. Before you do, check on the customer's expectation for a solution, with questions such as:

Tips for Effective Listening

1. Use open-ended questions.
2. Take notes.
3. Never interrupt.
4. Probe for the problem beneath the problem; peel the onion.
5. Use nonverbal signs of encouragement such as nodding or leaning forward.
6. Encourage your customer to talk about feelings, but don't push if there is resistance.
7. Pay attention. Make good eye contact.
8. Ask for clarification. Use "who," "what," "when," "where," and "how." Asking "why" can make people defensive.

- If you were to go ahead with _____ when might you want to do it?
- Who might be involved?
- What results might you expect?

Offer What They Want

Now it's your turn. You have all the language you need for a response from the questions your customer has been answering. Whether you respond at this point with a proposal or return in person at a later time is a judgment you as the salesperson will have to make.

Use your customer's words in developing your response. Your recognition and understanding of your customer's need will strengthen rapport and help you connect.

Nonverbal Connection Supports Effective Listening

Nonverbal communication includes how you dress and look; how you move, your voice tone, speed and pitch; and your mannerisms and expressions. Each of us has a set of nonverbal cues that we give out in an exchange with another person, often without being aware of the message we are conveying.

Your first step is to get a reading on how you come across to others. There are three ways to monitor this:

1. Become more aware of your mannerisms, posture, nervous habits, and expressions.

2. Ask others (friends) to give you feedback.

3. Videotape yourself in conversation with others and watch the videotape critically. Or audio tape and listen to your voice and speech patterns.

Eliminate mannerisms such as:
- eyes darting around the room, inability to focus on the speaker
- staring at the speaker, over-focusing
- fidgeting, drumming fingers, twiddling, twirling, and other nervous distracting habits
- grimacing, pursing lips, or other negative facial expressions
- speech pattern problems—excessive use of "ah," "like," "um," "ya know"
- talking softly so others must strain to hear you
- talking loudly so others recoil from the sound
- speech so rapid that others often ask you to repeat something

MATCHING BEHAVIORAL PROFILES

Behavioral profiles are the patterns that a person brings to a situation.

People adapt their behavior to different circumstances. But, unless there is a reason to change, many people will behave in more or less the same way in similar situations. These repeated patterns allow us to identify clues to their behavior and make some adjustments in our own behavior to increase rapport.

Assessing Behavioral Profiles

There are many good instruments on the market for assessing behavioral profiles. I use the Personal Profile System® (PPS), a copyrighted instrument of The Carlson Learning Company. It groups key behavioral traits into one of four dimensions: Dominance, Influence, Steadiness, and Conscientiousness.

The PPS provides you with a profile of your major goals; fears; likes and dislikes; decision style; behavior under pressure; and preferred buying, selling, and managing style. (If you'd like a self-scoring copy, please contact me. Cost is $12.)

Each of us has a preferred set of behaviors. There is no right or wrong, good or bad styles. But there are some styles that fit together better than others. Knowing your behavioral tendencies and adapting to your customer's preferences allows you to improve that fit.

Clues To A Customer's Profile

Which of these descriptions fit your customer?

Dominance Behavior. These results-oriented people are quick, decisive, want to remain in control, and may be curt.

Influencing Behavior. Influencers enjoy being involved with people. Influencers like being recognized by others and fear the loss of that acceptance or approval. An Influencer doesn't like detail or working alone but is often quick to see the possibilities in an idea or new approach and to say, "Let's do it." The Influencer responds best to ideas that do not carry a lot of detail with them and which are supported by the endorsements of others.

Steadiness Behavior. Some people exhibit Steadiness tendencies. This person doesn't like change or having to make decisions quickly. He or she requires lots of reassurance that it's the right decision and lots of personal attention and support. If you pressure Steadiness types, they will become even more indecisive. With patience and support, they can be encouraged to move toward the recommended change. Once they embrace something, they will be uncritical and unswerving in their support.

Conscientious Behavior. Like the people who exhibit Dominance behavior, the Conscientious focuses on the task at hand and shows little interest in the people side of the issue. Where the Dominant is quick to decide and impatient with details, the Conscientious people can't seem to get enough details and may, at times, want to study an idea to death. They are most concerned about making an incorrect decision and can be very stubborn if you push them to decide when they haven't studied something thoroughly.

See the chart on the next page for how to recognize and work with Dominant, Influencing, Steadiness, and Conscientious behaviors.

How To Recognize And Work With Dominance, Influencing, Steadiness, and Conscientious Behaviors*

	Verbal cues	Nonverbal cues	Will respond best if you:
Dominance Behaviors	Gets right to the point Avoids small talk, personal references Speaks rapidly Strong voice, possibly even loud Lots of voice inflection Controls conversation Delivers a lot of information May not listen attentively May interrupt Asks "what" questions	Closed posture (arms folded) Sits behind desk Face impassive, hard to read May not smile Brisk, formal Impatient, wants to get to bottom line	Give them options Provide an efficient solution
Influencing Behaviors	Verbal, emotional speaker Open and approachable Easily distracted Interested in making small talk Concerned about feelings; hears emotional voice tones Asks "who" questions	Open posture Smiles easily May prefer to eliminate desk barrier Lots of gestures	Provide lots of testimonials Save them personal effort
Steadiness Behaviors	Slow, even tentative speech Soft voice, lacking in expression Questioning, perhaps apologetic Uses words that emphasize feelings, stability, cooperation Asks "how" questions	Listens attentively Open posture Shows feelings on face Casual	Give them lots of personal attention Assure them of stability
Conscientious Behaviors	Asks a lot of questions Demands documentation, proof Seems unwilling to be convinced Seems hesitant to commit or decide Asks "why" questions	Closed posture Little facial expression Matter-of-fact voice tone Reveals little personal feeling or response	Use logical approaches Show evidence of quality and accuracy

*Based on The Personal Profiles System®, a copyrighted instrument of The Carlson Learning Company.

MATCHING THE COMMUNICATION STYLE OF YOUR CUSTOMER

You also connect to customers and prospects at the nonverbal level. To do this effectively requires reading the communication styles of the person to whom you are talking. Understanding their behavioral styles will be a good start.

Nonverbal cues govern your first impression with a client or customer and set a tone for the rest of the meeting. Without mimicking to the point of calling attention to what you are doing, notice whether your customer is:

- talking softly or loudly
- talking rapidly or slowly
- sitting formally or in a relaxed fashion
- moving around or staying in one place

Match as many of the nonverbal cues as you can without becoming awkward and you will notice a positive response from the person with whom you are communicating. They will sense a compatible rhythm in your communications style and will identify you as "someone like them."

Verbal Cues

Verbal cues come next. While talking with a customer, note whether:

- the tone is formal and impersonal or informal and personal—match this tone. Do not become personal and in-

---

Tips For Increasing Rapport With Customers

1 Try to schedule the meeting away from the customer's office, in a place where you will not be interrupted and where positional power is suspended temporarily. Meals or coffee offer well-tested occasions. If you are unsuccessful in hosting your customer for any of these, try to move the meeting into a conference room or other area away from the customer's desk to remove distractions.

2 If you were referred by a mutual friend or acquaintance, mention that referral and ask if the client knows why so-and-so referred you. You can take your lead on what to say next from the answer.

formal when the customer's words have not set such a tone.

- your customer says "I think" or "I feel." "I think" people are looking for facts, numbers, and supporting documentation. "I feel" people are looking for solutions that will address their emotional needs or the perceived emotional needs of others.

- your customer uses technical jargon. Follow the customer's lead. If technical jargon is a part of the conversation, and if you're comfortable with it, you can use it. Otherwise, explain technical concepts in a professional but understandable way if they are necessary to the conversation.

Once again, when you speak to them as they like to speak, you make them more comfortable. When you continue to build on this rapport, the relationship develops.

What Do Customers Want?

SURVEY

☐ Did an employee greet you within a minute of you're entering the store?

☐ Was the employee who greeted you able to answer your question or direct you to the appropriate associate?

☐ Did the employee thank you for your business?

The American Society for Quality Control (ASQC) asked 1,005 adult consumers what quality factors they considered important when purchasing a product or service.

For manufactured items, they ranked: performance, durability, ease of repair, service availability, warranty, and ease of use. Price was ranked seventh out of nine factors!

The same survey defined good quality service as courteous, prompt, responding to one's basic needs, and being provided by someone with a good attitude. Customers will be more forgiving of difficulties if they perceive that they are being treated with personal care and respect.

CUSTOMER NEEDS SHOULD COME FIRST

How do you treat customers in your business? Do customer needs take precedence over internal needs? Are you sure?

- If you design products and then look for customers, you are guilty of *inside-out* thinking.
- If you measure your progress in terms of how many products you sell or how

many units of service you deliver, you are product-centered, not customer-centered.

- If your business hours suit your schedule, rather than your customers', you are thinking from the inside-out.
- If you spend your customer-contact time touting the features of your products or the programs you can offer, you are thinking about your need for a sale, not your customer's need for a solution.

SUMMARY

The point of this chapter is that building rapport with prospects and customers will make you successful. Among the many ways to build rapport are thinking from the customers' viewpoint, focusing on value, not transactions, and going beyond customer satisfaction. Other ways to develop rapport include better listening, awareness of behavioral styles, and nonverbal communications. Many new behaviors can be used to improve your rapport with your customers. Start by sincerely placing the customer at the center of your focus and concern. Then gradually add new approaches that enhance your effectiveness.

10 ACTION SECRETS

FULL SPEED AHEAD

1 Develop a specific checklist to build relationships with people who buy from you. This could include a schedule of contacts, gathering information about their interests, etc.

2 Change something to make your company more convenient for customers. If you can't influence company policy, start by giving

customers your home phone number or starting your own fax newsletter.

3 List the ways you add value to your products or services.

4 Do some research on customers now. Start with an informal survey or by gathering testimonials.

5 Write down your policy for dealing with unhappy customers. Do you thank them when they complain? Sincerely? What are you authorized to do to make up for a mistake?

6 List the "moments of truth" when prospects or customers form an impression of your company.

7 How can you be a better listener? Write down good questions that you can use to build rapport and understand customer needs better.

8 Videotape yourself giving a sales presentation and list your nonverbal habits that you can improve.

9 Identify your behavioral profile and note the profiles you relate to most effectively.

10 Decide how can you work better with styles that are different from yours.

Chapter 8

THE INCREDIBLE POWER OF GIVE VS. GET

Jeff Locker

Jeff Locker, president of Speaking with Spirit!, is a speaker and productivity trainer, specializing in working with salespeople, managers, and executives, predominantly in the financial services industry. He has worked with some of the top corporations, including Xerox, Merrill Lynch, Guardian Life Insurance, Time-Life, Allstate, Rockwell International, and Fireman's Fund. He has spoken to, and trained thousands of, individuals throughout the US and internationally.

Mr. Locker speaks and provides training sessions for top sales producer conferences, leadership conferences, awards banquets, executive and manager conferences, management symposiums, and home office sales events. Each presentation is customized to meet the specific needs of the audience he addresses.

He has written articles for numerous domestic and international publications. His new book, *Teachings for a New World*, will be published Spring 1997. He belongs to various professional organizations including the National Speakers Association, National Association of Life Underwriters, General Agents and Managers Association, International Association of Financial Planners, Women's Life Underwriters, and Meeting Planners International.

Jeff Locker, Speaking with Spirit!, 52 Halyard Road, Suite 111, North Woodmere, NY 11581; phone (516) 791-3457; fax (516) 791-2177.

Chapter 8

THE INCREDIBLE POWER OF GIVE VS. GET

Jeff Locker

"The same level of thinking that got you to this point in your life can't possibly be the same level of thinking that will get you to the next point in your life."
—Albert Einstein

Marketing, prospecting, selling, life...they all boil down to relationship building.

"Give vs. Get" is an incredibly powerful concept I use as a productivity trainer and motivational speaker. It is the one thing that will most quickly helps you create strong long-term relationships with just about every person you meet or with whom you want to do business.

CHOOSING A MARKET TO BE INVOLVED WITH— THE FIRST STEP

The concept of Give vs. Get fits right in with identifying and choosing your market. I am a big proponent of a concept called "niche market focus and saturation." Often I see sales-people wasting their marketing efforts in a shotgun, general approach. In each market, they are recreating new efforts. They don't have today's efforts tie right in with yesterday's and the day before's, etc.

Realize the power in being perceived as a specialist versus a generalist to a particular market. Identify a marketplace or industry that has a need for the product or service you offer. They must have the financial wherewithal to afford this product or service and they must be the type of people with whom you can visualize yourself spending large amounts of time.

Find Industry Associations

The industry or marketplace you choose should have an association that unites the members, either in your local area, regionally, or nationally. It is very helpful if the organization has trade journals or newsletters that are read by the members. Additionally, you should find out if the organization allows associate or affiliate members to join their association.

Trade Group Newsletter

MARKETING WITH "SOCIAL PROOF"

One way to determine some of these potential marketplaces is to look through your existing client files to see if there are any industries or marketplaces that you have already worked with that might fit these criteria. This is called "Marketing with Social Proof." The concept is that you may have already created the basis for potential markets without even realizing it.

Often when we go through our existing client files (as you will do in the "Top 50 Existing Clients Exercise" later in this chapter), we begin to see existing client marketplaces that will fit our profile. Being able to utilize these existing clients as "social proof" is very powerful.

Social proof alleviates the sell portion of the relationship-building process. Instead of hearing from you how great you are and what a fabulous job you believe you can do for them, prospects hear these exact same things from someone they know and with whom they already have a relationship. When prospects or "suspects" hear these claims from you, they filter your statements through a screen that says, "Well, you're just trying to sell me something." They disregard about 50% of what you say.

Being able to use your social proof in conversations with prospects and suspects also answers one of the common unspoken objections that exists in the minds of many people you approach to do business. They think, "What do you know about *my* specific needs? What do you know about *my* industry or specific market needs?" Being able to begin your conversations with how you have already helped all your current clients who are in the same business is very powerful. This will drastically cut down the time it takes for prospects and suspects to want to do business with you!

A Market Survey

Existing clients are also prime candidates for you to approach to do a market survey to find out more about additional nuances of their markets. (See the form on the diskette at the back of this book for an example.)

This market survey will provide answers to questions about your prospect's or client's industry, such as whether affiliate members are allowed to join their industry association, or where and when meetings are held locally or regionally, who is the membership chairman to talk with about joining, whether they have a trade journal or publication that the members read, etc.

You'll want to identify more than one potential market for two reasons. First, you may not feel an affinity, a chemistry, or a fit with the people in a particular market once you start spending time around them. The other reason stems from the adage, "Don't put all your eggs in one basket." I have watched people put all their efforts into one marketplace, but after becoming part of the industry, they wind up with nothing. In each case, timing and unforeseen occurrences

Don't Put All Your Eggs In One Basket!

caused the industry or marketplace to wind up in trouble. To alleviate the possibility of this occurring, once you have determined a few potential markets that fit your criteria, choose one as a primary market, one as a secondary market, and a third as a backup. Spend time in these markets accordingly.

Membership Roster

Darrell Amalluh 1718 Lynwood Perkins, NV 87123 (555) 555-1288	Cynthia Coldwater 92 Del Mar Ave. Mattis, CA 91111 (555) 555-2109
Keith Anastasi 537 S. Fourth Ave. Bell, MS 38888 (555) 555-7929	James Cullen 977 Davis Dr. Surrey, OK 79284 (555) 555-2983
Rodney Bell 3817 W. Biddison Grove, FL 32100 (555) 555-2899	Kim Daworth 11 Roxie Blvd. New York, NY 10022 (555) 289-6663
James Brocco 32 Chestnut St. Merr, IA 50973 (555) 555-3924	Joseph Downey 22 Deist Road Fern, OR 92888 (555) 555-0165
Charles Carney 8500 Fulton Lane Storr, MO 63943 (555) 555-8923	Ellen Dulles 9 Rustin Lane Elk, NM 83928 (555) 283-4382

Join And Give

Begin with your primary market and join its association. Once you join any association or organization, what is the first thing you receive as a new member? Right, the membership roster. Now, here is where you need to use restraint. Don't make the fatal error that salespeople often make when they first join a new association. They begin mailing and marketing to every name in the membership directory. Do you think this fits under the category of "Give" behavior or "Get" behavior? It's pure unadulterated Get!

The Give way to approach this same situation is to position yourself as a resource. Go to your first meeting or event and ask some key members what they believe are some of the problems that the association or organization is currently experiencing that you could potentially help them resolve. I'll tell you one problem that almost every organization or association is experiencing that you could help greatly with: membership.

Affiliate yourself with the membership committee as soon as possible. Begin by talking to prospective new members about the benefits of membership.

An Insurance Example

As an example, I recently had this experience with Tony, one of the life insurance producers with whom I was working. He decided he wanted to work with restaurant owners in his local area, so I suggested he join the local restaurant owners association. Once he joined, he received his membership directory. He began to salivate and wanted to immediately start a marketing campaign. I had to hog-tie him and muzzle him to keep him from doing it. Instead, I got him to join the membership committee. As it turned out, the association was in the midst of a membership drive so they were delighted when Tony offered his help.

Tony began to spend all his spare time calling on nonmember restaurants and talking to restaurant owners about the benefits of membership in the restaurant association. Their first question to Tony was usually, "What do you sell?" His standard answer was "I'm a life insurance salesperson, but that's not what I am here to talk to you about today. Let's talk about the benefits of membership." He was so successful that over the next six weeks he signed up more new members than anyone had ever enrolled.

Tony and his wife won a weeklong cruise to the Caribbean based on his membership work. The association was so pleased, they also invited him to join the membership committee and everyone began to talk about him as the "membership machine."

New Friends. When each of these new members came to the meetings every month, who was the only person in the room they knew? Right. Tony. And, he would take them over and introduce them to the chapter president and other officers. He was their first exposure.

Tony ended up doing an amazing amount of business with these restaurant owners. He was a resource to them; then he became their friend. When people need something that their friend or resource sells, they buy it from him. As an added reward for his Give behavior, Tony was eventually named sole supplier of insurance, benefits programs, and group health for the entire association.

SELLING FROM GIVE VS. GET

"The Incredible Power of Give vs. Get" is the one thing that can separate you from the pack faster than most anything. Do you think the average salesperson comes from Give first or from Get, Get, Get???

If you said Get, you are 100% correct. The average sales professional meets a prospect for the first time and sees dollar signs on the person's forehead! The salesperson thinks, "How much money am I going to get from selling this person something?"

When you come from a what-you-can-Get-for-yourself perspective, you project a certain energy. It's the energy of a salivating dog—a Pavlovian dog after the bell has rung! You may not give your prospects and suspects credit for a lot of things, but the one thing you had better give them credit for is knowing whose best interest you truly have at heart!

What Prospects Want To Know

Let me share with you the three questions people ask themselves about you when they first meet you in an opening interview:

#1   WIIFM (What's in it for me?)

#2   Why you, why your company? (Why would I want to buy something from you and why would I want to buy something from your company?)

#3   And, #3 is for all the marbles: Whose best interest do you have at heart? (Are you more interested in helping me solve my problems and satisfying my needs, or are you only interested in the money you might get from selling me something?)

Here's the important thing to ask yourself. If their answer to the third question is that they believe you are only interested in the money you might make (the Get), do you think for one minute that you are going to get very far with them? No shot. But some of them will let you get to first base. They will use you for what you are worth and then will buy from someone they believe cares about them.

BE A RESOURCE

This is where the Give vs. Get philosophy comes in. Focus on what you can give to people in a way that is over and above your core products and services. Position yourself as a resource to

"The most powerful way to network is to enhance the revenue of opinion leaders. Realize that before receiving business-related endorsements, you must first 'send business.'"
—Thomas J. Stanley, *Networking With the Affluent and their Advisors*

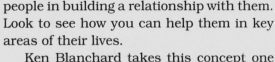

people in building a relationship with them. Look to see how you can help them in key areas of their lives.

Ken Blanchard takes this concept one step further. He talks about why creating satisfied customers is no longer enough. Instead, we must turn our customers and clients into "Raving Fans."

"People don't care what you know, until they know how much you care."

—Ken Blanchard,
The One Minute Manager

The key is to be viewed as a resource to people we meet and help them in ways that have nothing to do with our core products and services. When you are a resource to people and give to them in this manner, they become Raving Fans. They are out telling everyone about you as if you were a great movie they had just seen or a fabulous Italian restaurant they had just found.

Now I'm sure that it wouldn't break your heart if your best clients were out telling everyone they know and meet about how you are the best thing since sliced bread. This comes from focusing on "Give vs. Get" in every aspect of your business life.

Give, Give, Give!

Each time you are in a position to choose whether you come from Give or Get, choose to focus on how you can give to that person. What can you do to help that person in a way that has nothing to do with how you get paid? Focus on Give, Give, Give.

Some of you might be saying, "That's easy for you to say, but I've got a mortgage payment, credit card debt, a car payment, and three hungry teenagers. I've got to focus on what I can Get."

Let me share something with you that one of my early mentors, Zig Ziglar, taught me 18 years ago. He said, "You can get everything in this world that you want if you're willing to help enough other people get exactly what they want...FIRST." I say this to myself seven to eight times a day to keep from ever looking at people as having dollar signs on their foreheads.

All that is necessary for you to implement this is to first believe that Give vs. Get is the way that will help you build stronger, longer lasting relationships that will convert your satisfied clients into

Raving Fans. The more that people feel you are interested in helping them solve their problems and satisfy their needs, the quicker they feel comfortable with you and will buy from you.

NETWORKING FROM GIVE VS. GET

A powerful way to utilize the concept of Give vs. Get is in networking. When you meet someone for the first time, work to find out how you can be of assitance in ways that have nothing to do with your core products and services.

Let's say this weekend I'm at a party and I get into a conversation with somebody. In networking from Give vs. Get, what I want to do is ask some questions about their business. Let's say the man I'm talking with turns out to be an architectural engineer. I say to him, "You're the first architectural engineer that I've had a chance to speak with. Tell me a little bit about your business."

Here's where the networking from Give vs. Get comes in. I say for example, "I'm in the financial services industry. I work with business owners of all types. What type of people might you get value out of being introduced to? What type of people could I introduce you to where both you and they would get some value?"

I'll guarantee nobody else at that party asked that kind of a question. I will try to get together with this individual at a later time to discuss some of the things I might be able to do to help him. In networking relationships, you want to be looked at as a resource. You want to try to help in specific areas, like building your new contacts' busi- nesses, that have nothing to do with your core product or service.

Introduce Others

You can start to show your "Give" attitude by introducing a new contact at a networking group or party to people right there. If you're well established because of your giving to the group, you can at least introduce these new contacts to the officers, if not to a possible customer, immediately.

How To Be A Resource

Tom Stanley—who specializes in working with the affluent marketplace—tells us that when we are looking to be a resource to business owners (and professionals in particular), there are two main areas on which to focus. The first is to help them generate revenue, and the second is to have empathy for their problems.

Stop and think about it. What's the most important thing to the average business owner or professional? Generating revenue. So as a resource, you want to help generate revenue through referrals, direct business, or other means.

The second thing you can do is to have empathy for their problems. Everyone wants to be understood. Being able to do this for people puts you head and shoulders above the average producer. It also helps in creating Raving Fans.

Once we get to be a resource to people, they start to become excited referrers. Stop and think about how this relates to networking from Give vs. Get. I ask this architectural engineer, "Who could I introduce you to?" He tells me, and then I go out looking for some of these people. I bring him one or two potential clients.

What do you think he starts to believe about me? That I'm interested in him; I'm interested in giving to him. What starts to happen is the law of reciprocity. He quickly realizes that he's going to need to reciprocate in some fashion and bring me some people to work with or I may not continue to look out for him in the same way.

TOP 50 EXISTING CLIENTS EXERCISE

Let's take this resource concept to the next level. I have an exercise that has been successful for the people with whom I work. It's called the top 50 existing clients' exercise.

Go through your existing client files and pull out the top 50 clients with whom you've worked. What I mean by the top 50 are the clients with whom you have the best and closest relationships. These are the ones whom you've done the most business with, or whom you feel the most affinity for.

If you haven't been in business long enough to have 50 such clients, it can be the top 30, or top 20. The number isn't important. If you've been in the business long enough, make it 50.

I want you to put down their telephone numbers and industry affiliations on your list. Then, prioritize the list from the warmest and fuzziest of the 50 all the way down to the coldest of the 50, which is still pretty warm in relation to your other clients.

Start to look at this list in two particular areas. The first is as a prime list to go back to and ask for referrals. The second is something called "cross fertilization of existing clients" that is an extremely powerful concept in being a resource.

Client Cross-fertilization

I recently had a salesperson in New York City who did this exercise. When we looked at his list, we saw #5 was a real estate developer who was just completing a very large hotel renovation project in the city. We looked further down on his list and at about #15 was the CEO of one of the largest advertising and public relations agencies, specializing in real estate development projects.

We scheduled a luncheon with the four of us. We sat down, made introductions, had a very nice lunch, and they wound up being able to work together.

Over a six-month period of time, more than $200,000 worth of fees were generated for the public relations firm for an extremely successful launch of the hotel project. That's cross-fertilization.

Who do you think got the kudos for all the value and ben-

Provide Social Value

Another way to connect with people is to help them with their personal interests. Harvey Mackay provides a list of 66 things to learn about prospects and customers. One potential customer's son was a big hockey fan. When the boy was injured in an accident, Mackay got a hockey stick signed by the local professional players and delivered to the hospital. That personal gesture changed his relationship with the prospect.

efits that happened in this relationship? My client did. Do you think they still looked at my client as just a salesperson? No. He very quickly become a powerful resource and they became Raving Fans (or as I call them, "excited referrers").

Beyond the value of the referrals and cross fertilization opportunities you have, there's another possibility. I have my producers add one additional thing to this list. I have them go back in their files and research the birthdays of these top 50 clients. The commitment is that once a week, they have a breakfast or a lunch with one of these top 50 clients for his or her birthday. This helps get their relationships to the next level.

IMMEDIATE REFERRALS FROM GIVE VS. GET

The concept of asking someone to whom you have just sold something for the names of additional people you can call upon to sell your products and services makes the average sales producer feel very uncomfortable. You have just earned a commission of $100 to $50,000. Now you are asking to get a name you can call to get another commission. No matter what your background is, you feel guilty with this type of an approach.

Such thinking is a "limiting mindset." This is a conversation we have with ourselves that becomes a rule that holds us back from doing something. In this case, it is asking for a referral.

Why Not Ask For Referrals?

There are many limiting mindsets that hold sales producers back from asking for referrals. These include: "If I ask you for a referral, you might not think I am as successful as I want you to think I am" or "People don't feel comfortable giving referrals; they don't want to sic a sales producer on their friends," or my favorite: "I'll wait until they are really, really satisfied with my product or service, then I'll ask." We all know when our time comes and they are nailing us in that wooden box, we think, "Gee, I never got those referrals from so and so." Not a very good time to remember!

The first limiting mindset that stops a lot of sales producers is, "If I ask you for a referral, you might not think I am as successful as I would like for you to think I am." To be rid of this limiting mindset, replace it with the empowering mindset that says, "One of the reasons I am so successful in this business is because everyone I work with wants to introduce me to the people they care most about who can benefit from the products and services I offer."

You Are A Resource

Can you see the difference? The first mindset sets you up to feel like you will look unsuccessful if you ask for referrals. The second mindset is that you are successful because you do such a good job for people. Thus, clients are anxious to introduce you to the people they know who you can help with your products and services.

Another limiting mindset that stops sales producers is the one that says, "If I ask for a referral, I may blow my deal. It's the closing interview, I have just made my presentation. They want to buy what I am offering. They have given me the completed application and a check, and now I'm supposed to ask for more names of people I can call to sell? I don't think so. They're happy and I have the check. I'll just get the heck out of Dodge City before they change their minds!"

New Mindsets

The key to feeling comfortable with the process of asking for referrals is to reframe the way you look at this whole referral issue. You must find a way to alter these limiting mindsets. One of my main mentors is a gentleman by the name of Og Mandino. Og wrote a must-read book for every sales professional entitled, *The Greatest*  *Salesman in the World.* It is a book about ten scrolls handed down from ancient times. Each scroll has a principle that will help overcome some potential limitation of human behavior. For example, "I will greet this day with love in my heart," "I will persist until I succeed," "I am Nature's greatest miracle," or "I will act now."

Og taught me many years ago that you cannot just eliminate a bad habit. The way to permanently put a bad habit to rest is to replace it with a good habit. It is the same exact procedure when we are talking about stopping a limiting mindset. To rid ourselves of a limiting mindset for the long term, we must replace it with an empowering mindset.

What's A Referral Worth?

For instance, here's how to be rid of the limiting scenario of not asking for a referral when you make a sale. We must replace the limiting mindset, "If I ask for a referral now, I may blow my deal," with an empowering mindset that says, "The referral is as important, if not more important, than the sale itself."

Let me explain. Let's say your average commission is $500, and you close a sale and don't ask for a referral. What is the maximum amount of money you could expect to earn from that sale? Right, $500. You didn't need your calculator for that one!

But now, let's say you have the new mindset that says, "The

referral is as, if not more, important than the sale itself." And, an additional mindset that says, "I get two or three quality referrals from every person I work with." And, you get two or three quality referrals from those two or three people, and so on and so on. It becomes an infinite supply of referrals—very powerful!

Few people will choose to not buy from you because you asked to be of service to the two or three people in their life who they care enough about to want to see get value from your products and services. That rare person will wind up cancelling their order after the third month with some buyer's remorse story anyway. I don't know about you, but the type of salesperson I am, I would much prefer to have nothing from this person in the way of commissions, than to have my commission taken away from me after I have already spent it.

Referrals: Give Or Get?

The other main reason that most sales producers feel uncomfortable asking for the referral is that they assume it is a Get. No matter how hard they try, the whole concept makes them feel guilty.

I believe that the referral process is actually a Give not a Get. You must begin the process by truly believing that you did something beneficial and valuable for the person to whom you sold your products or services. Then you must look at them and ask yourself, "If I did such a good job for them and they are truly satisfied with me and our relationship, then I could give them more by helping their friends who could benefit from the products and services I offer." You would be giving them the opportunity to help someone they truly care about get the same level of satisfaction from you, your products and services.

"High-performance networkers gain endorsements for reasons that go beyond the basic product or service they offer. They do extraordinary things."
—Thomas J. Stanley, *Networking With the Affluent and Their Advisors*

Chatting Builds Connections

Research shows that friendly people talk about topics not directly connected to the business transaction at hand. This makes the interaction a little more personal. (Sports and the weather are innocuous topics.)

—Ken Blanchard and Sheldon Bowles, *Raving Fans*

SOCIAL MARKETING

Being able to get our relationships to deeper levels with people is crucial. It's all based upon strong client connections, getting people to look at us as more than just a sales professional. Social marketing means getting involved in nonbusiness areas with both our existing clients, and with people we would like to turn into clients.

I advise my clients to buy tickets to special sporting events and invite their existing clients and existing clients' friends. As an example, one of my producers arranges for a trip to take some of his top clients and their friends to the Super Bowl. He pays for the tickets, they pay for all their travel plans, but his people make all the arrangements.

Another client does that for the US Open Tennis Tournament in New York. He buys front row box seats and does the same type of process there. The key is to look for any opportunity to take one of these people to something special.

Impressing Prospects

It also stands to reason that the bigger the fish you are looking to catch, the bigger the bait. As an example, recently one of my producers was looking to woo an extremely wealthy individual. He knew the guy was a real hockey fan. So as the hockey season was winding down, he made arrangements through a ticket broker to get center ice seats for game 7 of the Stanley Cup Finals. He arranged for a stretch limousine to pick this individual and him up, and take them to the game. They sat through game 7 and had an incredible bonding experience.

About two months later, when a need arose for this individual to do some estate planning, my producer wound up writing about $200,000 worth of premium purely because he was looked at as more than just a life insurance agent. He was looked at as a resource. He became someone who was able to go above and beyond and be involved in a social situation with somebody, not just business.

Meet New People

I want you to start thinking the same way. I want you to start thinking of the words "being socially visible." Start to think about being involved in private country clubs. For instance, at golf or tennis clubs, you can start to meet some of these affluent individuals on a social basis.

Get more involved in your community. Maybe it's being involved in your church or your temple, or some other association like the Red Cross or the American Cancer Society where successful individuals give time.

The stronger you can build long-term relationships from Give vs. Get, the easier time you are going to have building your business to amazing heights. The key question to ask yourself is: How badly do you want to move your business to the next level?

If you want it badly enough, do what has to be done when it has to be done and don't take no for an answer, especially from yourself.

CONCLUSION: PUTTING IDEAS TO WORK

The words that you just read in this chapter could turn out to be worthless or they could turn out to be worth thousands of dollars for you.

One word is going to make the difference for you: Implementation! (See also Chapter 22.) Too many people read a chapter or book like this and then get wrapped up in their busy lives. They do nothing with the suggestions.

The other alternative is to commit right now to one idea that you are willing to take into your busy day and utilize.

Getting Help

You can undertake a process that will help you to continue this implementation in your life. It's called establishing a "requested accountability relationship" with someone you respect. The process is to find someone you respect. It could be someone you work with or someone in a completely different business. Call them and ask if they would be willing to establish an accountability relationship with you. Preferably it will be a two-sided accountability process. Each Sunday night you will speak by telephone and make a commitment to do certain marketing, prospecting, or relationship-building activities by the following Sunday evening.

Give the agreement some weight by putting up a cost or consequence for not fulfilling the commitment. It could be money (a large enough sum to be painful), or something else that would be painful to have to do or give up. The trick is to make the cost or consequence more painful than the activity you are committing to do.

To Thine Own Self Be True

Before I end this chapter, I would like to leave you with a gift. It's a gift that has been amazingly meaningful to me—a poem entitled "The Face in the Glass" that has been handed down through the generations. Unfortunately it was handed down anonymously so I can't give anyone credit for it. However, it is as powerful today as the day it was written.

The moral to this poem is To Thine Own Self Be True. Go to your nearest mirror, turn your eyeballs around, and look as honestly and openly as you possibly can into your life. Ask yourself, "Am I truly a Giver or have I thus far come from Get?" While this process I am suggesting may not be comfortable, I guarantee you it will be amazingly worth the effort. All that is necessary is for you to take the first step.

My wish for each and every one of you is successful implementations of these marketing ideas—and even more—

The Face In The Glass

When you get what you want in your struggle for self
    and the world makes you king for a day,
Just go to a mirror and look at yourself and see what that
    face has to say.

For it isn't your father or mother or spouse whose
    judgment upon you must pass,
The person whose verdict counts most in your life, is the
    one staring back from the glass.

Some people might think you're a straight shooting
    chum, and call you a great guy or gal,
But the face in the glass says you're only a bum if you
    can't stare it straight in the eye.

That's the one you must please, never mind all the rest,
    that's the one with you clear to the end,
And you know you have passed your most dangerous
    test when the face in the glass is your friend.

You may fool the whole world through the pathway of
    years, and get pats on your back as you pass,
But your final reward will be heartache and tears if
    you've cheated the face in the glass.

---

health, happiness, prosperity and, most importantly, inner peace and mental well-being.

10 ACTION SECRETS

FULL SPEED AHEAD

1 Focus on building multiple relationships in a few markets. Become part of these markets by joining the associations and contributing.

2 Study each marketplace you work in. Use a survey to gain more information.

3 Join the membership committee of each group and use your sales skills to recruit new members.

4 When you meet people, work on what you can do for them before you ask for anything. Ask them who they'd like to be introduced to.

5 You can immediately help others by generating revenue for them, or giving them human warmth, acceptance and empathy. Find out about their personal interests too.

6 Look for links you can create among your clients that will help them both.

7 Get comfortable asking for more referrals. If you truely help others, you are a valuable resource they can share.

8 Use the old traditional "tickets to events" for clients who like sports or other events. Make it a special outing. Go with them to build your social relationship.

9 Join new groups where you'll meet successful people you could work with. Donate time to charities.

10 Pick at least one idea to implement now. Look for a partner so that you can reinforce each other for keeping a regular program of new action going.

Chapter 9

LOVE THEM OR LOSE THEM:
Customer Retention in Action!

Lynn M. Thomas

Lynn M. Thomas
is president of 21st Century
Management Consulting. Her
firm specializes in Customer
Retention, which plugs the "leaky customer bucket" and thereby increases a
company's profitability.

Ms. Thomas' unique skill set stems from her formal training as a tax attorney
with Arthur Andersen & Co., and then her work with Bank of Boston, initially as
a Private Banker and then as a Change Agent for a massive reorganization of
an 1,800-person division.

Ms. Thomas works with companies of all sizes, in diverse industries
including accounting, advertising, auto services, education, finance, high-
technology, hotel, insurance, law, real estate, restaurant, and oil and gas
management. She employs an innovative and successful methodology, using a
three-pronged approach to *attract, retain,* and *reclaim* a company's most
profitable customers.

Ms. Thomas has written articles for numerous publications in many industries
and is a nationally-known speaker on customer retention.

Ms. Thomas serves on the Omega Board of Directors.

Lynn M. Thomas, 21st Century Management Consulting, 56A Charlesbank Way,
Waltham, MA 02154; phone (617) 899-4210; fax (617) 899-0707.

Chapter 9

LOVE THEM OR LOSE THEM:
Customer Retention in Action!

Lynn M. Thomas

"An effective salesperson first seeks to understand the needs...of the customer."
—Stephen Covey

Here is the bottom line of customer retention: You have a choice—one choice. Love your customers or lose them. Period, end of story!

There is no longer any middle ground or gray area. Customer retention is a 100% passionate commitment to keep your customers for life. This will dramatically improve your profitability and your enjoyment of your business.

Are you 100% committed to your customers? If so, read on. If not, are you willing to be?

Customer retention is not customer satisfaction. It is not customer service. Customers can be well serviced and satisfied, and still leave because they receive a better offer elsewhere.

Customer retention is moving from customer satisfaction as a company's goal to customer profitability: Who are the customers that your company can serve profitably?

THE NEW GAME OF BUSINESS

There is a set of new rules in the game of business:

1 **Businesses are experiencing an epoch change.** They happen every hundred years. The last one was the industrial revolution. The manifestation of this technology revolution is downsizing which will be continuous and permanent. Why? Because the basic pyramid structure of how businesses operate has become archaic. It is evolving to a more flat and market-driven structure which will resemble the structure of DNA.

2 **There is a limited supply of customers.** In the 1980s, many companies operated on the assumption that there was an unlimited supply of customers. It wasn't true. The customer of the 1990s is worth his or her weight in gold.

3 **Time is today's precious commodity.** We are working approximately 10 more hours a month than we did five years ago. Customers want to speak with us when they want to, not when it is convenient for us.

4 **The buying cycle is becoming longer, which increases customer acquisition costs.** Despite the hurry-up pace of today, customers often take longer to make a decision. Customers may take longer because their attention is divided among competing options, or they may take longer to change vendors.

5 **Mass production is being replaced with mass customization.** For example, Seiko makes 3,000 watch bands, M&Ms are sold in 88 different packages, and Nike makes over 400 different types of sneakers. These companies are making a product for a smaller group of people—mass customization.

6 **Automation and technology are permanent new methods of organizing and communicating large amounts of information.**

"Tomorrow's share-of-customer market will... sell [one] customer as many products as possible over the customer's lifetime."

—Don Peppers & Martha Rogers, *The One to One Future: Building Relationships One Customer at a Time*

Customer Retention And Growth

What do the companies on the New York and American Stock Exchanges that had double digit growth for ten or more years have in common? They have all had 90% or higher customer retention rates.

WIN BY RETAINING CUSTOMERS

Why is customer retention important? The top five companies in any industry have a 93–95% customer retention rate.

Most companies have a 78–82% customer retention rate. If average companies are annually losing approximately 20% of their customer base, that means over 50% of a company's customer base will be replaced every two-and-one-half years.

This is an inefficient and very expensive way to operate. It is not necessary to have a "leaky customer bucket." Plug the holes and you'll see your customer bucket expand.

A study of 17 different industries determined what positively correlated with long-term profitability. It was not sales volume. It was not market share. It was not low-cost production. It was customer retention!

Customer retention was the sole correlation with long-term profitability. Yet, most companies measure sales, costs, and profits but *not* retention. I believe this is because the potency of retention is not well understood.

10 KEYS TO CUSTOMER RETENTION

There are necessary key points to understand customer retention. I'll discuss 10 here to help you get a basic grasp.

1 Retain your most profitable customers. The 20% of your customers that produce 80% of your revenue determine your company's long-term profitability. In contrast to the fascination in this country with sales as the way to produce a highly successful company, I view sales as a two-part process. The first is acquiring the customers; the second is keeping the customer. Since a customer is the most valuable asset a company ever creates, profitable selling is not "making a sale" but "creating a customer and keeping that customer for life."

Spending additional resources to secure your assets—your customers—is a prudent and economically sound investment. In turn, they will become more loyal and assist you as your *unpaid sales force.*

"Marketing is anything you do to get OR keep a customer."
—Michael Porter, Harvard University

2 **First, identify how many customer bases (homogenous groups of customers) your company has.** Then tier each customer segment "A," "B,"and "C." Every company has three customer segments, your A, B, and C customers. Your A customers are your most profitable and coveted customers. These valuable customers produce 80% of your revenue and will be the source of your company's growth over the next five years. Thus, it is imperative to spend 30–50% of your time and resources to attract, cultivate, retain—and if necessary—win back these profitable customers.

Since your company cannot be all things to all people, focus on what you do well. What do you do that "Wows!" your A customers? What keeps them coming back again and again and again? In other words, identify those customers you want to keep and go about the business of keeping them!

Customer Report Card	
Abbot Mfg.	B
James Rustin & Assoc.	A
ARC Consulting	A
T.R. Baskin	C
Craig Nestor	B
Austin Hopper Co.	A
Mac A. Katten	C
BenterRubin, Inc.	B

3 **Cut operating costs by increasing retention.** High operating costs are a symptom of a low customer retention rate. In service industries 30–50% of a company's budget is consumed

by "rework." Rework does not appear on the financials and thus is disguised in service business. Rework is:
- pricing and billing errors
- wasted time
- low employee morale
- excess supervision
- premium delivery (e.g., Federal Express)
- excess overtime
- decreased productivity
- losing customers and market share
- customer complaints
- excess field service
- angry customers telling 8–10 others

4 Measure customer lifetime value. We tend not to look at the lifetime value of a customer but at the annual revenue that they generate.

The more accurately you assess the true economic value of your customers, the easier it becomes to make better business decisions. Your company needs to roughly calculate the average lifetime value for an A, B, and C customer. Determine what an average A customer generates in a year. Then multiply that by the average number of years a customer stays with your business. This number will assist you in making more accurate, astute, and profitable decisions.

Repeat Customer Value

At Sewell Cadillac in Dallas, they know that the lifetime value of a customer can easily be $300,000. With that in mind, they go out of their way to provide little extras to make customers feel special.

Taco Bell has determined that a repeat customer is worth about $11,000 in lifetime total sales.

Xerox has learned that a *very satisfied* customer is six times more likely to repurchase Xerox equipment than a merely *satisfied* customer.

One study found that reducing customer defections by just 5% resulted in:

- an 85% profit increase in a bank's branch system,
- a 50% profit increase in an insurance brokerage, and
- a 30% increase in an auto service chain.

Achieving Breakthrough Service (Harvard Business School Press).

5 It costs a company five to seven times more to acquire a new customer than to retain an existing customer. With a longer buying cycle, the acquisition costs of customers continue to increase. It is becoming more urgent for companies to plug their leaky customer buckets. The steady stream of lost customers will place many companies in financial jeopardy.

6 Measure the Service-Profit Chain. The Service-Profit Chain is a fascinating concept which illustrates the interrelationships among profit, service, employees, and customers. Customer profitability is rooted in customer delight, which in turn, is rooted in employee satisfaction.

Why? Because the glue of any company is the relationships between its employees and customers. When an employee leaves, the customers' expectations and bonds of trust are broken.

One of management's primary goals must be to "Wow!" its employees. They, in turn, will Wow! their customers, producing high profits. Then the cycle repeats.

How does a company Wow! its employees?

First, it must truly empower them. Empowerment has been overused, so I want to clearly define it: Provide your employees with the tools, equipment, and training that they need to superbly serve customers without impediments from management.

Employees need to know how much time, money, and other resources are available for them to do what is neces-

The Service-Profit Chain

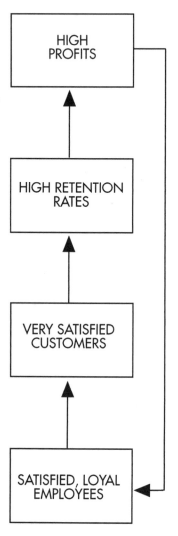

sary to serve and retain customers. Then get out of their way and let them Wow! your customers!

Second, create a win-win situation: Financially reward employees for higher retention rates. Retention bonuses have been used successfully by many companies to motivate and create employees who want to retain customers.

7 Work for referrals. What is the best source of your most profitable new customers? Referrals from your existing A customers.

Why? First, they are the least expensive way to attract new customers. This reduces your customer acquisition costs. These customers become almost immediately profitable.

Second, referrals have a 92% retention rate over two to three years versus 67% from any other marketing source. This 25% increase arises because they are prescreened by your A customers.

Since we tend to know people like ourselves, A customers will tend to know potential As; Bs will know more Bs; and Cs will know more Cs.

8 Thrill your customers. The goal of any company is to produce highly satisfied customers. They are six times— that is *six times*—more likely to repurchase, cross-buy, and refer new customers.

Statistics show that we repeatedly seek new prospects who are the least likely to become customers, are the most costly to acquire, and have the lowest retention rates. What a paradigm we are stuck in!

It is interesting to note that, on average, one out of 20 prospects will become a customer. One out of 10 former customers will become a customer. One out of six referrals will become a customer, and one out of four existing customers will buy additional products.

These new customers will, in turn, become loyal, be retained, and refer new customers. This

"It takes 'great service,' not just 'good service' to insure differentiation from competitors, to build solid customer relationships, to compete on value without competitng on price, and to inspire employees to create repeat business."

—Leonard Berry, *On Great Service*

perpetuates a very profitable cycle.

Satisfaction is no longer adequate. If your customers are merely satisfied, 50% will leave your company within two to three years. Satisfaction is a very expensive way to operate a business. Customers need to be delighted, astounded, and Wowed! to become highly satisfied customers.

Most companies have been striving to satisfy their customers. This goal is based on two inaccurate assumptions: that if a customer is satisfied, he or she will not only stay with us but also will buy again.

When AT&T was broken into the Baby Bells, it was puzzled why it was losing market share when 94% of its customers were satisfied. They learned that satisfaction is not enough. For instance, in the automobile industry, 85% of us are satisfied with our present cars and yet only 41% of us will buy the same car next time. Satisfaction does not correlate with retention. "Highly satisfied," which is also called "delighted," "astounded," or "Wowed!" does correlate positively with customer retention.

Ask Customers

The only way to know how satisfied customers are is to ASK them. When I have asked identi-

Tom Peters On Wow-ing Customers

In his book *The Tom Peters Seminar: Crazy Times Call for Crazy Organizations,* Tom Peters suggests that all organizations should be in the business of Wow-ing their customers.

He gives the example of how the respected healthcare futurist Leland Kaiser looks at healthcare delivery: "When I meet a friend who has just returned from a visit to the hospital, clinic, or doctor's office," wrote Kaiser in *Healthcare Forum Journal,* "I ask, 'Did you have a good time.' This is the same question I might ask a friend if she or he just returned from a trip to Disneyland. A visit to a healthcare facility should be a great experience."

* * *

Peters also recounts the tale of University of Texas marketing professor Robert Peterson who had studied customer satisfaction for years, but couldn't find significant correlations between customer satisfaction and repeat business.

Peterson was puzzled by the lack of relationship, but kept studying the problem. What he found was, that in order for a customer's experience to lead to repeat business, an emotional link must exist between the consumer and the product or service.

cal questions of management, employees, and customers, it was apparent that the internal staff knew only about 60% of their customers' perspectives, needs, and wants—and were blind to 40%.

Since the internal staff are not customers, they have not had the customers' experiences. This blindness is unavoidable. The only way to correct it is to actively and regularly seek your customers' opinions and experiences.

How can a company gather its customers' input? There are three qualitative methods to gather customer data: telephone, in-person interviews, and focus groups. The method needs to be tied to the goals of the company. Each method has different biases. In general, the more methods utilized, the more accurate the data.

A survey is the main quantitative method utilized to gather customer data. Most surveys are designed without adequate qualitative data. Thus, the results of the survey don't generate clear next-action steps. For example, if customers say the company needs to act more "professionally," what exactly are they requesting?

- Is it to be more accessible when the customer telephones?
- Is it to have more knowledgeable and experienced people?
- Is it that they do not wear appropriate business attire?
- Is it they do not shake the customers hand when they meet?

These different interpretations translate into different ways for the company to change.

> "If you ask our customers about SAS, they won't tell you about our planes or our offices....Instead, they'll talk about their experiences with the people at SAS."
>
> —Jan Carlzon,
> *Moments of Truth*

HOW CUSTOMERS JUDGE QUALITY

A company needs to identify its customers' "Moments of Truth" to be able to create highly satisfied customers and repeatedly reap the benefits of these efforts. A moment of truth is when a passenger pulls down the tray on an airplane and sees a coffee stain that should have been cleaned up and was not. What conclusions could a person draw from this specific piece of information? Some people may think that if the airline cannot maintain its trays, it is sloppy at all maintenance and probably does not maintain its engines! Therefore, the passenger may conclude that the airline is not safe and will choose to patronize other airlines.

Customers Overgeneralize

People overgeneralize all the time. How do we evaluate a new restaurant, department store, product, doctor, service station, etc.? We take whatever information we have and generalize it throughout a company.

Your customers are doing the same thing. You need to identify the four to five pieces of data that your A, B, and C customers are using to decide if they want to do business with your company. The As will likely differ from the Bs and the Cs. The reasons are not general, such as "good products." They are similar to the coffee stain—small and precise.

Ask Your Customers

Ask your customers, and listen carefully to their words. They will tell you why and how they make decisions about coming to, staying with, and leaving your company.

What is the overall reason that customers leave any business? It is the perception that no one cares if they stay or not. About 67% of customers

---

What Do Customers Want?

You don't know what customers want until you ask them. Sometimes the answers might surprise you.

Ken Blanchard, author of *The One Minute Manager*, worked with a bank to improve customer service. What did the customers want? They wanted tellers who smiled, referred to the customer by name, processed the transaction as quickly as possible, mentioned a non-business topic like the weather, and thanked them for their business.

We often assume customers want all sorts of fancy bells and whistles when all they really want is to be acknowledged and treated with respect.

leave any business because of the perception of indifference exhibited by some person at the company. This statement is based on three separate studies by *U.S. News and World Report*, *Fortune*, and the American Bar Association. It was not the costs, the results of litigation, or other factors. It was indifference.

Think of the last time you were in your grocery store, pharmacy, doctor's or dentist's office, etc. Did you get the feeling that they really cared whether or not you came back? Rather than genuinely saying something to show their gratitude for your patronage, businesses act indifferent and then wonder why customers leave. Do you show the same indifference?

9 Negative factors add up. Customers leave a business because they have experienced four to five negative events. Most customers say they leave because of price. Yet I have interviewed over 300 former customers of various businesses, and only two left solely because of price.

There are always other factors. These tend not to be mentioned because with price the salesperson cannot present a counteroffer. Thus the customer avoids a conflict.

We are loyal by nature. We do not want to find another dry cleaner, service station, grocery store, lawyer, etc. We have better and more rewarding things to do with our time!

This is also true for your customers. *Your customers want to stay with your company.* Do not create reasons for them to even think of leaving.

How can you do this?

Create Extra Positive Contacts

When a customer first purchases a product or service, the customer is 100% loyal. After that, every contact will either increase or decrease the customer's loyalty by 20%, depending if it is positive or negative from the customer's point of view.

Over long periods of time, negative events will occur. You need to proactively create positive contacts.

American Express, Polaroid, General Motors, and General Electric lead the way in creating customer contact programs. They have been inordinately successful, producing measured 15% to 401% returns on their investments.

These companies proactively call customers to ask how everything is going with their products. For example, General Electric calls 14,000 customers weekly and asks them about their experiences with their GE appliances.

"Hello, this is Bill at Fairview Auto. I'm just calling to see how you like your new car. If there's anything I can help you with..."

If you have bought a new car in the past few years, you might recall that about a week after your purchase, and then six months later, the car dealer called you.

The dealer knows nothing is wrong with the car. What are these car dealers doing? They want to increase your loyalty by building in positive contacts. This helps ensure that when negative events do occur, your opinion of the dealer will not fall so low that you are unlikely to repurchase the same make of car.

10 Complaints are gold mines. Complaints are pure gold! Ninety-six percent of all customers do not complain, they just walk away quietly. Only 4% complain. When a customer calls and complains, imagine that your customer is the spokesperson for 25 people, and you will have a more accurate perspective.

Love Your Complainers

Guess what? Complainers are your MOST loyal customers. When they complain, they are saying, "I do not want to leave your company; please help me stay." They cared enough to take the time to complain and have provided you with free market research. Give complainers the royal treatment: Taking the time to listen and remedy the situation will produce a Wow! for the customer.

In contrast, your least loyal customers are

"Complaints offer companies the opportunity to demonstrate their appreciation of, and interest in, the customer which can turn a disgruntled client into a satisfied, loyal, and vocal advocate."

—Janelle Barlow and Claus Møller, A Complaint Is a Gift

noncomplainers. Call your A noncomplainers. They may just about be ready to leave.

Make it easy for your customers to complain. Provide 24-hour hotlines. Place your telephone number on all correspondence. Staff telephone lines adequately to avoid long waits.

You want customers' input. In fact, you need their opinions to remain profitable.

> "If you're trying to set a goal that every customer service rep can aspire to, how about this: Solve every customer problem in one phone call!"
> —David Bowen, Arizona State University, co-author, *Winning the Service Game*

It Takes Empowered Employees To Wow Customers

Empower your employees to answer 90% of customer queries on-the-spot—no waits, return telephone calls, or transfers allowed. On-the-spot.

With time becoming a more precious commodity, customers have become less willing to wait for a response. Give them what they want and do it now.

Former Customers

How can you win back former customers?

Here are some powerful and proven techniques. First, when you know a customer is thinking of leaving or has decided to leave, immediately call him or her. Ask what it would take for the customer to continue to do business with you.

The second method is to systematically conduct exit interviews with all defecting customers. Probe underneath their initial responses to unearth their real reasons for leaving. By tracking the reasons and then remedying the root causes, you will lose fewer and fewer customers.

Third, continue to regularly contact former customers. At some point, they may become unhappy with their new supplier and be very open to returning to your company. About 30% of the former customers responded to my question, "What would it take for you to become a customer of XYZ again?" with "Just ask me. They haven't called, and thus they do not care."

Ask former customers for their advice, ask

them for the referral, ask them for their input—and ask them to come back.

IMPLEMENTATION SUGGESTIONS

1. List your top ten customers. Then call them and ask the three magic questions:

- What did I do well, that you would like me to do again?
- What could I do differently next time?
- If you could change one thing about our business, what would it be?

Record their responses. Then select the next 10 A customers and continue the process for about half of your As.

2. Select about five to ten objective criteria that determine who your A, B, and C customers are. Then segment the customer base into these categories. Ask the As what they need to be Wowed!, then the Bs, and then the Cs.

3. Calculate the lifetime value of your average A, B, and C customer. This will assist you in making more profitable business decisions.

Sample Programs

We have helped companies with many programs which have been successful in raising customer retention rates. These programs are simple and easy to implement and many have produced dramatic results. Here are a few examples:

Welcome Aboard Programs provide customer orientations. Think how many organizations have orientation programs. Colleges have welcome programs, companies have programs for new employees, hotels for new guests, and health clubs for new members.

You need to decide to which customer segments (A, B, C) you want to offer this program . Then create one that will Wow! your new customers and let them know how delighted you are to have them aboard.

Customer Contact Programs increase customers' loyalty by proactively contacting them when they expect to be contacted. Decide which customer segments you want to target.

Send a written survey or use focus groups to find out when, or for what events, customers want your company to call them.

Write out some possibilities and then let customers fill in the blanks. Some possibilities are:

- after a major complaint
- when their service person leaves and they are reassigned
- when they send something back
- when they move, etc.

Collect and analyze the results and then create your Customer Contact Program to address their needs.

Wow!-The-Customer Programs focus on what a company can do to Wow! its present customers, with a special emphasis on uncovering customers' emerging or unmet needs. This allows you to leap ahead of your competitors. You will have already identified and addressed customers' needs before customers and competitors even know they exist.

The best method to achieve these goals is to hold focus groups with present A customers. Gather and analyze the results, then implement what your customers want and what your company can achieve profitably.

Welcome Back Programs aim to attract back former profitable customers. This begins with a telephone call to your former customers to identify why they left and what it would take to regain their business. If possible, give them what they want and then make a big fuss when they return.

CONCLUSION

As mentioned in the beginning of this chapter, customer retention requires a 100% passionate commitment to your customers. Are you ready to get aboard the customer retention train that is leaving now?

Do you want to be way ahead of your competitors? If you keep on doing what you are doing, you will keep getting the same results. Be bold. Be daring. Take risks in proven new innovative areas.

Customer retention is the most potent and highly leveraged activity any organization can undertake. Waiting can be fatal, since time is no longer on your side. Do it and do it NOW.

FULL SPEED AHEAD

10 ACTION SECRETS

1 Calculate your customer retention rate. Calculate it for different types of customers and for different points in customers' histories with you.

2 Identify how many customer bases your company has.

3 Rate your customers as A, B, and C. Decide on the criteria for classifying them, including the amount of time they take, the referrals they bring you, and the ideas they give you for new products and services.

4 Break out your A customers who are worth the most to you. Decide what you can do to thrill them soon. Then do it.

5 Calculate the lifetime value of a customer.

6 Ask former customers why they left and probe under their initial responses. Make a list of the main reasons you lose customers. Look for "holes in the bucket."

7 Survey your employees about both their satisfaction and their suggestions to improve your customer retention rate.

8 Ask your A customers for referrals. If appropriate, reward them. (See also Chapter 12 on referrals.)

9 Find out the difference between a satisfied customer and one who loves you. Identify your moments of truth when customers or prospects form their impressions of your company. Do a customer survey.

10 Develop a list of things you can do to build up extra credit with your customers against those times when they are unhappy and don't tell you.

Bonus Tip: Work hard to get complaints. Have a 24-hour hotline. Consider paying customers for complaints.

Chapter 10

DON'T <u>CLOSE</u> THE SALE: <u>Open</u> <u>Up</u> The Customer

Stephanie Davis & Wajed Salam

Stephanie Davis is the president of Leapfrog Performance Systems, Inc., a training and consulting firm that helps companies increase sales, keep happier customers, retain higher profits, and develop better employees. She specializes in determining how you can *leapfrog the competition*—by jumping off the top of a success curve (before decline sets in) and onto a new one, with creative ideas, new strategies, and fresh growth. She stays on top of sociographic, demographic, and business trends that affect the marketplace mindset.

Ms. Davis has delivered thousands of speeches, and conducted hundreds of seminars throughout the US, Canada, and Southeast Asia.

Wajed "Waj" Salam is president of Foresight International, an international training and consulting firm with offices in Tampa and London. He is a peak performance consultant to individuals and organizations. He is frequently called upon to speak to and to develop companies' field sales teams. Before founding Foresight International, Salam was, for five years, the number one field sales manager and trainer for Anthony Robbins Seminars.

He has delivered over 3,500 talks to large and small businesses, educational institutions, and nonprofit organizations in North America and Europe.

Stephanie Davis, Leapfrog Performance Systems, Inc., 5973 Avenida Encinas, Suite 218, Carlsbad, CA 92008; phone (619) 438-4333 or (888) LEAPFROG; fax (619) 438-9596.

Wajed (Waj) Salam, Foresight International, 2202 West Azeele, Tampa, FL 33600; phone (813) 258-8744; fax (813) 258-8747.

Chapter 10

DON'T <u>CLOSE</u> THE SALE:
 <u>Open</u> <u>Up</u> The Customer

Stephanie Davis & Wajed Salam

The names of the marketing game in the 1990s and beyond are relationships and service...it takes time to nurture the customer relationships and render superlative service.
—Jay Conrad Levinson

Customers are tuning out marketing hype more than ever before. Salespeople don't seem to notice that nobody wants to be "closed" any more. But if you know how to earn customers' trust, you don't have to worry about closing—doing business together will happen naturally.

You've probably noticed that influencing people isn't getting any easier. Many customers today feel deceived, duped, annoyed, manipulated, and even "stalked" by sales and marketing executives.

Today, trying to influence people using *traditional* methods of persuasion is like trying to catch fish by flinging bait into a raging river.

Yet ineffective sales tactics are everywhere. If salespeople bothered to do a reality check on the effectiveness of their tactics, it would probably bounce!

The *good news* is, it's not your fault. You don't need to brush up on sales skills. (It would probably make things worse.) And you certainly don't need to scream louder, persist longer, or resort to hornswoggling. None of that will help.

The *bad news* is the game of persuasion *has* changed so radically that you'll have to learn some new rules.

MAJOR CHANGES IN THE MARKETPLACE

Here are a just a few of the changes and our recommendations for how to play by the new rules.

Change #1. Seeing Double

For every option, there is an equal or identical competitive option! Quality standards have raised the bar so high that almost all suppliers try to "offer the highest quality at the lowest price." Everything looks and sounds so similar that people think they are seeing double.

When asked to identify which product an ad campaign represented, consumers performed poorly. To make matters worse, other research has clearly shown that when a customer can't differentiate between two options, he or she suffers "analysis paralysis" and puts off the decision until different information becomes available.

Having a distinct personality is the best way to position yourself. You want your customers to feel that "people like them like stuff like this." An example is the large California furniture store called IKEA. IKEA projects a *persona* that appeals to people who like to be different, have fun, and make shopping an experience.

In contrast is the Levitz furniture store chain. The only persona that Levitz projects is as a haven for people strapped for cash who need to defer their payments for six months or more.

IKEA customers feel a bond with the

store, and often just "stop by" to see what's new. Levitz customers only think of the store if they are in immediate need of furniture and they see an ad in the newspaper.

Recommendation: You *must* find a way to differentiate yourself! Decide what niche (no matter how small) you can excel at, and find a way to creatively communicate it to the masses. (See other chapters for great ideas.)

Change #2. "Plethoriasis"

People are overloaded and overwhelmed with a plethora of options. In the last 10 years, "offers" have multiplied faster than rabbits, for example:

- The number of items now available in the average supermarket has tripled to over 30,000.
- Coupon offerings rose to 300 billion per year in the US alone.
- The number of messages the average person is exposed to each day has skyrocketed to 3,000 or more.
- We now have over 600 types of cars, and even 118 brands of vodka, to choose from!

Recommendation: Learn to think and communicate in "holographic soundbites." If you shatter a holographic film plate, each little splinter still contains the entire image. Make sure that every piece of your communication is complete and compelling so even if people only catch bits and pieces of what you're saying, they'll get the message.

Change #3. Procrastination Pays

Scarcity has always been a best friend of sales and marketing executives. However, "the price may go up tomorrow," doesn't pack a very powerful punch in a world where people know that competitors offer to "meet or beat any price."

One-of-a-kind designer clothes don't have nearly the appeal when knockoffs are sure to hit the streets within weeks. The latest greatest techno-toy loses its ability to excite when a more advanced version comes out within months.

The bottom line is that, today, procrastination pays. Why would anyone go through the agony of making a decision today—when the item will probably be on sale, out of style, or obsolete tomorrow?

Recommendation: When customers learn that you invented a deadline just to close the sale, they'll never trust you again. Instead, use only real reasons and personal conviction to move them to action. If you've established a good relationship, your advice will be welcome, and your passionate "pressure" will not be annoying. In the age of skepticism, never, never, never stoop to falsehood!

Change #4. "New And Improved" Is Getting Old

Although newness, freshness, and curiosity will always have their appeal, people are saturated. Nostalgia is popular because people yearn to go back to when life was less complicated, less confusing, and less frightening.

Recommendation: Don't tout how "new" your product or service is unless, #1—it really *is* new (no lying, remember?) and #2—you are certain that the "newness" won't tax their threshold for change. If you want to be on the safe side, focus on getting them *away* from boredom, pressure, unhappiness, etc., rather than *toward* what might be perceived as overwhelming new territory.

Change #5. Power Shift

In the field of persuasion, you used to be able to make an offer and the customers would come running. It was a sellers' market. Today, you have to make an offer*ing* at the altar of the almighty customer because the power has completely shifted! For every action, there is an equal and opposite reaction. Consider the following:

Action: Just after World War II, selling was easy. Customers were eager to improve their lifestyles and were easily dazzled by mesmerizing entertainers. The practice of selling the "pizzazz" became an art form. ➜ ➜ ➜ *Sales soared.*

Reaction: As products became commonplace, consumers began to tire of being "sold" with razzle-dazzle, and became concerned with differences and utility. ➜ ➜ ➜ *Sales began to decline.*

Action: Savvy salespeople switched from the dog-and-pony show to "features and benefits." They diligently pointed out how their features translated to benefits, and how those benefits would greatly enhance the lives of their prospects. If you could address the question, "What's in it for me?" it was argued you could score a touchdown every time. ➜ ➜ ➜ *Sales soared.*

Reaction: Alas, even benefits can get stale. Customers caught on and quickly realized that if it sounded good, it was probably hype. In a massive study conducted in the '70s and '80s, it was discovered that when salespeople named benefits—it *caused* objections! A salesperson or commercial mouthing, "You'll love blah blah because of blah blah blah…" causes the customer to think, "Yeah yeah yeah…sure…you don't *know* me!" ➜ ➜ ➜ *Skepticism rose; sales declined.*

Action: Most salespeople floundered in the face of this new customer resistance and upped the ante by making even bigger, bolder benefit claims. Savvy renegades discovered that by using consultative, or collaborative selling, they could uncover an individual customer's *personal* needs. By uncovering these personalized needs before starting the pitching process, they found they could bypass most skepticism because it's pretty hard for a customer to talk back to his or her own words. ➜ ➜ ➜ *Sales soared.*

Reaction: At first, customers liked the personalized attention. Then they realized that the questions helped "lead them to the slaughter," and took up a lot of their time. So they closed their mouths and minds and began to say, "*Just tell me what you've got; I don't want to answer any questions.*" ➜ ➜ ➜ *Sales declined.*

So here we are...in the age of skepticism. We want to personalize, but customers refuse to answer questions. They back talk to our benefits, distrust our claims, and resent our recommendations. And thanks to technology, they'll soon have the ability to block our contacts. Customers will be able to avoid any exposure to news, commercials, telephone calls, or sales calls in which they aren't interested. You will have to get their permission and, in many cases, *pay* them to listen to your pitch!

Recommendation: Make sure whatever you are selling is something that people want to buy. Then make sure you only talk to qualified prospects. Finally, master the art of "resonating" so that you can get people to open up to you. People will buy what they **need** from those who clearly know what they want. If they believe you *really* understand them, they will slam the door in everyone *else's* faces, and open it wide for you.

> "A consultant's problem-solving approach to selling requires helping customers improve their profits, not persuading them to purchase products and services....The ideal positioning for a consultative seller is *customer profit improver.*"
> —Mack Hanan, *Consultative Selling*

CHANGES IN CUSTOMER PSYCHOLOGY
Change #6.
The Spin Doctors Have Created Monster Customers

Thanks to millions of messages promulgated by the spin doctors of advertising, a generation grew up learning that they're "worth it" and that they can have it "their way" and that they can "just do it." Customer service slogans and mission

I WANT IT ALL

LIFE'S MENU

© 1992,1994 CHARLES BARSOTTI

statements have created customers who expect perfection...NOW. We now have seen a dramatic rise in selfishness, hedonism, and impatience.

The real Catch-22 here is that the same hedonistic and impatient people we're trying to please also work for us and wait on our customers!

Recommendation: Don't insult, annoy, or disappoint the customer! Use mystery shopper tests to ensure that your employees aren't scolding, annoying, or patronizing your customers.

One study done at a bank found that 41% of poor service incidents occurred as a result of impertinent employee actions. For example, tellers scolded customers for improperly completed deposit slips, and ridiculed them for not understanding that a 6% interest, three-month CD would not earn the full 6% in only three months.

If you don't have any employees to worry about, check your *own* speech patterns and written literature to be sure that nothing can be interpreted as patronizing or insulting.

Change #7. Social Saturation

When they needed advice, people used to ask a few immediate relatives and friends, and that would be it.

Today, thanks to fax machines, cell phones, e-mail, and the Internet, people have instant access to every person they have ever met and millions of people they don't even know.

In today's information age, people are checking with more people *before* deciding, and face a lot more potential criticism *after* deciding—so they're much more cautious as a result.

Recommendation: Realize that more and more people are consulting other people before they make decisions. In many cases, especially with technology, these advisors are young and savvy. (In 1994, kids influenced buying decisions in the US to the tune of $400 billion!) Put some serious effort into determining where your biggest enemies and allies are on all those "advisory boards" and strategize accordingly.

Change #8. Life's A Pitch

Benefit claims are so common, so inflated, and so pompous that even the truth sounds like hype. Very few people believe advertising claims anymore.

Members of Generation X (people born between 1964 and 1981), have made skepticism an art form. The first time they did what the TV told them to, and convinced mommy or daddy to buy them that special toy, *and it didn't change their lives like the ads promised*, a little light went on that said, "stuff they say on TV isn't really true." Generation X-ers learned to mistrust at an early age, and the mistrust runs deeper each day.

Recommendation: Try the truth. In fact, how about the *real* truth. Some of the most powerful ad campaigns and sales lines are brutally honest statements about the suppliers' intentions or about how "hype-ish" the world has become. You're better off saying, "*You know, this very well may not be right for you...*" or "*The bottom line is, we want your money, and you want to look good, so why not try our cool shirts?*" Blunt honesty will often beat out hollow benefit claims.

Change #9. Irrationality Is On The Rise!

Ten years ago, people made decisions in a reasonably rational fashion. More recent tests have shown that decision makers are using shortcuts that are very irrational.

One of the most interesting decision patterns is that people use entirely different criteria to choose between options than they do to reject an option. Take

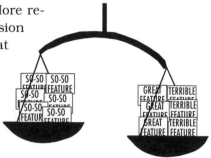

the case where Option A has six "pretty good" features, and Option B has three fantastic features and three terrible features. Research shows that when asked to *choose* one of the options, the majority of the people will choose B.

The shocking thing is that when asked to *reject* one of the options, the majority will *reject* B!

The reason for this paradox is because when the challenge is framed as *choosing*, people use the shortcut of only comparing the positive features. The three fantastic features weigh more than the six "pretty good" ones, so they choose B without even considering the negative features! Conversely, when the challenge is framed as *rejecting*, people take a shortcut and focus on the negative features. The three terrible features outweigh the six "pretty good" ones and B is rejected.

Recommendation: Master the art of framing! Study your strengths and weaknesses, and those of your competitors. If you have a few negatives, but your strengths far outweigh your competitors', focus your efforts on framing the customer's decision as *choosing* between you and your competition. On the other hand, if a competitor outshines you in many areas, but has a glaring weakness, frame the customer's decision-making process as *rejecting* the worst option. Only give the customer what he or she wants and nothing more.

Additional Features Frame Choices

Another interesting study showed that when faced with two options that weighed equally in the mind, a person will suffer analysis paralysis and defer the decision. But if one of the options suddenly develops an "additional feature" (i.e., one store decides to throw in a free toaster with the washing machine), *the decision will be made based on the reaction to the additional feature!*

In other words, if the person likes and wants the toaster, they will go for that option, but if they don't like the toaster...they'll buy the other washing machine!!!

The mind was deadlocked until the toaster came along. The toaster "framed" the decision and biased the mind to *choose* or *reject* based on its merit alone since the other features had already been determined to be equal.

Whatever you do...*don't give them anything they can reject!*

Change #10. Overdosing On Overdrive

With lives getting more and
more complicated, and less and
less secure, people's attention
spans have shrunk several sizes!
People are working more hours,
taking on more projects, getting
more involved in their communities, and if they are parents,
signing their kids up for several
activities each. Stress claims have
more than tripled, and over 50% of work-
ing women report "extreme stress." If people can't even handle what
they've got on their plates, why would they want any more?

The average American:

- hears 3,000 "messages" a day (600 of which are advertisements)
- gets interrupted 73 times a day
- commutes 45 minutes every day

In a lifetime, consumers will:

- spend 8 months opening junk mail
- spend 2 years trying to reach people who aren't in, or
  whose line is busy
- spend 6 months sitting at traffic lights
- spend 1 year searching for misplaced objects
- spend 5 years waiting in lines
- spend 3 years in meetings
- learn how to operate 20,000 machines
- watch over 120,000 hours of television!

Recommendation: If you want to get someone's attention,
you'd better have something *really* important to say. The average
person is already spoken for! Make sure you have a *very* compelling
or intriguing 10-second statement that will capture attention and
warrant further investigation. Become a master at being concise,
captivating, and compelling.

Change #11. Speed Decisions, Or Jury Bias

People are sorting information faster. They decide "for" or
"against" something in less than a minute.

Overloaded and overstimulated, people have learned the power of "remote control"—anything that does not capture their interest within seconds is zapped away. They *speed-sort* information and judge instantaneously; you get *instant approval* or *instant disapproval.* Research has revealed just how fast this judgment occurs:

- 18-36 seconds in-person
- 16-21 seconds over the phone
- after reading 11 words of a letter
- 9-20 seconds when perusing a packet of information
- 4-11 seconds when viewing a print ad

Even more shocking is how "set in stone" these judgments are. After making the initial decision, people actually listen and observe information differently. They are "biased" to prove that their initial judgment was correct. If a prospect decides "for" you in the first few seconds, you have a 93% chance of closing the sale. (Why only 93%? Because there's a 7% chance that you will say something stupid, or that the prospect will smell commission on your breath and run away.) But the really frightening thing is that if you get off on the wrong foot, you have a 99% chance of failure!

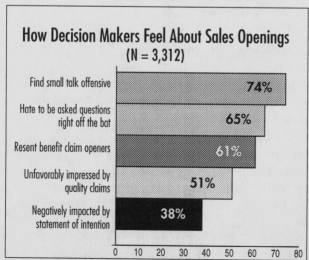

How Decision Makers Feel About Sales Openings (N = 3,312)

- Find small talk offensive — 74%
- Hate to be asked questions right off the bat — 65%
- Resent benefit claim openers — 61%
- Unfavorably impressed by quality claims — 51%
- Negatively impacted by statement of intention — 38%

Recommendation: The only reliable thing that gets you an instant "for" judgment is a resonating statement that rings true for them. *Scrap all other openings.* We cannot stress this enough! It takes a bit more work to resonate because you have to learn with whom you're dealing before you go into the meeting. However, the effort is well worth it.

Our research has shown that if you make an appropriate resonating statement, not only do all the walls of mistrust come tumbling down, but the reaction is nothing short of *gushing*. After hearing a resonating statement, a person may say, "*You're darn right! In fact, just the other day...*" (and proceed to spill his or her guts out to you). The net result of this interaction is that the person now feels a strong emotional closeness to you and senses "*You know me*"—which garners trust and earns you the right to influence.

With a new entrepreneur, just starting his or her business, the statement could be:

> "*There's nothing like being your own person...having the freedom to call your own shots and get the job done without anyone looking over your shoulder or restricting you....*"

With a computer programmer, you could say:

> "*It must be interesting...working through all those obstacles...it probably takes an awful lot of patience and concentration—I bet you hate getting interrupted!*"

Resonating Statements. The key to resonating successfully is finding a way to tie your statement into the moment. If you get a chance to start the conversation, you can comment on their occupation, and then deliver the statement as a sort of "thinking out loud" about what it must be like to be in their shoes.

If you *can't* start the conversation that way, then when asked what you do, or what you sell,

---

So How Do You Resonate?

You make a comment or statement that summarizes either their deepest desires, or their worst nightmares. The statement has to be specific enough that the person recognizes its truth intimately, but general enough that you won't be accused of being a spy.

Don't Be Self-Serving

The most important thing to remember about resonating is that the statement will backfire if it is in any way, shape, or form connected to your product or service.

you can turn the question around by saying:

*"Actually, what I do, isn't nearly as important as **why** I do it. My customers are business owners who believe that you gotta be your own person and have the freedom to call your own shots and get the job done—without restrictions. Is that true for you?"*

After they've agreed with your statement (and preferably gushed forth with examples), you can begin your Socratic questioning process by saying:

"Well, in order for me to determine if I can help you, I'll need to ask you a few quick questions. May I start by asking you...?"

The resonating statement goes with the customer, not the product or service. The same statement can be used on the prospect whether you are selling widgets, or trying to get a date. So a statement like, *"If you have a production line, you're probably experiencing a lot of wastage due to overruns, aren't you?"* will not resonate! In fact, it will send you off on the 99%-chance-of-failure-path with the majority of prospects.

A resonating statement is emotional because people react before they think. Emotions are faster than rational thoughts. A good resonating statement for a production manager might be something like this:

"It seems like you're really on the hot seat here. It's your neck on the line, and you deserve to have things go smoothly."

Strike a chord, hit an emotion, get them to **feel** one of their deepest feelings and show them that you empathize with them.

Change #12. People Are Lovin' Em <u>And</u> Leavin' Em.

Is brand loyalty dead? There is strong evidence that says it is. And there is strong evidence that says it isn't. Customers seem to be notoriously unfaithful—jumping from one supplier to the next depending on who's got the better deal going at the moment...or they are hopelessly devoted to their suppliers, through thick and thin in an almost zealous fashion.

AT&T and MCI routinely pay $50-$75 for customers to "switch back" while Harley Davidson owners wouldn't be caught dead on a Kawasaki. Retail establishments routinely offer to accept competitor's coupons and offers, while thousands of Starbucks' fans feel guilty and "unfaithful" if they drink any other kind of coffee!

Recommendation: If you don't make much of an impression, consumers have no loyalty whatsoever to you. Make a good impression, and consumers will want to settle down and stop shopping around. They will want to use you as their prime resource for any related products and services because they don't want to deal with the "wolves out there."

Will Decision Makers Switch Vendors?

Decision makers were asked: "Would you consider buying from anyone else?"

Bought because of FEATURES	Bought because of BENEFITS	Bought because of HELPFUL SALESPERSON
↓	↓	↓
94% Certainly	91% Probably	99% Absolutely Not!

SUMMARY

Your tactics are not the problem. Customers' reactions are the problem. Today, you must *earn the right to influence.* If you prove yourself worthy of being a consultant, *then* you can probe, prescribe, and even entertain your way to the sale.

How do you earn that right? You start from the inside-out. You have to *be* the kind of person who

Consultative Selling™ Is More Than Consulting

Mack Hanan, in his book, *Consultative Selling*, says you earn the right to work with people by bringing them proposals that provide a superior return on their investment.

you would want to do business with. Then you have to get inside the customer and establish that you can *empathize* with what it's like to be in their shoes.

Once you've resonated with empathy and they really "get" that you are the type of person (or company) who they can trust and want to do business with, you have a 93% chance of success with them.

The key to loyalty is to *resonate* when selling, and project a *persona* when marketing. A *persona* gets your customers to think, "*People like me like stuff like that.*"

How do you know if your company projects a *persona*? Ask yourself if a customer would ever say, "*I'm a [name of your company] kind of person.*" *Persona* is to a company what a personality is to a person. It creates relationships, rapport, and loyalty.

Think about Macintosh users. They are like a species all to themselves. They say things like, "*We 'Mac people' like to do things this way...*" They *love* to be with other "Mac users." Think of Harley Davidson owners. They could say, "*I'm a Harley kind of guy (or gal)*" and it would mean something. That's *persona*.

10 ACTION SECRETS

FULL SPEED AHEAD

1 Be **bluntly honest**. People can see through BS and appreciate being given credit for intelligence.

2 Be **choosy**. Don't waste your time with people who don't want or need what you're offering.

3 Be **compelling**. Study advertising. The basic formula for a compelling case is:

    A. What you have, own, or are is not O.K. You can do better.

    B. Doing (this) helps many people like you do better.

    C. Try it, you'll like it.

    D. Imagine the future the way it "ought" to be.

    E. This is guaranteed—you are safe. You've nothing to lose and **everything** to gain.

4 Be **credible**. Don't exaggerate claims. Don't use false scare tactics. In fact, downplay the **truth** if it seems too good to be true!

5 Be **concise**. Speak or write in "soundbites" that flow together but can be understood separately.

6 Demonstrate **competence**. Try to put a little sample of what you have to offer in everything you do so that people don't have to take it on faith that you can perform when the time comes.

7 Be **congruent**. Make sure that your actions are speaking louder than your words, and that they're saying the same thing!

8 Be a **consultant**. Don't run around with pre-determined ideas. Roll with reality. See what **is**, imagine what **could be**, and **then** design a path to get there.

9 Be **unique**. Work hard to develop a clear personality that your customers can understand, remember, and identify with.

10 Make sure your employees represent your values and position.

Chapter 11

THE CREATION FACTOR:
Beyond Customer Service

James A. Ray

James A. Ray
is a professional speaker, author, and business transformation consultant. During his 17
years of experience, Mr. Ray
has created Design Technolo-
gies™ to assist individuals and organizations in creating the lasting results they
desire.

After achieving top recognition at AT&T for sales and management, for
building and leading AT&T's National Telemarketing operation, and a four-year
alliance with the Stephen Covey Leadership Institute, Mr. Ray left to start his own
consulting practice. Since that time, Mr. Ray has worked with such companies
as Bell Canada, Boeing Aircraft, Dow Chemical, IBM, and Tropicana to create
outcomes based on timeless principles that foster creativity, leadership, communication, and teamwork within the organizational culture. He is a master of
motivational techniques to inspire individuals to action.

A member of the National Speakers Association, Mr. Ray launched his
speaking career after working with corporate leadership for over 15 years. He
is committed to balancing his motivation training with practical applications that
participants can immediately apply in their own work environments.

James A. Ray, Ray Transformation Technologies, 7319 Brodiaea Way, Suite 100,
La Jolla, CA, 92037; phone (619) 459-6909; fax (619) 459-9186; e-mail
JRaySpeaks@AOL.com; www.JamesRay.com.

Chapter 11

THE CREATION FACTOR
Beyond Customer Service

James A. Ray

"Success is dangerous. One begins to copy oneself, and to copy oneself is more dangerous than to copy others. It leads to sterility."
—Pablo Picasso

Nothing fails like yesterday's success.

Now, more than any time in our history, we must begin to adopt new approaches and new ways of doing business. Knowledge is doubling every three to five years. A good many of the things you will use on a daily basis in five years have *not even been invented yet.*

This may seem extreme, but check your own experience. Think about how many items have become commonplace in your own life that did not exist five to ten years ago. Those things that produced results in the past will no longer bring success in the present and into the new millennium. If you are running your life or your business as you did twenty, ten, even five years ago...you are going out of business.

To be outstanding in the marketplace of the future, we must continually "re-think our thinking" in every area of our lives...every moment of every day.

What does this have to do with customer service? I'm glad you asked.

THE WORLD HAS CHANGED

The world of yesterday is gone forever. No longer will customer service alone, or even excellent customer service, differentiate you in the marketplace. Again, we must re-think our thinking. Customer service and satisfaction have become the expected standard in the marketplace. To truly set ourselves apart from our competitors, we must go *beyond customer service*...to the "creation factor." How do we do this?

Excellence Is Not Enough

A multitude of individuals are excellent at what they do. They are excellent at customer service and satisfying customer needs. But 99 times out of 100, these individuals are not the people making the major impacts. The individuals who receive the accolades are those who are more than excellent...they are *outstanding.*

THE CREATION FACTOR

"Excellent" managers, sales people, and business owners operate very well within *current* paradigms. Conversely, outstanding leaders *create* new paradigms. In other words, they *go beyond* the current trends;

they create new trends. They don't serve and satisfy customer needs, they break through these thresholds to surprise and delight their customers through *design, innovation,* and *creation.*

In a world where customer service and satisfaction are much talked about, a paradox exists. We are often told things like "The customer is always right" or "We must satisfy all our customers' wants and desires." This is true, isn't it?

Maybe. I would like to submit to you that customer service is a paradox in that it is absolutely necessary, but in-and-of-itself it is insufficient. In fact, in many cases, customer service is actually a *disservice.*

How can this be?

ARE YOU REACTING, COMPETING, OR DESIGNING?

The prime objective of my consulting practice and our Design Technologies™ (Personal, Interpersonal, and Cultural) is to assist individuals and organizations in designing and creating the lives and businesses they truly desire, both now and in the future. I will address this in a moment. But first, let's understand how the vast majority approach their lives and the outcomes they produce as a result.

The Reactive Approach

Many people live a substantial portion of their lives in a reactive/competitive mode. They have become absolutely excellent in this mode of operation. But unless they change their approach, they will never become outstanding.

When we live a life of reaction, we are living the *effect* of an outer stimulus. For example, a customer may want a particular service, product, or benefit. In a reactive mode, we hurriedly scramble

"If you're not willing to impose your terms on the future, you have to be willing to let it impose its terms on you."
—T.S. Eliot

to provide exactly what customers have requested.

We may react quickly and efficiently; we may do so with warmth and kindness. It may endear us to our customers; however, it will *never* truly set us apart or drastically increase our market share. At best, the reactive approach will satisfy and serve, but in-and-of-itself, it will *never* increase business for the long term.

The Competitive Approach

What about the competitive approach? Not only do the truly outstanding not react—they do not compete. For the outstanding creators of the future, competition *does not even exist!*

To fully understand this idea, let's look at how the competitor operates. The competitive person expends a great amount of energy and effort measuring his competition (hence the rise of the "benchmarking" movement). Competitors are constantly concerned with meeting, matching, or beating the competition.

Perceived success or failure is measured in relation to the accomplishments of others. For example, a new product or service enters the market, and those in the competitive mode rush to develop a similar product or service. Consequently, these individuals and organizations are continuously at the mercy of the "designers and creators." They will always be searching for a way to be like, or to differentiate themselves from, the market leader...the one who *created* the new need. They are, and always will be, "behind the curve."

The Design Approach

Conversely, when designer/creators' products hits the market, they become the market

ORIGINALITY PUSHES
YOU OFF THE CHARTS

leaders because they "create the curve." When you create the curve, you own the market. You stand alone in a world of reactors and competitors.

Designer/creators can set the market price for their products as well, since no precedent has been established. Their products are most often viewed as the top of the line or the highest in quality. Because of their foresight, they can continue to charge a premium as long as they maintain strong perceived value in the mind of the consumer.

Be An Original

The reactor/competitor's product is frequently viewed as a take-off on the market owner's product. And, as if this were not enough, the second and third to market typically have to compete at a lower price...versus designer/creators who can charge whatever they want.

Think about it. When you consider where to go to buy athletic shoes...what comes to mind? Probably Foot Locker, the number one shoe chain in the world. Foot Locker designed and created a market; consequently, they own the market.

When you think of facial tissue, what comes to mind? Kleenex, of course. Kleenex created and now owns the market. Not only do they own the market...their brand name has become the *descriptor* of the product line.

Last but not least, when you think of buying high-end gourmet coffee—where do you go? Starbucks, of course! Starbucks is one of our country's most recent success stories—the designer, creator, leader, and owner of their market.

I could go on and on but the point is this: Each of these designer/creators is doing more than satisfying and serving customer needs—they are designing and creating *new* customer needs. As a result, they have the ability to charge a premium for their products. They design, create, and own their markets!

SO WHAT'S THE PROBLEM?

Unfortunately, the majority of us are still caught in the customer service/customer satisfaction mind-set.

It's an okay start to ask our customers what they want and then provide those exact products and services. In fact, this reactive and competitive mind-set has been the major contributing factor to the entire quality movement (more on this to come).

Solving Problems Is Only A Start

Both the reactive and competitive approaches are interrelated. Often, these approaches manifest themselves as "problem solving." When problem solving, we are focusing on what *we don't want* versus designing, creating, and focusing on what *we want*.

We problem-solve all the time. But problem solving will *never* guarantee that you design, create, or achieve what you *truly want*. And it certainly won't make you a market leader or a market owner. When solving problems, you are limited by the innovation and foresight (or lack thereof) of others—not a very empowering position from which to design your future. Let's explore this further.

WHERE'S YOUR FOCUS?

In his excellent book *Leaders, Strategies for Taking Charge*, Warren Bennis speaks of the

"Conventional wisdom, by definition, favors that which has come before. That's great if you're building a house, but it's useless—even dangerously misleading—in creative positions."
—Barry Diller, founder, Fox Television Network

"Wallenda Principle." You may recall the high-wire family known as "The Flying Wallendas." You may also remember that Carl Wallenda fell to his death.

An interesting interview was done with Carl's widow several months after he died. In this telling conversation, Mrs. Wallenda speaks of how her husband had always been totally fearless. She spoke of how he was always thinking of his next event, always attempting to make it bigger and better.

"It's the strangest thing though," she recounted, "something shifted in Carl." She then proceeded to tell how a few weeks before his demise, he had awakened from a nightmare in a cold sweat. "He had a dream that he had fallen to his death, and from that moment on he became totally consumed with safety." She continued, "We would see him checking the wires, making sure they were taut. He was so afraid of falling." Unfortunately, Carl's worst fear became his reality.

You Get What You Focus On

The Wallenda principle asserts that *you will move toward (and create) your continual point of focus.*

Your point of focus is critical to your outcomes. Individuals and organizations who function in the problem solving mode focus a major portion of their energy and effort upon the very things they *don't want.*

Getting back to customer service—aren't we most often fixing problems and dealing with things that our clients *don't want* instead of designing and creating what they do want or *will want* in the future? Of course we are!

This may seem confusing. However, if you will take the time to understand it, this distinction between problem solving and designing/creating will *massively* impact upon your personal life, your professional life, and your position in the marketplace. We must understand that the results we get today are the direct outcome of the decisions and actions of *yesterday.* Consequently, when we problem-solve, we are dealing with the effects of a past cause.

People tend to move away from problems (or things they don't want) instead of designing, creating and *moving toward* what they ultimately want to achieve. Sadly, this is how the majority of individuals live their lives and make their daily decisions. Compare this mentality to driving your car while looking into the rear view mirror instead of out the windshield (don't try this, it is just a metaphor!). This type of thinking causes us to literally "back into the future with our eyes on the past."

Problem solving will never get you what you want. It will never make you outstanding in your personal or professional life. And yet, this is the typical approach to customer service. We literally do ourselves and our clients a disservice by constantly living out of memory rather than possibility.

WHAT YOU THINK ABOUT...COMES ABOUT

In 1991 I was brought into a manufacturing organization to improve employee morale, which had hit an all-time low. Although this type of request was not that unusual, when they described the situation to me, they left out one small piece of information.

It seems the entire plant was scheduled to close and the employees had been told that soon they would all be out of a job! It was obvious why morale was so low. (Talk about a challenge!)

Upon arrival, the primary point of discussion was the fact they were going out of business. At the time, I was in the early stages of creating what are now Design Technologies™, but I knew that in order to change morale, I had to help them change their thinking. They were uti-lizing the Wallenda Principle to their own demise.

I passionately began to tell them that they had to change their focus. I told them repeatedly, "If you continue to focus and con-centrate on what you don't want (going out of busi-ness), you will tend to further it and possibly ex-pedite it."

GOALS

Believe me, this was a hard-sell. Almost every day without fail, I would encourage them to "Focus on what you want to create." After much energy and effort, they finally accepted the message.

I constantly asked them, "What do you want?" When they would come back with something they didn't want, I would not accept it and would ask again, "What do you want?" We finally began to set goals. Instead of focusing on not going out of business, we began to focus on becoming profitable and getting new customers. Instead of focusing on how poorly we had been treated, we began to ask, "How can we make today a fun and productive day?"

Positive Thinking Leads To Positive Results

You see, concentrating on how terrible it is that "we are closing" or the fact that "we really don't want to close our doors" was debilitating and deadly. And the fact of the matter is, they had been told they were going out of business so it couldn't get any worse. We collectively agreed to re-think our thinking by deciding that "if we were going to go out...we would go out in style." With this mentality, two things could happen:

- At the very least, they would feel good about themselves and their accomplishments.
- They may have opportunities to transfer to other parts of the business that were not closing by being highly attractive and productive employees.

Could it be possible that the situation would be reversed?

Little by little we began to see positive things occur. The primary production line met its quota for the first time in months; and this was the turning point. People began to take pride in their work again, and a new slogan started circulating around the plant: "We're going to make it happen no matter what!" Slowly we began to celebrate the small successes and talk about how to make them bigger and better. And then the big announcement came...they had recruited a new client and signed a two-year contract as a result! The plant was going to stay open.

WE'RE GOING TO MAKE IT HAPPEN NO MATTER WHAT!

It was a long road to shift the mentality of an entire organization, but I'm happy to say that at the time of this writing, they are still open and viable as a business. Part of this condition is directly correlated to the fact that they began to focus on and create what they wanted (a thriving and lasting business) versus what they didn't want.

There are obviously many factors that were involved, but the learning point is two-fold: First, we could have given good customer service by fixing morale in the short term (which could have been done in numerous ways). Instead, we went *Beyond Customer Service* to make a lasting difference in the organization.

Secondly, this is a great example of the Wallenda Principle. And how by changing your focus to creating what you really want, you can go *Beyond Customer Service* with yourself and your clients.

Don't Predict The Future From The Past

In a recent survey, American managers were asked, "What will it take to be successful in the new millennium?"

Eighty-five percent of the managers polled answered, "Quality."

They're wrong! Quality is no longer a highly differentiating factor in today's environment—quality, like customer service, is *expected*.

The truth is, America ran W. Edwards Deming out of our country with his quality principles, so he went where there were future-thinkers at the time...Japan. Because of this, the Americans fell behind on the innovation curve and, following the success of Japan, began playing "reactive catch-up" to the quality movement.

Ironically enough, in a management survey with Japanese managers, the same question was asked, "What will it take to be successful in the new millennium?" Not surprisingly, approximately 90% of their managers had a different answer—"new products."

Chances are that you have been exposed to or involved with the quality movement. Never before has there been a movement so widely accepted in corporate America. Guess what? Continuing to make quality a primary focus in the future is reactive—it is problem solving. This approach will not make you more outstanding!

QUALITY IS ONLY A START

I am by no means suggesting that quality is unimportant. Quality is imperative. But, let me ask you a question: Will quality sell your products or allow you to highly differentiate yourself from your competition? Of course not!

Likewise, will great customer service sell your products or allow you to differentiate yourself from your competition? Same answer.

Why? Because these attributes have become the norm. They are expected. Products and services must be of high quality and customers must be well served just to be considered in the market—just to *maintain* market share.

> "Many change programs are so general and standardized that they don't speak to the day-to-day realities of particular units. Buzzwords like 'quality,' 'participation,' 'empowerment,' and 'leadership' become a substitute for a detailed understanding of the business."
> —Michael Beer, professor, Harvard Business School

Good Service Isn't Enough

Customer service is very similar to the quality issue.

I have worked in many organizations which were heavily vested in some new customer service program. Unfortunately, they were not involved in this program because of its design or innovation capabilities. Rather, they were in the race to react to their customers' perceived needs or to "out-service" their competitors.

The sad truth is, when (and if) they achieve the level of customer satisfaction they are targeting, it will not provide a sustainable leading edge in the market place.

CREATE NEW ADVANTAGES

I strongly believe that if we do not begin moving toward a creation mentality, it will be the major factor that leaves us behind both in individual and business arenas. We must differentiate ourselves through creation rather than through reaction and competition. We must get beyond customer service to the creation factor.

> "The best way to predict the future is to create it."
> —Peter Drucker

Those individuals and organizations who understand and apply this truth will be the leaders in the new millennium. Understanding this distinction will differentiate and catapult them into a new arena. They will have no competition in an arena and a market that *they create and own.* This is the imperative that will cause all of us to thrive versus merely survive in the years ahead.

Not Just Creativity

Many people in our workshops say, "Okay, I understand, but isn't this just about being creative?" The answer is no.

There are distinct differences between being

The Difference Between Creativity And Innovation

There is a distinction between "creativity" and "innovation." I don't use the terms synonymously. I think of creativity as the generative side. It's coming up with the ideas. They are a dime a dozen. There are zillions of ideas and all sorts of games one can play to elicit them from others or from yourself. That's the easy part, although for some people even that is tough. The tougher part is the innovation side. Taking the idea to the marketplace is the execution side. Real innovation is such that it not only creates a new product, it furthers the industry itself.

— Louis Patler, co-author of *If It Ain't Broke, BREAK IT!*, interviewed in *Executive Edge* newsletter

creative and being a creator, even though they are related. Many individuals are creative. They have great ideas, but they never put their creativity into *action*.

The difference is that creators have creative ideas which are followed by immediate, intelligent, and consistent action. Being a creator necessitates an end product. In other words, *creators get results!*

Being a creator is about bringing something out of nothing—creating a need where none is currently perceived. Creators are, and most often will continue to be, the "owners" of their markets.

An Example Of Applied Creativity

General Electric holds the worldwide patent on the self-cleaning oven. This one patent alone generates literally *billions* of dollars for them. How many people would even *consider* buying an oven in this day and age that isn't self-cleaning? Slim to none. The self-cleaning oven has become a staple in our society. For those who use an oven, it is an absolute necessity.

Guess what?

No one ever asked GE for a self-cleaning oven. If GE had been reactive, they would have waited for a request—and, in all actuality, would probably still be waiting. Instead, GE was a creator—not only of a new product feature, but of a *need*. GE went beyond customer service to the creation factor.

Why Didn't They Think Of That?

Let's look at an opposite situation.

Dan Burris, the author of the best-seller *Techno-Trends*, speaks of multi-speed windshield wipers. If you have purchased a new car within the last ten years, it would be a safe bet that your car has multi-speed windshield wipers as standard equipment.

Do you need them? Of course you do! There are days that are foggy; there are days that are drizzling; there are days when it's a virtual downpour. Multi-speed wipers are an absolute necessity!

If this feature is so valuable, how is it that we had single-speed wipers for over thirty years?

Dan Burris went to the chairman of Chrysler, Ford, and General Motors and posed this very question. Guess what answer he was given?

"No one ever asked."

The point is that for over thirty years the American auto industry was extremely *reactive* in the area of wipers. Waiting for someone to ask is deadly! Think about how much potential revenue was lost with this one simple feature. All because no one asked! This is truly customer disservice!

Countless companies are asking their customers what they want. This is a faulty approach. In many cases, customers don't *know* what they want. In fact, if a customer had been asked what they wanted in windshield wipers, the answer may likely have been, "I don't know...how about blue?"

But We Could Have Thought Of It!

Not only did the car companies around the world not think of the intermittent windshield wiper, but when a small inventor got a patent on it, they all stole the idea. Their defense was that it was common knowledge because it didn't involve anything new. Only after many years, did the inventor win his court case and millions in damages from every car company.

"Other players skate to where the puck is...I skate to where the puck is going."
—Wayne Gretsky, hockey great

TAKE THE INITIATIVE

Market leaders are creators. They don't ask the market what they want, they create new needs. They *tell* the market what they want!

That's why they are leaders. When you are measuring and following the market, you are invariably following one or more of the market leaders.

I'm not suggesting that measuring customer satisfaction and needs should not be done, only that it should not be viewed as sufficient. *Satisfying* customer needs is reacting. *Generating* customer needs is creating.

Becoming designers and creators is about becoming futurists. It's about looking ahead and creating need where there currently is no perceived need.

HOW TO BECOME A CREATOR

How do we make this shift? How do we design and create customer needs? How do we get beyond customer service to the creation factor?

Creating this shift is the main thrust of Design Technologies™. This is where our leadership and consulting practice spends a large portion of its time. Although there is no way to teach all the methodologies in this one chapter, there are three things you can begin to put into practice immediately.

Questions For The Innovation Generation

1. How can I best provide for or satisfy this need?
2. What is the cause of this need? Or what purpose is this need satisfying?
3. How can I provide more value by addressing the cause of this need?
4. What is a different or a better way I could do that?
5. What is another example of that? (Continue asking yourself until you run out of ideas.)

Your Current Approach

First, you must understand your normal tendencies and your normal approach. It is important to honestly assess your current way of operating before you can begin to consider a different way.

One thing is certain: We are all doing everything absolutely perfectly to get the results we are currently getting! To get different results, we must re-think our thinking—and more importantly, follow new thought with new action!

The Pareto Principle (80/20 Rule)

The majority of us spend approximately 80% of our time problem solving. This will *never* set us apart.

Remember the 80/20 rule? The rule basically says that 80% of our results come from 20% of our efforts. If we apply the 80/20 rule to our day-to-day activities, we will find that we are typically problem-solving 80% of the time and spending no more than 20% of our time designing and creating.

Even though problem solving is where most of our energies and efforts are spent, we make the assumption that we can surprise and delight our customers with this approach. This is faulty logic.

Remember the Wallenda Principle—you move toward your primary point of focus. Put another way, "What you think about, comes about."

Don't Be Reactive

Second, realizing that reaction and competition is the norm, you must begin to break your old patterns of behavior. You will then be able to develop new habits which will foster your creative

> "The definition of insanity is doing the same thing over and over and expecting a new result."
> —Albert Einstein

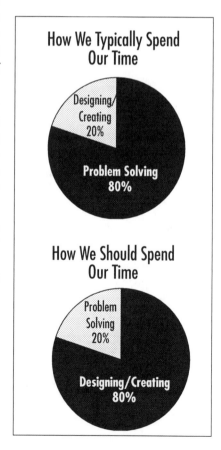

How We Typically Spend Our Time

Designing/Creating 20%

Problem Solving 80%

How We Should Spend Our Time

Problem Solving 20%

Designing/Creating 80%

What! No Problem Solving?

Many people ask, "Are you suggesting that problem solving is something we should *never* do?" Not at all. But just suppose for a moment you were to flip the percentage.

What would happen if you spent 80% of your time designing and creating and 20% problem-solving? How much would that improve your business and your results? How would that improve your personal life? Obviously it would make a *dramatic* difference! As we begin to spend 80% of our time designing and creating, and no more than 20% of our time problem-solving, we will be guaranteed that the Wallenda Principle is working in our favor. This is truly the *creation factor*.

ability. This is not as easy as it may sound. I consistently spend a great deal of time with this very issue when teaching the Design Technologies™ to individuals and organizations.

Designing and creating what we want is not how the majority of us think. I challenge you to become a student of yourself and others, and I guarantee you will find this to be true.

Ask The Right Questions

When I ask someone what they want in their organization, a frequent response is, "Well, I *don't want* all this fighting and lack of teamwork." I will respond "Wait a minute, that's not what I asked you...what do you *want*?" Or I may ask, "What do you want in your job?" Often the answer is something like, "Well, I know I *don't want* to work for this boss anymore!" Once again I will respond, "That's not what I asked you...what do you *want*?"

The Million Dollar Question?

What do I really want?

Create Positive Images

Unfortunately, this is not only present in question and answer scenarios. Audit your language and the language of others. How frequently do we tell our children, "Don't spill the milk."

Now think about it: What do they have to focus on to make sense out of your request? They have to access a visual image of what you don't want them to do!

What if you said, "Make sure to keep all the milk in the glass."

Or how often do you tell a guest when leaving your home in the dead of winter, "Don't slip on the ice"?

What visual image do they access? Instead, what if you said, "Walk carefully on the ice." These positive outcome statements may sound a bit strange at first, but think about the images they create versus those of the first statements. Is it possible these positive statements would create a much greater success ratio?

I wonder how often, because of our way of thinking and communicating, we set the Wallenda Principle in motion to the disadvantage of ourselves, our loved ones, and our clients. You can never truly become an outstanding creator—you will never skate to where the puck is going—until you first break out of this ineffective pattern.

> "Problems we face today cannot be solved with the same level of thinking we were at when we created them."
> —Albert Einstein

Change Your Thinking

The first step in this process is listening to your own language and auditing your own thinking. When you catch yourself focusing on what you or your customer *don't want* versus what you *do want* (and you will), you must interrupt the old pattern and begin to condition a new habit.

I challenge you for the next thirty days to commit to heightening your awareness of your language and your thinking. As you begin to notice your old disempowering patterns, immediately re-think and re-state what you *want* instead of what you don't want.

FOCUS ON FUTURE POSSIBILITIES

Finally, we must follow the immortal knowledge of Albert Einstein and realize that

"Imagination is more important than knowledge."

Put another way, we must begin to live out of imagination rather than memory. No longer can we afford to limit ourselves by what we have achieved or created in the past. I like to say, "We must not re-live the past but pre-live the future."

The past *does not* equal the future.

We must become the Wayne Gretsky's of our industries. Like General Electric, we must begin to anticipate customer needs; but even more importantly, we must design and create customer needs. To do this we must overcome our own self-imposed limitations. We must discontinue our reactive/competitive problem-solving behaviors and begin to utilize our true capabilities.

CONCLUSION

It is widely known that we only use 10% of our true potential. You must begin to tap into your human uniqueness and power by believing in yourself and trusting your intuition.

If you understand and apply this, you will join the ranks of the absolutely outstanding in the new world ahead. You will begin to create, live, and work in a world where there is no competition. You, and you alone, will lead and *own* your industry.

The rare individuals and organizations who operate this way will set the standards. They will create the curve, and they will have the abundant rewards that follow. Be one of them!

FULL SPEED AHEAD

10 ACTION SECRETS

1 List things that you are doing that you know are habits from the past. Drop the ones that are unproductive.

2 Great customer service is a good basis for success with your current approach. What could you do that would immediately improve things for customers? How about speed up responses, offer a great guarantee, call your best customers now, or start a free newsletter?

3 Analyze any segments of your business that are shrinking. Is there anything you can do about them? Are they profitable to ride down?

4 Analyze the segments of your business that are growing. Do they represent new trends that you can ride up?

5 If you could create the ideal new product or service, what would it be? How could you move toward it now?

6 Create a customer advisory group. Ask them what an ideal new product would be for them. Talk to customers who have complained or left. Do their reasons give you any new ideas?

7 Hold a brainstorming session with a cross-section of your employees (include customers, suppliers and others if you're too small). Explicitly ask for the wildest ideas, stupidest ideas, and ideas that could never work. Often these will be your jumping-off point for a breakthrough product or service.

8 Instead of competing with competitors, how can you cooperate with them? Call three today and set up a lunch with at least one.

9 What are you focusing on now that you're trying to avoid? Change your negative focus to a positive one about something you want to accomplish.

10 If you started a new business today, without any investment in your old infrastructure, what would it be? Why not start inventing that new business now?

Part Three

SALES SECRETS

Chapter 12

SECRETS OF SUCCESSFUL REFERRAL SOURCE MANAGEMENT

Jim Rhode

Jim Rhode, BME, CSP, president of SmartPractice, has developed and presented hundreds of seminars and workshops on practice administration and professional marketing for two decades. He has spoken to thousands of progressive dentists, and their spouses and staff members.

From his years in industry as a long-range planner with American Can Company and Celanese Corporation, Mr. Rhode brings to the dental profession scores of practice-building techniques and the motivation for timely implementation. His extensive business experience includes team building, financial analysis, operation streamlining, and long-range planning.

He is a member of the Society for Advancement of Management, and the National Speakers Association. Mr. Rhode was honored with the prestigious Arizona Entrepreneur of the Year award for 1990. He has given talks in all 50 states, and 13 foreign countries. In addition, he is the publisher of *PracticeSmart: Dentistry's Marketing and Management Newsletter.*

Jim's philosophy is best summarized by the proverb: "Any enterprise is built by wise planning...becomes strong through common sense...and profits wonderfully by keeping abreast of the facts."

Jim Rhode, SmartPractice, 3400 East McDowell, Phoenix, AZ 85008-7899; phone (602) 225-9090; fax (602) 225-0599.

Chapter 12

SECRETS OF SUCCESSFUL REFERRAL SOURCE MANAGEMENT

Jim Rhode

> *"Satisfied customers are an organization's most successful salespeople, because they do not stand to benefit financially from recommending the organization to others."*
>
> —Eberhard E. Scheuing,
> *Creating Customers for Life*

Getting referrals is the most effective marketing you can do. Most companies wish they had more referrals, but they don't have a program to produce them consistently. Generating new referrals can grow your business into the next millennium. This chapter will show you how.

WHAT YOU WILL LEARN IN THIS CHAPTER

In this chapter, you will learn proven secrets of successful referral source management that will work in your business.

- seven reasons why clients refer
- seven reasons why they don't

- eight actions you must take to keep customers wanting to return
- nine ways to make your office or business more "client-friendly"
- five dramatic concepts to differentiate your business from others
- eight ways to encourage your clients, staff, and friends to refer

At the end of this chapter, you will also find 10 Action Secrets you can put to work in your practice or business today to increase your bottom line through effective referral source management.

HOW *WHAT* YOU LEARN WILL INCREASE YOUR REFERRALS

Using the strategies presented here, you will be able to significantly increase your business through referrals by:

- implementing cost-effective ideas immediately;
- reducing or eliminating those concepts that don't work for you;
- using word-of-mouth marketing to your best advantage.

WHAT IS WORD-OF-MOUTH MARKETING?

Word-of-mouth marketing is creating an experience that will keep other people talking about you. For example, a friend of yours comes into your office and happens to mention what a fabulous meal he had last night at a new restaurant in town. His positive influence or recommendation—his word-of-mouth endorsement about the restaurant—might significantly influence you to try out that restaurant in the near future.

Word-of-mouth marketing tools can keep others talking about you, too. For example, if you provide a novel value-added giveaway, such as an imprinted gift, it will give the recipient something to mention to his or her friends in normal, everyday conversation.

SEVEN REASONS WHY CLIENTS REFER

First, it's important to know why your existing clients refer others to you. There's no real magic to it, just common sense. Here are the seven reasons I have found why clients give referrals.

1 **They are the referral type.** In other words, they are sociable, like to be liked, and enjoy helping other people. Often, these are the most successful people in business.

2 **They expect referrals in return.** If they own or run a successful practice or business, they look to other professionals like you to help increase their business. One hand washes the other!

3 **They like you (somehow, you really pleased them).** People like others who treat them well, often by pleasing them with excellent service or by delivering a greater than expected result. Some of your best referrals sources are the people you pleased the most—people you've really helped in a crisis or time of need.

4 **They like a particular part of your business.** The likelihood of repeat business and referrals often lies in how your staff treats customers. I cannot underscore this principle enough! In a landmark publication (*Marketing Strategies: A Guide to Practice Growth*), Stephen W. Brown, PhD, renowned professor at Arizona State University, presented the concept that:

A Legend In Their Own Time

Nordstrom department stores encourage employees to satisfy customer needs that you wouldn't expect. Their goal is to create word-of-mouth legends—about their services.

Just how legendary Nordstrom's service has become was shown by the results of a survey in Phoenix. Residents were asked to name their favorite department stores. As usual, Nordstrom was number one. The extraordinary thing is that Nordstrom didn't have a department store in Phoenix!

- 68% of lost clients are the direct result of staff discourtesy
- 16% are lost due to product/service dissatisfaction
- 11% are lost to competitive inroads
- 4% simply move away
- 1% pass away (see diagram)

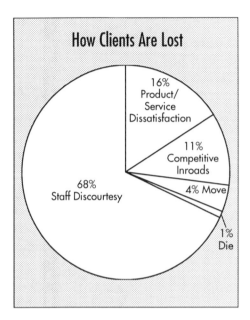

Imagine if every business in America reduced that 68% to 0%!

5 They think you are fair and competent. Most everybody I know likes to feel treated fairly, in both business and personal relationships. They also enjoy a sense of security being in the hands of a competent practitioner or professional.

As one neighbor of ours recently commented, "When I sit in Kelly's chair (she happened to be referring to her stylist), I know that I will be well taken care of. She's an excellent hair dresser. I wouldn't leave Kelly for anything!" She'd follow Kelly to a new shop. This is the classic, word-of-mouth type of referral.

As long as Kelly's fees remain fair in the market and she continues to deliver the same high level of competent service, my neighbor will never leave her salon! And, what's more important, she'll make lots of referrals to Kelly!

6 You are convenient and easily accessible. People on the go today like things quick and easy. That's why more fast-food restaurants prepare complete family meals that can be picked up on the way home after a long day at work. That's why grocery stores are going back to offering home delivery. That's why franchises are springing up on every busy intersection. Customers who find it easy to get to you, with ample parking and no hassles, are more likely to (a) keep coming back and (b) refer their friends.

7 **You refer to them first.** The notion of reciprocity is not a new one. Setting up a mutual referral system is a quick, easy and painless way to generate more referrals. It's fair and it works!

SEVEN REASONS WHY THEY DON'T REFER

You'd be surprised to discover why people don't refer to you!

1 **They think you are already too busy.** Tell them the truth—that you always welcome new customers. People move, retire, etc.

2 **They think you are too expensive.** Tell them you're in the "high-average" fee range. Truth be told, although people say they look to low price first, psychologically, they're afraid of it for fear that quality will be compromised.

3 **It never occurred to them to refer.** Plant the seeds in their minds that you welcome referrals from people as nice as they are.

4 **They think you are "elitist" and don't care to do business with "rank and file" society members.** Discuss this with them.

5 **They don't refer to anybody—ever!** They are afraid to be responsible for a mismatch that would reflect poorly on their judgment. Now's a great time to suggest it—when they feel most satisfied with your service or product line.

6 **They don't want to share you with others.** They like and want to keep your exclusivity. You need to reassure them that they'll always be a "preferred client."

7 **They're afraid that if you get too busy, you'll lower your quality or level of service.** That's why they want to keep you for themselves! Actually, that's quite flattering, isn't it? But, if you need new clients, this reason can hurt you, so identify and discuss this "business-buster."

EIGHT ACTIONS YOU MUST TAKE TO KEEP CUSTOMERS WANTING TO RETURN

Now that you know why your best clients refer to you and why some don't, you need to know what you must do to keep them wanting to return.

1 Believe in your quality and service level. As one of the basic criteria for the Malcolm Baldrige Awards, commitment to continued quality and improvement is essential for all businesses and services to grow and to continue to thrive into the next millennium. If you don't commit to quality, why should anyone refer you?

2 Be convinced that your customers or clients need what you present to them. Who is better and more qualified than YOU to know what your customers need and want, and what is in their best interests over the long-term? One of our best customers recently shared with me that when he gives a case presentation, he always includes a preface that goes something like: "If you were my mother/wife/sister/daughter/father/brother/son...I would recommend _____ because that's what is best for her/him." His case presentation acceptance rate is well above 80%! Note: This works only if you mean it.

3 Focus on the benefits to the client as a result of "buying" what you have to offer. This will vary, of course, depending upon the type of business or service you run. Some of the most successful marketing messages include: quality, endurance, self-indulgence ("you deserve the best"), increased satisfaction with self or performance, enhanced desirability, and feelings of power or control.

Benefit Messages
• Quality
• Endurance
• Indulge yourself

Dealing With Terrorist Customers

One of the rules at Disney is: If you argue with a customer, you're fired! But as we all know, there are people out there who will test anyone's patience. If one comes into your store or office, you and your employees should be aware of a technique called "fogging." Instead of getting upset or challenging the person, you can cool the person's intensity by saying things like: "Yes, that might be true" or "That's really interesting." This keeps you above the fray. It's like pouring water on the person instead of adding fuel to the customer's fire.

After such an encounter, employees should also be able to "take themselves out of the game." They need to know they can take time to re-energize.

—Ken Blanchard

"You'll be able to strut your smile," a highly successful cosmetic dentist tells her patients with confidence.

4 **All of your personnel must be courteous, even when difficult situations present themselves.** Face it, we've all had to deal with difficult people—paying customers—we'd just as soon went elsewhere. They make our day miserable. We can't seem to please them to their level of satisfaction. Staff, especially, often feel caught in the middle because they must strive to be pleasant and facilitating, often acting as a "gate-keeper go-between" of the business owner and the customer. Reaching a satisfactory level of performance expectation is both a skill and an art!

One of the most successful things I've found is to turn their concerns into a question. "So do I understand that you're upset?" By acknowledging their concerns, they will feel listened to, that you care, and they will relax.

5 **Ask questions to establish rapport.** I make it a point to ask open-ended questions, showing an interest in the other person. This gives me time to make assessments, to learn what's really important to the other party, and to make some mental notes of ways I can present solutions that can help him or her.

6 **Avoid showing anger or frustration.** This isn't always easy. When I feel myself getting tense or angry, I attempt to empathize with the

other person. I hold my breath and count very slowly from one to 10.

> ## Fire Customers
>
> If you can't satisfy a difficult customer, fire them! This will empower your staff who have been hassled by this customer. Plus, it will clear room for the quality customers you deserve.

I try to look at things from the other person's point of view by reflecting what he's telling me. I recap the situation by saying something like this, "John, help me understand this. I hear you telling me that you're upset about _____. Is that correct? I'm sorry this happened. Let's work together on this to reach an amicable solution. Will you work with me on this?" It almost always works.

7 **Give them your full attention.** How many times have you been "served" by uncaring people? If you're like me, the answer is "All too often." It's irritating and frustrating to have to wait your turn, only to have a service representative treat you like a non-person.

As one client's long-time office manager remarked to me at an entrepreneur's dinner one evening, "When a patient is in my doctor's dental chair, that patient is the most important person in the world at that time. My doctor strives to make each and every patient feel that way. That's why my boss is so successful in getting and keeping patients."

Wow! What a wonderful feeling, to be treated as if you are the most important person in the world! We all like to feel that way!

8 **Say "thank you" often!** One of the greatest feelings in the world is feeling appreciated. Think how often it made a difference to you when someone expressed appreciation for your effort or input.

A podiatrist client of ours recently shared a story with me about his success. He recalled having worked as an operating room technician early in his career. He had assisted a podiatrist in a particularly long and grueling operation. At the conclusion of the operation, the surgeon looked him directly in the eye and said, "Thank you, Jack. This operation would not have been a success without your help."

"To this day," said the podiatrist, "I think of him often and how his skill and his sense of appreciation helped me become a successful doctor today. There's not a day that goes by that I don't thank my staff or my patients. They make my success possible."

NINE WAYS TO MAKE YOUR OFFICE OR BUSINESS MORE "CLIENT-FRIENDLY"

Another element of successful referral management is making your business more "client-friendly." Everybody likes doing business with friendly people, from fast-food restaurants to dry cleaners. Your business is no exception. Here's how:

1 Make sure all of your staff members wear name tags. The expense is minimal and the return is immeasurable! Customers and clients feel more comfortable when they know who they are doing business with. Instead of "the tall fellow behind the service counter" or "the redhead who does my nails," putting a name with a face makes people more accountable and more approachable. It's a friendly sort of feeling.

2 Hang pictures of your staff on the wall of your business. This makes you more human to clients and prospective clients. It increases your "hospitality factor." It's nice to know what people who will be serving you look like.

A newsletter subscriber of ours

has named his photo display, "Dr. Kramer's Hall of Famers." Car dealers and supermarket chains are especially good at providing employees' pictures. But just about any business can do this.

Staff photos are on display in the emergency waiting room at a Kaiser Permanente hospital. In this situation where patients will likely be treated by a doctor they haven't dealt with before, it's easy to imagine that patients might be put more at ease even while they're waiting, seeing the faces of the staff who will be treating them.

3 **Make sure your reception area is wide open and airy.** Gone are the days of fogged, sliding glass doors with a mysterious employee lurking somewhere in the shadows. Today's service industries are warm, friendly, open, approachable. They set goals, for example, to acknowledge everyone who enters within 30 seconds!

4 **Provide a comfort level of background music.** It helps people feel at ease. Psychologically, it puts them in a relaxed state of mind by mentally transferring them somewhere else. If you're unsure about the type of music best suited to your clients' tastes, find out by asking them. You can include a question or two on your client survey, or simply ask them at a service point.

Gauging your audience and adjusting to their preferences can have a dramatic effect on your business and in generating new referrals.

An office manager in Colorado called me recently, frantic as to what to do. It seemed her boss preferred very loud rock

---

A Client "Music Questionnaire"

1. Did you notice the music in our office?
   ☐ Yes
   ☐ No

2. Was the volume...
   ☐ too loud
   ☐ too soft
   ☐ just right?

3. Please rank order your preference from the following:
   ___ classical
   ___ contemporary
   ___ country
   ___ disco
   ___ gospel
   ___ show tunes
   ___ opera
   ___ New Age

music, to the point of distraction for the staff and patients. She asked me what I could recommend.

I suggested they discuss developing a patient satisfaction survey at their next staff meeting. They came up with a variety of questions about the levels of service provided in their office. Mixing in one question about the music and weighing the results from the fact-driven perspective of paying clients could make a dramatic impact upon the doctor's preference for loud rock music.

The office manager called me back two months later. It seemed that more than one-third of the patients mentioned the loud music. The doctor, somewhat reluctantly at first, agreed to turn it down for awhile.

5 Create a "living" environment in your reception room or intake area. We all like to feel comfortable in the living rooms of our own homes. It's true in many professional settings, as well, and can generate increased referrals.

Many professional practices feature fish tanks (proven to reduce blood pressure); or scenic videos of wildlife, nature scenes, crackling fires, rain forests, or ocean sound effects. Living environments serve as focal points of interest that gently distract customers from some of their anxieties or inhibitions.

The focal point of a professional group practice in Tempe, Arizona, features a built-in aviary with several dozen colorful breeds of feathered friends. Clients, and especially their children, enjoy watching and listening to the birds, which are housed in a safety-glass-enclosed, climate-controlled, professionally cared for environment.

6 Have a professional logo that carries throughout every aspect of communica-

tion with your clients. For example, scrubs or uniforms, your stationery and business cards, your billing invoices, your newsletter, shipping labels, your doormat and your outdoor signage. You will be surprised at how much people do notice!

A successful client of ours in Spring, Texas, told me recently, "My patients comment positively every day about my staff's matching, professional look. Carrying a logo throughout the office has been a great boost to my practice," said the doctor.

7 **Provide cosmetics and "creature comforts" in your reception area and rest rooms.** Customers will be impressed with your forethought and consideration for their comfort. Such amenities as scents to hide medicinal smells, a boot tray and umbrella stand in cold climates, designer hand soaps, hair spray, alcohol-free mouthwash and complementary single-use toothbrushes in the rest rooms all send a message of "We care about your personal comfort."

A prosthodontist friend in Santa Fe, New Mexico, gives patients warm, lemon-scented towels to refresh their faces at the end of impression appointments. "This is one thing I wouldn't dare give up," he says, "patients like the lemon towels so much, they'd say something if I didn't offer them anymore."

8 **Have a "no waiting" policy in your "reception" room.** Whether in a restaurant or scheduling a haircut, we all like to be acknowledged and taken care of promptly. A pediatric dentist in Sierra Vista, Arizona, has the perfect system worked out. Even if he has several children already seated in the treatment rooms, he always has his assistant admit children promptly at the appointed time. He provides an assortment of video games, tapes, and other hands-on activities for the children while he finishes up his current patients.

The parents and grandparents in the reception area like it because their children are taken in on time. The kids like it because they have lots of fun things to look forward to in the treat-

"It's our waiter. He's stuck on the George Washington Bridge— would we care to order drinks while we wait."

ment area. And the doctor likes it because he doesn't feel rushed when running behind schedule. "It's a 'win-win' situation for everyone!" he says.

9 **Call "serious" or "involved" clients throughout a job or service.** Many doctors call their patients at home the evening of an invasive procedure just to see that they're doing all right. A neighbor of ours who runs one of the most successful floor covering business in the Phoenix area makes a personal site visit to every installation, regardless of the size (from the Biltmore Hotel to a guest house) just to make sure customers are being taken care of courteously and that his workers are doing a satisfactory job.

Most restaurants also make it a policy to have their servers inquire within 90 seconds to three minutes of placing an order in front of the patron if the meal is satisfactory and is there anything the patron requires. Simple, isn't it? And you can bet they get repeat and referral business through word-of-mouth marketing from satisfied customers!

FIVE DRAMATIC CONCEPTS TO DIFFERENTIATE YOUR BUSINESS FROM OTHERS

Distinguishing your business from others will also keep referrals coming your way.

1 **Understand the "out of sight, out of mind" syndrome.** To keep clients referring to you, you have to stay in front of them *between* professional contacts.

One of the easiest ways to do this is with cost-effective, personalized giveaways they'll associate with you. Items such as a personalized mug filled with flowers or jelly beans delivered to their workplace or car sun shades (great because they're seen by everyone in the mall parking lot every time they're used) are all great ways to keep your name in front of people. Personalized calendars, key rings, and magnets "stick around" all year, too!

DEAN JAMES, DDS
Taking Care
of Your Smile

2 **Keep your workplace updated.** Keep your "operation" in style. The look of your workplace is a direct reflection on your business savvy and currency within your profession. If your business look seems outdated, clients may perceive your business practices as equally outdated!

If in doubt, ask several of your closest friends or business associates to do an informal "walk-through" of your establishment. Ask them to play devil's advocate by pointing out things a first-time visitor might notice. Be sure to thank them, especially, for pointing out ways you can improve your business's look.

3 **Be generous in all things.** Be willing to go the extra mile. I like the term, "lagniappe"—meaning a small gift given a customer by a merchant at the time of a purchase. It is an unexpected extra. In marketing and merchandising, the term is "value added." I also like to call it a "Cracker Jack"—something you get free when you get down to the bottom of the box.

Think of that "new car smell" at the car wash that's added at no extra charge; or a baker's dozen at your favorite bagel shop; or chocolates on your pillow at a fine hotel. Today's professionals are learning from yesterday's merchandisers! Face it, everyone likes a free gift or an unexpected courtesy.

4 **Feed word-of-mouth marketing.** Be willing to ask for favors from others in the form of referrals, just as you are willing to give referrals.

5 **Recruit and keep a well-trained staff.** In most professions, the staff members are the first and last contact for clients. They can "make or break" your business in a hurry!

I've found that hiring the best, being fair, and rewarding equitably help ensure low turnover of

One Person Sets The Tone
by Tom Peters

Our staff is loaded to the gills with résumés to die for. Then there's Leslie McKee, the receptionist. I've never seen her résumé. But she has taken our company and turned it around. You see, Leslie is amazingly upbeat, courteous, funny, patient, upstanding and professional, smart, outrageous, and helpful. I don't know what our official "core values" are. We've never written them down. (Whoops.) But I know what they are unofficially: They're Leslie.

CUSTOMER SERVICE WONDER

Clients love Leslie. She, of course, is our Commander-in-Chief of Client Service. Among other things, she takes most incoming calls. Here's her customer-service magic:

Her manner per se—energetically cheerful—gives us a foot in the door with whoever is calling. Leslie makes sure you end up talking to the right person (no small thing), or are otherwise handled efficiently and effectively and feel good about it.

Once a week or more, it seems, she takes some totally amazing personal initiative to research something for a client. Often as not, it's unrelated to anything we do; it's just plain helpfulness. (Reading "praise Leslie letters" from clients eats up a lot of my time these days.)

© 1995 TPG Communications. Reprinted with permission of Tribune Media Services, Inc.

valued and loyal staff. Make a long-term investment in them by offering to sponsor their continuing education, upgrading their existing skills, and by expressing your appreciation to them. As an employer, it is to your benefit to share your vision and to empower them to support it.

EIGHT WAYS TO ENCOURAGE CLIENTS, STAFF, AND FRIENDS TO REFER

By now, you've discovered that much of the success of referral source management lies in common sense. Here are ways to encourage referrals from clients, staff, and friends:

1 **Ask them!** Develop your own technique, with which you feel most comfortable.

2 **Reward them each time.** Remember that behavior that gets rewarded gets repeated.

3 **Thank them** (when it finally happens). A simple verbal thank-you may be sufficient. Other times, a written note or card from you may be just the right touch. Try to send an unusual card that will be saved or displayed and has your name, logo, address and phone number in full view.

4 **Extend a "$0" fee or "no charge" at their next visit;** or at least consider it, depending upon the type of business you're in.

5 **Refer business to them.** Everyone likes to feel he or she is getting what he or she wants or needs. Help them get it. To paraphrase Zig Ziglar, "Eventually you'll get what you want, if you help enough other people get what they want."

6 **Give them your magnet or picture frame to hold pictures of their children, grandchildren, nieces or nephews as a thank-you for referring.** They'll look at it forever! (Remember, out of sight, out of mind.)

7 **Reward them with something special for a certain number of referrals.** For example, employees can receive dinner for two, flowers, theater tickets, etc.

A client of ours has generated more than 600 new patients from referrals during the last 12 months. To acknowledge and thank them, he sends a personalized letter of thanks and informs the referral that he is making a donation in that person's name to a local charity. Wow!

8 **Be sure your staff know that client referrers are "VIPs" of your business, so staff will give them proper recognition and attention.** Acknowledging staff referrers also reinforces the message.

Other Referral Sources

COMPETITOR REFERRALS
Some of your best referrals can come from your apparent "competitors." For instance, general practice dentists will refer to orthodontists. One landscaper gets more than half his business from a tree and a patio contractor.

"TIPS" GROUPS
In most communities, groups exist just to provide members will referrals. These organizations are often called "Tips" or "Leads" groups. Only one person per business category is allowed to join to avoid competition. Members are required to bring a lead for someone to each weekly meeting.

The Most Aggressive Referral Program

You should have at least one friend or client who will open his or her Rolodex to you and send a letter to everyone who could use your services. (You can do the same for them.)

—Rick Crandall, *Marketing Your Services: For People Who HATE to Sell*

SAMPLE LETTERS PROVEN TO ENCOURAGE, REINFORCE, AND THANK REFERRALS

Through the years, I've also found that referrals need to be tracked and reinforced. It's crucial that you keep a computerized list of your top 10 referral sources, monitor it periodically, and always, always, always, take time to express your thanks.

Following are excerpts from one of our best-selling books, *The Complete Dental Letter Handbook: Your Fingertip Resource for Practice Communications.* You are welcome to adapt and add to them to suit your professional needs. We've received rave reviews on them and I'm confident you will, too. (There are more examples you can use on the computer disk.)

Dear Betty,

You recently referred (name of new client) to our office. Referrals like this are the nicest compliments we could receive. We appreciate your confidence in us.

Through referrals by patients like you we have created a positive work environment. A thank-you seems hardly enough for your trust and consideration.

Thank you for your confidence. It's our pleasure to give you the best available care.

Sincerely,

John Dentist

Dear Judy and George,

You are two of our most valuable patients! We again have the opportunity to thank you for referring (name of new client) to our office. You express so much confidence in our practice by these referrals that we would like to extend a special thanks to you.

We would be honored to treat you to a complimentary dinner for two at (name of restaurant) at (location). Just present this letter to the manager and have a wonderful dinner--on us!

My staff and I hope you enjoy this evening out. Thank you again for your continued confidence.

Sincerely,
Susan Doctor

10 ACTION SECRETS

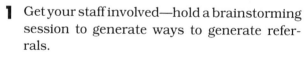

Following are Action Goals you can put to work today to begin your successful referral source management program. You'll have success using common sense, staff commitment, and a solid philosophy of word of mouth marketing.

1 Get your staff involved—hold a brainstorming session to generate ways to generate referrals.

2 Schedule a staff meeting to review how you provide high quality and good service—use examples from happy customers or satisfied patients. Collect written testimonials to use.

3 Reward staff—encourage and reward all ideas, not just the ones you actually implement.

4 Set target dates with new business goals—by _____(date) we will experience a (percent) increase in new referrals. We will track the source of all new client referrals and reward them promptly.

5 Implement a referral source tracking guide (see sample on page 246)—to track and reinforce referrals.

6 Have a surprise contest—give a prize to the staffperson who comes closest to naming the top 10 referrers to your business.

7 Make a list of professionals you feel comfortable referring to— create a list with phone numbers.

8 Identify one of your top referrers—invite him or her to have lunch with your staff as a special birthday present.

9 Make a list of 10 people who your practice or business needs to thank—then do it for special reasons.

10 Order a quantity of appropriate giveaways—this will keep your name in front of your client base.

Bonus Tip: Use the guide on the next page to track referrals and your responses.

REFERRAL SOURCE TRACKING GUIDE

"Whom may we thank for referring you to our office?"

DIRECTIONS

When tracking your new patient sources use the following letters to denote referral codes:

P – Patient
D – Other Dentist
DS – Dental Specialist
ST – Staff

M – MD Referral
W – Walk-in
YP – Yellow Pages
O – Other

Use the following letters to denote the thank you action taken:

1 – No Action
2 – Thank-You Note/Card
3 – Flowers to Workplace
4 – Flowers to Home

5 – Poster
6 – Restaurant Gift Certificate
7 – Professional Courtesy
8 – Other

DATE	NEW PATIENT'S NAME	REFERRAL CODE	REFERRAL NAME	THANK-YOU CODE

Chapter 13

STOP PRESENTING, START PERSUADING

Chip Eichelberger

Chip Eichelberger
is an expert on sales, customer service, team building, and motivation.

Mr. Eichelberger was an award-winning salesperson for Jantzen Sportswear. He followed this success by quickly becoming Anthony Robbins's top salesperson in his six years there. Then, as the principle international point man, he pioneered new markets for the Robbins organization in the United Kingdom and Australia.

He then began his own speaking career, and has spoken to over 200,000 people. He presents over 50 programs annually to corporations and organizations worldwide. He is known for his humor, strong content, and ingenious integration tools. His clients have included Toyota, ADP, Century 21, and FAI Security. His unique programs are "Gaining the Edge! Inspiring People to Take Action and Be Accountable;" "Who You Are Makes a Difference: The Magic of Acknowledgment and Team Spirit;" and "The Critical Conversion: Transforming Your Customers Into Raving Fans."

Mr. Eichelberger is a lifelong student of business and personal development. He has interviewed hundreds of business leaders and constantly does research on the challenges and opportunities facing the busy professional of the '90s.

Chip Eichelberger, 325 La Veta Avenue, Encinitas, CA 92024; phone (619) 943-8122; fax (619) 944-5298.

Chapter 13

STOP PRESENTING, START PERSUADING

Chip Eichelberger

Present. Verb: To bring forward and quote for formal consideration; advance, cite.

Persuade. Verb: To succeed in causing (a person) to act in a certain way. To sell, convince, bring around, induce, talk into, prevail on.

Anyone can learn to be a persuader and effective speaker. Emerson knew this, and it prompted him to say, "All the great speakers were bad speakers at first." That was certainly true in my case. My experience, working with Jantzen Sportswear for four years (showing their clothing line to a few buyers at a time), did not prepare me for the challenge ahead.

I started working with motivational guru Anthony Robbins in the fall of 1988 when he was just beginning to put on his one-day programs for business people. At that time, there was very little training on how to sell this program from the front of the room, and almost no one knew who Tony Robbins was.

My teams and I would speak to all types of companies. I eventually spoke in 20 major cities in the US, and throughout the United Kingdom and Australia, giving well over 1,000 talks. **Perfected repetition is power.** I was the top salesperson each year when I was on the road, and I was able to help train many leaders in the organization.

The difference between presentation and persuasion was very simple. If I was a presenter, people at the end of the my talk would say, "Hey, that was great, thanks for coming in." If I was a persuader, they would say, "Who do I make the check out to?"

If they had experienced both talks, few would have noticed much difference. The line between success and failure is just as fine for you whether you are addressing your employees, your clients, or your children.

WHY DO PEOPLE BUY?

From the beginning, I was fascinated with why some people purchased a ticket to the Tony Robbins seminars I was selling while others didn't. Initially, if they didn't buy, I thought it was them. I bought into their stories of lack of time, no money, or no desire to attend.

My life quickly changed when I accepted that it was me. It was my lack of skills and ability to transfer emotion and a feeling of absolute certainty that kept them from taking action.

THE 4% SOLUTION

The 4% Solution applies to every facet of your life. The key is to spend 4% of your day on yourself. That equates to just one hour each day in a balanced dose of reading, listening to tapes, reviewing your goals and action plans, prayer, meditation, and writing in your journal.

Save An Hour For Yourself

If you are a good persuader now, you will be measurably better when you finish reading and begin to apply some of these proven strategies using 4% of your time.

As motivational speaker Jim Rohn says, failure is a few errors in judgment repeated every day. Is it possible that a few subtle (or not so subtle) errors have crept into your performance without you knowing it? Those subtle errors, repeated day after day, client after client, if not caught and corrected will lead to **disaster**.

The power of the 4% ritual is in the repetition of one hour a day, every day.

ENTHUSIASM VS. EXPERIENCE

Many people make the mistake of equating years of working in an industry with years of experience. Because of a lack of commitment to improving their skills, people may think they have seven years of experience when, in reality, they actually have one year of experience repeated seven times over.

In many sales organizations, new people come on board in the midst of many veterans and take off with immediate success. They have not gotten a lot of training and may be new to the industry, but they are excited. By transferring that excitement to clients, they quickly do well.

They are **ignorance on fire**! They do not know what they don't know. They are not aware of all the "problems" the veterans are aware of and thinking about.

The veterans are often **knowledge on ice**! Many have lost their original passion. They now focus on their limitations instead of their blessings.

> The Law of Familiarity states that *the more you are around something, the more you tend to take it for granted.* It could be your presentation, your job, or your relationship.

Continuous Development Needed

If you are not constantly striving to challenge your current methods of operation, you will miss many opportunities to improve.

Persuaders consistently review their performances by video- and audiotaping.

It is amazing how many business people have never seen themselves on videotape, or even heard themselves on audiotape. The number is consistently less than 10% when I ask this question at my seminars.

To start today, here's all you have to say to your client: "To better serve you, I am constantly trying to improve the way I present myself. Would you mind if I tape myself for personal use only?" In most personal business situations, audiotaping will be the most realistic alternative.

Instant Feedback

You will double your effectiveness in thirty days by following the simple guidelines here.

Perhaps the most underused technique in training is videotaping your performance. It is a powerful tool when practicing in role-play situations. If you do any speaking in front of a group, videotaping should be easy to do.

Critique Yourself

It will take some courage when you sit down to review the tape. Once you see what you have been doing, you can no longer blame anyone else for your failures. It was not the quality of the leads you were receiving, or the audience, or the marketing materials. It was more than likely you.

Use the Napoleon Hill Master Mind principle. Review your tape with at least one person (preferably someone who is better than you).

Focus first on what you did well. The tendency is to immediately pick yourself apart. Use the new distinctions you will make in this chapter as your guide for areas to improve.

Videotape review works. Ask any top athlete in any sport if they consistently review their performance. Tony Gwynn of the San Diego Padres has been the best hitter for average in baseball this

The Master Mind alliance: "Two or more persons, actively engaged in pursuit of a definite purpose in a positive mental attitude, constitute an unbeatable force!"
—Napoleon Hill

decade and he regularly reviews his appearances at the plate, sometimes even during the game.

Ask More Questions

When presenting, determine if you are *asking* or *telling*. A persuader understands that the majority of the time should be spent asking the right questions.

Once we have been doing what we do for a while, the tendency for many of us is to tell people everything we know. But to get leverage to move people to action, you must ask questions.

Listen to your tape and make a list of all the questions you are asking. Are you getting the commitments you must have with this set of questions? Did you do the necessary research up front to be prepared for the situation? Are you overcoming the key objections up front? After the customer made the decision to go ahead, did you solidify their actions by asking about all the positive ramifications of going ahead now?

Follow A System

If you want to reach your ultimate potential as a persuader, do not let more than a few weeks go by without some type of audio or video review. You will take the guesswork out of what you do and be much more consistent.

Most people's success in sales is inconsistent because they have not developed a system they can rely on to produce almost guaranteed results.

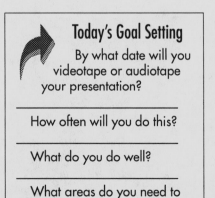

Today's Goal Setting

By what date will you videotape or audiotape your presentation?

_____

How often will you do this?

_____

What do you do well?

_____

What areas do you need to work on the most? _____

A persuader is never satisfied with the effectiveness of getting his or her message across. As the motivational speaker Les Brown would say, "They are HUNGRY!"

DO IT NOW

I get unanimous agreement that regular audio or video recording can help you improve. But I know that only 20%, at best, will actually do it.

Taping may be difficult for you to do. If it is difficult, you can still find a way to tape yourself consistently if you are committed to reaching your potential.

A persuader has a flexible delivery and exhibits a variety of emotions. Every audience you present to is unique, whether it is one person or three thousand. People you deal with will process information in one of three ways:

- **Visual:** what they see and picture to themselves.
- **Auditory:** what they hear and say to themselves.
- **Kinesthetic** (or feeling): what they feel and have emotions about.

We all use each of these systems to one degree or another, but each of us uses one more than the other two. A persuader understands this and has practiced, drilled, reviewed, and rehearsed to be effective in all three modes.

Persuaders understand that they have be flexible to reach all three types of people. To become an effective persuader *one-on-one*, you must assume that the person you are addressing has a *different processing system* than you do.

HOW TO READ OTHERS

How do you find out which is someone's dominant system? Become a detective and look for the simple clues.

If someone talks quicker and louder than normal, moves a little faster, gestures a lot and describes things while looking up, it is a good bet they are visual. They will says things like, "That looks good to me" or, "I see what you are saying."

If their voice is more melodic and even paced and they often move their eyes from side to side, they are probably auditory. They will say things like, "Sounds good to me" or, "I said to myself."

If they move a little slower with less gestures, speak slower and often speak while looking down, tend to have less eye contact, wear cardigan sweaters and touch themselves and everything

around them a lot, they are feeling-oriented. They will say, "It just feels right" or, "Can I have a hug?"

AN AUTOMOBILE EXAMPLE

I will give you an example I often use when training in the auto industry.

Presenters go into automatic pilot and begin their onslaught of verbal diarrhea.

Persuaders use their skills as a detective to size up the prospect:

- what car are they driving,
- how are they dressed,
- how quickly do they walk and talk,
- are they paying special attention to the way the door closes or the way the steering wheel or interior feels,
- what are they looking at specifically about the car?

A presenter will begin to tell the prospect all about the car without taking the time to determine how the person likes to process information. A persuader asks questions in a non-threatening way.

Ask Good Questions

Ask questions. "I'm curious, what do you like the most about the car you are driving now?"

If they say they way it looks—bingo—they are more visual.

If they say the sound of the engine and the terrific stereo, they are auditory.

If they say the leather interior and the way the car feels on the road, guess what, they are likely feeling-oriented.

Follow questions like that with this question, "Not to say that you would, but if you did buy a new car today (point to yourself), what would be the three most important features the car must have?" If you do not know their primary mode after they answer this, you are not listening.

Show the Product Differently

Begin to concentrate your discussion in the appropriate mode they like to process information. For example:

Visual: Show visually-oriented people features like special wheels, paint colors, interior color options, dashboard features. Pay special attention to the "walk around," pointing out specific ways the car has been improved over last year's model.

Show them what special aftermarket features are available to make the car look even better. Show them pictures of other happy customers with new cars purchased from you. Tell them how they look in the car. Ask them if they can they see themselves driving this car every day.

Auditory: Auditory people will like the sound of the engine, how quiet the car is when running, and the solid sound of the door or trunk closing. Demonstrate the special six-disc CD changer (have special CDs ready to play—pop, jazz, classical, etc.). Ask them what they'll say to themselves driving this car.

Kinesthetic: Get them in the car for a test drive ASAP. Suggest that they feel the leather or special fabric interior, the special memory seat adjustments, the feel of the seat, and the feel of the car taking a corner. Show

Today's Goals

What are the key visual aspects of your product or service?

_____   _____

_____   _____

What are the key auditory aspects of your product or service?

_____   _____

_____   _____

What are the key feeling aspects of your product or service?

_____   _____

_____   _____

them the special safety features that will protect them and their families and give them peace of mind. Ask them how they would feel driving this car compared to their old car.

What is the biggest complaint about buying a car or most sales situations? It is the high pressure sometimes used to close the deal.

This happens when a salesperson is too lazy to find out how to enter their customer's world. If you want to make it easy on both of you, take the time to discover the customer's dominant mode of processing and use it.

A Persuader Uses Stories And Third Party Testimonials To Elegantly Move People To Action

Another difference between presenters and persuaders is stories. Presenters "present" information, facts, and opinions. Persuaders involve listeners with great stories.

There is nothing like an effective story followed by the right questions to lock in the message. Become someone who captures stories and is able to capture your audience with them.

Stories are powerful to use in  any business or speaking situation. I regularly use stories from *Chicken Soup for the Soul* (by Mark Victor Hansen and Jack Canfield) to make a point.

THE VALUE OF A JOURNAL

Keep a hard-bound journal with you at all times to capture stories and magic moments. The major benefit of the journal is that it is a **permanent** place to record these nuggets.

Many people write things on a yellow pad or loose paper. What happens to it eventually? Right! It is lost or buried with that drawer full of pictures and other items you promised yourself you would one day organize.

Make that day today. Go buy your first journal today. I recommend the full size with 8½" x 11" pages. Call me if you can't find one.

Tony Robbins gave me my first journal and he said Jim Rohn taught him that "If life is worth living, it is worth recording." Journals are a place to record your life (and your child's).

Fill it with pictures, goals, action plans, seminar or church notes, magical cards and letters you are given, tickets from concerts and movies you attend. It is a diary and scrapbook of events and lessons that have shaped who you are and what you will become. You will draw from this to find your stories in the future.

> ### Journal Action Steps
> Start a journal to capture your stories.
> - I will buy a book by _____.(date)
>
> - Brainstorm the most powerful stories you have that you can use.

Persuaders Creatively Capture Their Success Stories For Maximum Impact

Capture your business success stories in a Raving Fan book. It is an old cliche that, "Stories sell and facts tell." I am a raving fan of Ken Blanchard's book *Raving Fans* (with Sheldon Bowles) and cannot recommend it highly enough.

When I was in Sydney for the second time in 1994, I met a great merchant who owned Monza, a men's clothing store. John and his family are now amongst my closest friends "down under". I asked him how he handled his referral business. His answer was very common for an Aussie and in the United States. He said, "I do not want to be too pushy."

I said, "That belief might be limiting your ability to expand your business. Try this belief on. You are cheating people if you do not find a way to help serve your current customers, friends, and associates because they will go somewhere else and get inferior service or a lower quality product." You should have seen his face.

> ### Creating Raving Fans
> Customers become raving fans only when they know they can count on you time and time again.
>
> Exceeding expectations is important, but it's even more important to consistently meet expectations. Meet first. Exceed second. Tattoo that on the inside eyelids of your managers.
>
> Limit the number of areas where you want to make a difference. Do a bang-up job, taking one improvement at a time, instead of trying to do everything at once.
>
> If it serves a customer's need, it's valid. There's no such thing as too good.
>
> From *Raving Fans* by Ken Blanchard and Sheldon Bowles.

Raving Fans Books

I helped John put together books I called "My Raving Fans." They are made of thick leather, dyed to match the color of his business decor and are about 12" x 18".

You can apply this strategy to almost any business in a variety of ways. I had John have his nephew Nazo begin to take pictures *with* their customers—starting with me—of the happy customers after they had the final fitting for their new suits.

The photos worked equally well with women buying clothes for their husbands. I told John our outcome would be to create Raving Fans who were loyal and would tell others about how great he is.

Inside the My Raving Fans book is a three-ring binder and clear plastic, non-glare presentation sheets. We created a simple template on a full size paper that has a nicely drawn frame for the 4" x 6" picture at the top, a frame for the business card at the bottom and room to write in between the frames.

John tells the customer it would be an honor to have him or her in his My Raving Fans book. He has a picture taken of the two of them together. He gets two copies made, one for the book and the other to send the new Raving Fan with a thank you card. He places the business card on a fresh page and has the customer write in the open space what they like best about Monza.

Referrals From Fans

What do you think happened after the customer had his picture taken with John, placed his card and wrote in the My Raving Fan book?

You are right! The commitment and consistency of the

picture, business card, and writing in their own words locked them in as a Raving Fan. John also puts them in his new monthly newsletter and personal marketing brochure, along with his amazing follow up and Raving Fan recognition program.

His business is growing over 30% a year. Many of his competitors have already gone out of business, or are discounting themselves out of business.

A Sales Tool

John has captured hundreds of success stories this way, one at a time. He uses his My Raving Fans books as his principle way of showing first-time customers and referrals about his business. He puts the beautiful book in their hands and says these are a few of My Raving Fans. Take a moment to look through it. I would like to earn your business and have you in my book. He has many of the most recognizable business people and media celebrities in the front of each book.

Is that an amazing tool to showcase success stories or what?!

Start Your Own "Fan Club"

What could you do in your business to apply this strategy today?

Some restaurants like Taco Auctioneers in Cardiff, California take pictures of their customers wearing funny hats and having fun, and display them on the wall.

I met the top auto salesperson in Hawaii. He had pictures literally covering his entire office of people who had purchased at least two cars from him, standing with him in front of their new cars.

Other businesses like closet organizers and home improvement companies with whom I have consulted now use this strategy. They use letters, quotes, and effective before-and-after pictures.

High-Tech Testimonials

The technology and cost effectiveness is now there to capture your success stories in an audio, video, or even CD-ROM format. I captured some recent testimonials on video of companies who had amazing results after they brought me in. I put their stories in my new promotional video.

The letters and pictures in my book are powerful. But they pale in comparison to people telling their stories in their own words when you can hear the inflection of their voices and see their faces.

THE "ONE SHEET" BROCHURE

The minimum tool you must have as a persuader is a nice "one sheet," as they call it in the speaking business. It's one page that combines a résumé and a "brochure" to focus on some aspect of what you do. This can be applied in any business. You might have one, or several.

The one sheet should have the following components on one piece of paper (you can use one or both sides):

- **Picture,** either yours or perhaps your entire office or company.
- **Specific attributes which separate you from your competition** and what that means to your customer. Hours, extra services, exclusive information or knowledge, special financing or first time buyer's program, frequent buyer's program.
- **Specifics about what people can count on** when they work with you, your Code of Conduct.

- **Quotes from your best Raving Fans** about you and your product or service which help overcome your most frequently received objections.
- **How to reach you.** Your telephone numbers (home, office, cellular, pager), fax number, e-mail address, and street address.

> **Action Steps**
>
> Create your own Raving Fan book documenting your successes. Buy a binder and plastic sheets by _____ (date).
> Who can you ask for your first "fan" letters? _____
> Who can you show the new book to? _____
> Create or improve your one sheet. _____
> Who can you send a one sheet to now? _____

HOW TO INTERRUPT PATTERNS

Persuaders will do whatever is necessary to interrupt people's patterns of behavior, and change their states.

Persuaders know that often their success is dictated by their ability to lead the person or the audience from their current level of emotion to a higher level of emotion. This can be done by having a group stand up, sing, or dance—or by simply getting your prospect to take a walk with you.

Ask Questions

Another way to interrupt people's patterns is by asking a question. This changes what they are thinking about. Ask your customers what is the most fun they have had in the past month, or what they are most proud of in their lives.

Ask a question that has positive feelings attached to it. The right question, carefully placed up front, or when things are not going well, will save you in many tough situations.

Whatever question you ask, the answer will take the place of what they were previously thinking about. Our brains have a tough time holding two different thoughts at the same time.

Breaking The Pattern: An Example

As a politician Ronald Reagan was a persuader, and he understood the pattern-breaking technique.

Tony Robbins told me the following story.

President Bush (after his term was over) invited Tony to attend a special conference with Margaret Thatcher, François Mitterand, and other key leaders who would be meeting in New York. Bush asked if, as a favor, Tony could pick up Mikhail Gorbachev in his private jet on the way to New York since the Soviet Union was no longer picking up Gorbachev's expenses.

Tony had met Gorbachev before and expected to have a great conversation on the flight. But it seemed Mr. Gorbachev was not very talkative from the time Tony picked up him, his wife, and several staff members.

Tony was getting nowhere with Gorbachev, so Tony **ignored him** and focused all his attention on Mrs. Gorbachev. They really started to hit it off, and Gorby began to chime in with a comment now and then. Slowly, he became involved in the conversation.

Tony asked him, "What changed the Cold War?" Gorbachev gave a few pat answers, but Tony persisted—he wanted to know the precise moment the Cold War changed.

Gorbachev was silent for a few moments. Then he began to laugh and slapped his knee several times. Gorbachev told Tony of the time when he and Reagan were meeting and arguing over the nature of capitalism and communism. President Reagan tended to lecture Gorbachev and it did not go over very well. At one heated point in the debate, President Reagan rose abruptly, and walked away as if leaving. Then, he turned around, walked toward Gorbachev smiled, exended his hand, and said, "Let's start fresh! My name is Ron, may I call you Mikhail?" Gorbachev began to laugh, and from that moment their relationship changed. Gorbachev told Tony, "You just got to love the guy."

Other Pattern Breaks

Unexpected actions will interrupt the pattern of the person or audience you are trying to persuade. You might do this by getting the person to follow you to another part of the store, or getting them involved in the demonstration of your product or service.

I was in the Sydney Opera House watching Stephen Covey deliver a talk in front of a packed house in 1994. He was not at his best and he did not appear to be having much fun.

After a short break, he came back on stage and asked for a volunteer from the audience. Covey asked the gentleman volunteer to do 20 pushups. The man struggled to make the final three pushups to reach twenty. The audience applauded, and the man returned to his seat.

We all waited for a moral or metaphor from Dr. Covey. It never came. He simply said his wife had told him to have more fun. We all laughed, he loosened up, and he was much better from that moment on.

> **Action Notes**
>
> What are ways you can interrupt negative patterns people fall into? _____
> _____
>
> How can you interrupt your own non-productive patterns? _____
> _____

BE AN ENTERTAINER

A persuader knows that people would rather be entertained than educated.

This is a fundamental belief I adopted from Tony Robbins. It affects every decision he makes when planning an event. He uses wild, fun, upbeat music, and visual images, to get and keep people moving during the day.

I am amazed that more people do not use music that will effectively put people into the specific state they are looking for. Use music to put people in the right mood at lunch or during exercises they are completing.

Do not let people sit down for more than 45 minutes at a time. When I do a program of over an hour, I give a carefully chosen person in the audience a tambourine or clock to shake when she thinks we need to get up if I ever forget.

I have a big squirt gun I hand out to people I think are the most serious in audience. I tell them they are the enforcers if anybody gets out of line. I have various games I play and fun toys to keep things light. **People like to have fun!**

Switch On!

I think there is an element of entertainment in all of the top salespeople I have met. Most use a strategy I call being SWITCHED ON!

I first heard the term in Australia. You can tell if someone is switched on immediately, either on the phone or in person. You can tell in their handshake, posture, eye contact, smile, tone of voice, and how totally focused they are on you.

People judge us quickly. A persuader understands this and does not leave it to chance. Persuaders know they must transfer a feeling of certainty and excitement quickly.

How To Switch Off

Many people are *switched off.* If you wanted to get depressed or switched off, isn't there a specific **recipe** you have to follow with your body?

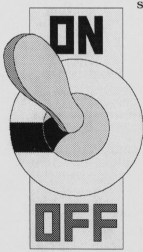

We can all recite it as if we had won a blue ribbon at the state fair for it: Head down, shoulders slumped, breathing shallow, eyes down, and unhappy look on your face. Either slump in the chair, lay down on the couch, or curl up in bed.

Combine that FIZZIOLOGY (as I call it) with picturing the worst case scenario over and over, and you have a good start on depression. Now add talking to yourself in a self-deprecating tone of voice, and you have a recipe for disaster.

Choose Your Energy Level

It is human to have some down moments. The key is how long do you feel that way? Help yourself and others get out of that state quickly.

A persuader knows that most people do not know they are choosing to feel a certain way because of how they use their body and the way they think about things.

Persuaders know that if they are to get their audience or customers switched on, they need to do it for themselves first, regardless of the circumstances happening around them. *You are the ultimate object of your persuasion.*

A Recipe For Energy!

Stand up right now and celebrate like you just won a million dollars in the lottery or made the biggest sale in a year. I bet you will quickly be up. Try it! That is a great feeling, isn't it?

Keep feeling that way and now look up with a big grin on your face. Don't read this, look up and grin!

Now keep looking up and smiling and try to get depressed without changing anything in your FIZZIOLOGY. It is almost impossible.

ZAP

Visualize Success

Picture the important events in your life in advance of them happening. Visualize them with certainty, happening just as you want each time, down to the smallest details of the contract being signed, etc. Relive those memories with emotion.

Focus on what you want to happen, not on all the things that could go wrong. I would always try to do this before a meeting selling Tony Robbins seminars. The times when I got clear on the specific number of enrollments and literally saw the people signing up, I always did better.

Develop A Routine

All athletes, entertainers, and persuaders have developed a personal routine to guarantee they will be at a level 10 when it is "showtime." Watch professional golfers before they hit the ball, or

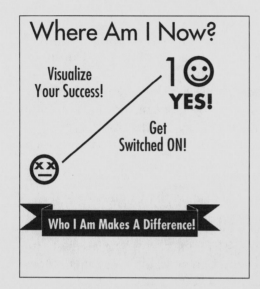

Where Am I Now?

Visualize
Your Success!

1 ☺
YES!

Get
Switched ON!

Who I Am Makes A Difference!

basketball players before they shoot free throws for examples of calm, focused preparation.

If you want to see intense, passionate preparation, go into the locker room of a football team before the game.

In the box to the left is a tool I created and have used almost every day over the past eight years. I have it in my briefcase and at eye level in my office.

The key question to ask is, **Where am I now?** Where are *you* on the scale of 0–10 of being switched on?

For myself, if the answer comes back less than 10, I quickly change my body to get to a 10. Ask this question consistently throughout your day.

Condition Yourself

You have to develop your own routine. I smile and move with certainty, stand tall, take deep powerful breaths and exhale strongly. I pump both fists and say "Yes!" with passion. I ask myself questions about what I am excited about and why I will succeed. I visualize exactly what I want to have happen.

It is amazing how well it works. You can get results very quickly after only a few dozen repetitions.

CONCLUSION

Your ability to persuade yourself and others is crucial to your success. Use the material in this chapter to push yourself to become the best persuader you can be. Do not fall into the trap that the Law of Familiarity can lay for you. A *presenter* tends to connect only with people who want to "think it over" and who often end up doing nothing.

Be a *persuader* who leads people to take action now and feel good about doing it. Make it easy by creating Raving Fans and creatively documenting your success so others can do your persuading for you. Live life **Switched On**, and induce that excitement in others!

10 ACTION SECRETS

1 Schedule 4% of your day—one hour—to improve yourself by reading, listening to tapes, and writing in your journal.

2 Start audio- and videotaping your presentation consistently to create a duplicable system of persuasion. Practice, drill, and rehearse.

3 Select a Master Mind partner you respect, one who is committed to improvement. Review the tapes together.

4 Practice being a detective to determine if your friends, family, and customers are visual, auditory, or kinesthetic types.

5 Work to recapture your early enthusiasms for what you sell. Change something in your approach.

6 Buy a full-sized journal and begin recording your life. Get one for each child, too!

7 Create a "Raving Fan" collection of testimonials, documenting your success with letters, quotes, business cards, and pictures of you and your Raving Fan together.

8 Create a "one sheet" to highlight your expertise and separate you from the competition.

9 Recognize when people are not "Switched On" and see if you can change their focus with a fun question or get them to move differently.

10 Make a commitment to ask, **"Where Am I Now?,"** before each important moment, sales call, presentation, or interaction with your family or friends. If you are not at level 10, get there.

Chapter 14

LOYALTY, THE SPICE OF LIFE

Robert McKim

Robert McKim
opened M\S Database
Marketing in 1991 with his
partner Evelyn Schlaphoff, fol-
lowing 25 years as a traditional marketing director with Gillette, Schick Electric,
and Bushnell Optical. As owner of Robert McKim Advertising, his innovative
strategies made marketing history. McKim is partner, strategic planning for M\S
Database Marketing, one of the nation's premier database marketing firms,
dedicated to giving clients a competitive advantage through advanced technology.

Robert McKim, M\S Database Marketing, 10982 Robbins Avenue, Suite 101, Los
Angeles, CA 90024; phone (310) 208-2024; fax (310) 208-5681; e-mail
RMcKim@www.MSDBM.com.

Chapter 14

LOYALTY, THE SPICE OF LIFE

Robert McKim

"The first step in managing a loyalty-based business system is finding and acquiring the right customers...."
—Frederick F. Reichheld, *The Loyalty Effect*

Loyalty marketing is nothing new. If you know who your customers are, you can treat them as they want to be treated (the Platinum Rule).

Years ago, the mom-and-pop corner grocery store owners had it all figured out. Old-time merchants didn't need a computer database to keep track of their customers. They knew their best customers and their not-so-good customers. They knew all their customers' names and could reward good customers with gifts and special attention. This built solid relationships.

This type of relationship building was abandoned during the 1960s and 1970s in favor of mass marketing. They may have had computer databases back then, but everyone was treated the same! Today, marketers struggle with how to develop a "personal" relationship with thousands, and even millions, of customers.

Database marketing is usually defined as

selecting the best segments from your records of customer and prospect characteristics to make sales. But it is also the tool that marketers can use to rekindle the loyalty that the mom-and-pop corner grocery store had with its customers. The decreasing costs of computer systems have made loyalty marketing the "new" reality again.

Loyalty marketing— to borrow a phrase from former New York Yankees baseball manager Casey Stengel—is "Déja vu all over again."

DEFINING LOYALTY MARKETING

Direct marketing, relationship marketing, and loyalty marketing are not the same things.

Direct marketing is transaction-driven. It sends messages to an intended audience to solicit a sale (e.g., "junk" mail). The effort is measured in terms of investment versus return on investment.

Relationship marketing is more like traditional advertising. It attempts to build a relationship and modify people's behavior over a period of time with structured communications. It's measured primarily in share-of-mind or the old traditional share-of-market terms.

Relationship building echoes the David Ogilvy advertising era and the brand equity notion that customers want a relationship with a brand. I personally struggle with the concept that people want a "relationship" with Crest toothpaste. People want relationships with other people, not with objects.

Loyalty marketing modifies people's behavior prior to and directly after a sale to increase incremental revenue. It's measured in return on investment (ROI) terms and increased purchases. Loyalty building within a brand, or even a company, works by reinforcing customers.

AN EXAMPLE OF SUCCESSFUL LOYALTY MARKETING

Travelers select the same hotel chain or rental car company on each trip. Why? Relationships and trust.

If marketers learn about customers' interests and preferences and deliver a level of service to meet these needs, the customers will trust that company to acknowledge and deliver future customized preferences.

An example is Pan Pacific Hotels and Resorts, an international "boutique" hotel chain with approximately 20 luxury properties in Europe, North America, and the Pacific Rim. Since Pan Pacific can't compete with the worldwide chains in number of properties, they look to loyalty marketing to cultivate increased revenue.

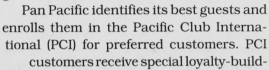

Pan Pacific identifies its best guests and enrolls them in the Pacific Club International (PCI) for preferred customers. PCI customers receive special loyalty-building benefits and services. The results have been good. Fifty-four percent of PCI members stayed in one or more Pan Pacific Hotels during the last year. Of those, 32% chose Pan Pacific hotels while visiting another country. PCI members' room nights averaged 2.48.

Pan Pacific has established a benchmark in personal service. At the Mauna Lani Bay Hotel and Bungalows, all staff members call the guests by name. A hostess welcomes preferred guests with a fruit punch in the lobby and escorts them directly to their rooms where she takes their registration information. Back home, guests receive a personal thank-you note and small gift from the hotel manager.

PREPARING A HIGH-PERFORMANCE DATABASE FOR THE NEW PARADIGM

Consumers only want information when they are interested in it. Information or solicitations that come at inappropriate times are regarded as "junk" mail. The direct marketing community believes that a 1–3% response is a good response. So, what happened to the other 97–98%?

Even with today's customer database information, it's still really a matter of happenstance as to whether a customer is ready to purchase. Marketers have been seduced by the incredible power and speed of the computer and the dizzying array of sophisticated database software that is available to manipulate customer records. Too frequently, marketers focus on shuffling around the customer database files and records simply to make it more efficient or convenient for themselves.

Understanding Your Customers

Our marketing priorities are not in order. We should not be preoccupied with speed. Our focus should be on gaining a deeper understanding of the customer. Today, if a company is to survive, knowledge about the customer is essential. The database marketing focus must be on understanding and knowing how to satisfy each individual customer's messaging and communications needs.

Today's marketing challenge should be how to collect knowledge about the customer and which information to collect. But it's not.

Traditions Needed

Most marketers preclude this from occurring through the blinders of tradition. Marketing tradition holds to three annual mailings (sometimes monthly) that "go for the gold" 2–3% response. All the activity surrounding the mailing is frenetic and the marketing personnel feel a sense of accomplishment once the mailing gets out.

Marketers are not taking enough advantage of the new enabling technology. By changing the paradigm, we might mail or communicate on a daily basis and change the

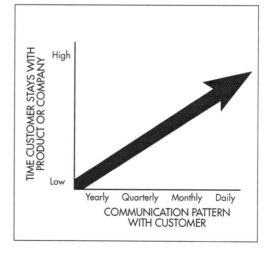

TIME CUSTOMER STAYS WITH PRODUCT OR COMPANY

High

Low

Yearly   Quarterly   Monthly   Daily
COMMUNICATION PATTERN
WITH CUSTOMER

offers and merchandise or communications to suit the receiver of the information.

Today's technology allows for a new marketing paradigm: mass customization that arrives to the consumer on a just-in-time basis.

How will we know if we succeed in this effort? The immediate indicator will be a double digit response, versus the ancient 1–3% figure.

The result will be higher revenues, a greater return on investment, and a more satisfied customer who will likely stay with the product or company for a longer period of time. Nothing wrong with that, right?

THE SEVEN MAJOR ASSUMPTIONS OF LOYALTY MARKETING

In order to create a "loyalty" tie between you and a customer, you need to be able to find and attract the right customers. Here are seven ways to make it work.

1 Past behavior is the best predictor of future behavior. Even if people become informed or suddenly acquire much wealth, their basic behavior changes only modestly over time, if at all. Remington Arms Company customers remain loyal because the Remington brand represents a special lifestyle and tradition which customers associate with themselves. Product loyalty runs high with the Isuzu Trooper Sports Utility Vehicle which has a high rate of repurchase.

2 Timing is key. A purchase is simply one event in a customer's life. It satisfies a momentary need. Once that purchase is completed, the consumer is looking to fulfill the next need.

Knowing exactly when to approach or contact the customer to meet that next need is the key to building lasting loyalty.

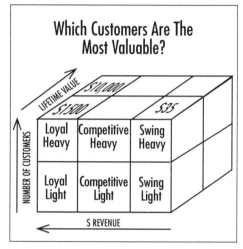

Which Customers Are The Most Valuable?

3 **To figure "worth," one needs to calculate "lifetime value."** Much like the mom-and-pop grocery store owners, marketers must know the dollar worth of each customer in order to reward and acknowledge that customer appropriately. The figure examines how a lifetime value set of complex issues can be looked at after the customer segmentation has taken place and groups of Loyal, Competitive (value-oriented), and Price-sensitive "Swing" customers are identified.

4 **Customers are more important than noncustomers.** Enough said!

5 **Certain customers are more important than others.** Some customers purchase more profitable products and require less support services than others. They deliver greater profit to the company. It makes marketing sense to identify these customers and reward them for their purchasing habits.

6 **Customers are likely to share certain characteristics with each other.** People have unique personalities. Multiple purchasers who purchase products or services from the same company over time are likely to share similar characteristics.

7 **Prospective customers are likely to look like current customers.** If marketers can define these customer characteristics, the information can be used to look for new prospects from other lists who possess similar characteristics.

DATABASE LOYALTY

One way that loyalty can also be generated is by retaining and retrieving detailed information. This enables marketers to deliver great customer service *by the customers' definition.* They can also respond to customer suggestions, follow through, resolve complaints and stay abreast of customers' changing needs.

The Ritz-Carlton network of 28 worldwide hotels maintains excellent follow-through with its Covia Travel Reservation database system of guest profiles. The system is so thorough that if a guest orders white wine with an ice cube from room service at the Ritz-Carlton in Cancun, Mexico, when that customer orders white wine months later at the Ritz-Carlton in Naples, Florida, room service will ask if he/she wants it with an ice cube.

GUEST: B. Nise
SMOKER: N
FOOD PREFS: Ice cube in white wine; salad dressing on side; substitute baked potato for fries
OTHER: Likes to have room made up early

Hertz generates loyalty with a driver who meets Hertz Gold Card members as they step off the plane and takes them directly to their cars. The member's name is on the driver's seat, the trunk is open, the motor is running, and the heater is on if it is cold. When customers are rewarded immediately for using products, they'll look forward to using them again.

Misloyalty Programs

When all customers are treated alike, as in most of our experiences as customers, loyalty and repeat business is less likely.

For the past three years, I've stayed twice a year, up to 10 days each time, at the Sheraton Chicago Towers Hotel. My "preferred customer" mailings say I will receive automatic room upgrades, daily newspapers, and other special amenities. Not once have these promises been fulfilled. With every stay, I give the front desk my "preferred customer" card. Each time, it's set aside and no one acknowledges that I've ever stayed there before. I don't plan to stay there again!

MANAGING CUSTOMER LOYALTY

Simply satisfying the customer is no longer the ultimate marketing virtue. Marketers must look for ways to increase loyalty. This includes extra services or things that customers perceive as adding value to their relationship with the company.

Managing customer loyalty requires an integrated process that:
- Provides accurate information about the customer value requirements that drive loyalty.
- Provides knowledge about how well the company provides value relative to its competitors.
- Funnels information about customer requirements into the organization's business systems and culture.

Five Steps To Managing Customer Loyalty

1 **Clearly define the objectives and communicate them.** Unless marketing begins with a precise statement of the objectives, loyalty efforts will readily dissolve. American Express approached the loyalty "game" in the same scientific way it dealt with customer acquisition. Prior to launching the successful Membership Miles program in November 1993, it set up three standards it believed defined loyalty: getting members to spend more, ensuring less membership attrition, and encouraging faster payments.

2 **Discover what the customers want.** Let customers define, in their own words, their criteria for quality, price, image, and value. Loyalty builders prompt a customer to give a larger share of their requirements to a company and encourage them to stick with a supplier even during difficult times.

3 **Conduct a critical needs and value assessment.** Armed with a qualitative understanding of the customers' needs, marketers can now set priorities among important customer requirements. Through database research, marketers can determine the relative importance of the many aspects of quality, innovation, price, and image that affect customer loyalty.

4 **Develop an action plan and implement it.** This turns customer loyalty management into a way of doing business. The voice of the customer must become the organizing principle around which cross-functional process and quality improvement initiatives are conducted.

5 **Monitor the marketplace and the company's results.** All the loyalty building components need to be regularly monitored to determine if the company's action plan and performance are continuing to be successful.

MINING THE DATABASE FOR THE BEST CUSTOMERS

Loyalty marketing is built on a foundation of existing customers which can be divided into a pyramid of customer profiles through database research. The pyramid consists of best customers, preferred customers, existing customers and the competition, category buyers, and potential customers.

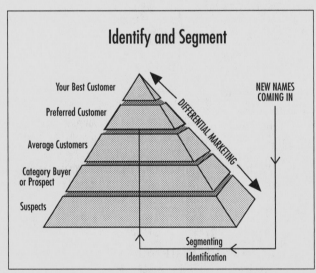

Identify and Segment

Your Best Customer

Preferred Customer

Average Customers

Category Buyer or Prospect

Suspects

DIFFERENTIAL MARKETING

NEW NAMES COMING IN

Segmenting

Identification

Defining Customer Models

Database research also shows marketers the most cost-effective methods for reaching the strong loyalty candidates. Use a combination of transaction and behavioral models to mine the database for past and future customers who are most likely to become loyal customers. The simplest approach to this has historically been to combine recency of purchase with frequency and monetary value to determine the best customers or prospects (RFM).

Discovering loyal customers goes beyond researching customers' purchasing behavior. Marketers must categorize customers by rank and status. This can be done by examining customers within the database on three activities:

• Transaction activities
• Frequencies of purchases
• Frequencies of responses

Identifying future loyal customers is equally important. However, future loyal customers are usually not in a position to demonstrate the most frequent or the largest purchases at their present age or economic level. Therefore, the best method to identify future loyal customers is through behavioral characteristics.

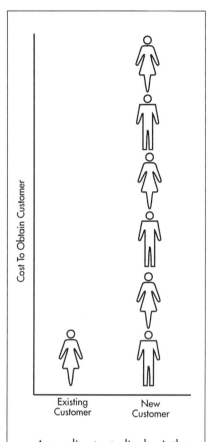

According to studies by Arthur Andersen and Deloitte & Touche, it costs six times as much to find a new customer as it does to retain an existing one.

Examining Lifetime Value

The next component is to examine customer potential Lifetime Value. This allows marketers to see which customers are more important than other customers to insure that the loyalty program is focused on the right customers. Marketers can then compare the value of existing customers with the potential value of prospective customers.

Once the best customers have been identified, the database model tracks each customer, updates their purchases by transaction and product, measures profitability, and forecasts what each customer is worth over time. The database becomes a major asset of the company.

Collecting Customer Data

Identifying behavioral characteristics is important to successful Lifetime Value analyses. This can be done through "data mining."

To achieve this, strategic data about the customers' past behavior, which provides insights into their future behavior, must be appended to the customer record. Such data can be purchased from outside data sources such as R.L. Polk or Donnelly Marketing, or collected by asking questions of the customer base and rewarding them for participating.

HOW TO CREATE LOYAL CUSTOMERS

Loyal customers are worth a lot of money to you compared to even slightly less loyal ones. In some cases, a financial reward to customers is well suited to a company's personality and sometimes easier to initiate. Financial rewards can be implemented immediately without changing a company product structure or culture.

"Raising customer retention rates by five percentage points could increase the value of an average customer by 25 to 100 percent."
—Frederick F. Reichheld, *The Loyalty Effect*

Many loyalty success stories use non-monetary rewards. American Express frequently seeks new products and services for its members from companies that want to get new prospects to try their products. Card holders appreciate being made aware of these offers even if they don't take advantage of them. Through statistical modeling, American Express insures that the offers it accepts are relevant to its members.

The Chicago Tribune offers a "Press Pass" card that gives *Tribune* preferred subscribers an opportunity to attend *Tribune*-hosted special events including parties, athletic events, and fashion shows. Saks Fifth Avenue hosts special parties for its preferred customers to celebrate new openings, designer introductions, teas, cocktail parties, and other get-togethers.

The highly competitive airline industry provides a contrast in successful strategies. US air carriers, which offer minimal in-flight special treatment, have used frequent flyer miles and bonus programs to achieve unprecedented customer loyalty.

Singapore Airlines, on the other hand, has only a minimal air points program, but has achieved celebrated success with in-flight loyalty-building treatment. For example, Singapore Airlines flight attendants in first and business class refer to each customer by name. The service is continuously exceptional and prime customers receive a special gift halfway through every flight.

CREATING A SUCCESSFUL LOYALTY PROGRAM

Companies with successful loyalty programs use the following procedures:

1 **The database is the essential element—without which a loyalty program cannot take place.** Identify the target customers and record their activity and progress toward the stated goals.

2 **Identify program objectives.** These should be stated in the context of the business objective and must fit with the company's overall objectives.

3 **Develop a plan with a timetable.** Set up milestones and measurement tactics to monitor the progress. Examine sales for increases in quantity and quality among the target audience.

4 **Identify the strategies used to modify behavior and stick with them.** Satisfaction surveys are one way to test the strategies to be sure they are working.

5 **Set specific interim goals.** The goals should be established with a time schedule and measurable results.

6 **Be specific about tactics by clearly writing down the specific steps in the process.** Be sure that everyone is brought

into the process to build team support for the program.

7 **Report the findings.** The boss will want to know how the program is progressing. Present the real information and describe the steps being taken to correct the course along the way.

LOYALTY PROGRAM DO'S AND DON'TS

The secret to building genuine customer loyalty is to let customer behavior drive the process.

Eight Rules to Follow

1 **Respect customers' wishes.** If they don't want to be contacted and want to know why they are in the program, make every effort to give them the information.

2 **Assign a customer advocate.** There needs to be someone inside the company who is watching out for the customer and insuring that the program is running smoothly.

3 **Understand the information and be sensitive.** Taking responsibility for the customer's information is a privilege and not a right. Guarding their privacy is essential to keeping customers happy.

4 **Be responsive and responsible.** If customers request something, be sure that the information is delivered within their expected time frames.

5 **Personalize where it makes sense.** Everyone likes to be called by his or her name. However, overuse in inappropriate ways will alienate the customer.

6 **Take customers seriously every step of the way.**

7 **Respect the customer's privacy.** Don't reveal customer health, sex, financial, or legal concerns. Blockbuster Video announced they planned to sell information about their viewers' habits and generated thousands of angry customer letters.

8 Develop a contact and response tracking system. Use the system to measure and identify what programs are working with which customer groups.

Seven Mistakes To Avoid

1 Don't treat a databased marketing program like a **promotion.** A loyalty marketing program takes time to implement and to change the consumer's behavior.

2 Don't focus exclusively on tangible results. Frequently in loyalty marketing, share of mind or attitude changes are meaningful precursors to later change in product usage, or up-sell or cross-sell activities.

3 Don't get the economics wrong. Having unrealistic expectations of the increases in incremental sales and poor knowledge of the expenses will result in unpleasant management surprises. Quaker Oats thought it could increase loyalty by providing coupons to the customers in its database. It mailed a million coupons. The effort resulted in no increase in loyalty and was much more expensive than other approaches.

4 Don't pretend to care more than you do. Customers are savvy. An insincere approach will be viewed by most as an unwelcome sales ploy. When AT&T sent $100 checks to prospective customers to entice them to switch service, it created disloyalty.

5 Don't try to sell customers on everything all of the time. Don't flood the customer's mailbox with nonrelevant offers just because the computer has the capability. Overselling tactics have the opposite effect of loyalty building.

6 Don't underestimate the degree of internal support necessary. A successful loyalty program demands total support from top management down to the fulfillment room personnel.

7 Not planning in advance for response. When 200,000 customers want something now, not having a planned reaction can be a disaster for your program and budget.

SO, WHY ISN'T EVERYBODY DOING DATABASE MARKETING?

The most consistent reason is that marketers have not done it that way in the past and they are happy with the current results. To many, this is a good reason for not changing!

An example from the June, 1996 issue of *Marketing Tools* magazine illustrates why the marketing blinders must come off:

> Adept Technology, a San Jose, California-based manufacturer of assembly line industrial robots, is an industry leader. Twice it's been named among the top 10 of *Inc.* magazine's 500 Fastest Growing Companies in the US. To continue the upward trend, Adept charged its marketing group with increasing sales and the return on marketing investment, without increasing costs. The firm correctly decided on a new database.

Like so many companies, Adept believed bigger was better. After asking what everyone in the company wanted the database to do, Adept purchased one that tried to do it all. The result was an expensive and highly complex database that cost too much, demanded too much time, and needed too many people to run it. Not surprisingly, the new database was eventually scrapped.

Changing Failure To Success

Why did the database fail? Because even with all of its high power, the database did not satisfy Adept's core needs:

- driving a prompt and effective communications process
- storing relevant customer information
- providing marketing with easy access

How did Adept correct the situation? Management stepped back and re-evaluated what it needed to accomplish its goals.

> "Many of life's failures are people who did not realize how close they were to success when they gave up."
> —Thomas Edison

First, management defined the database objectives:

- Inquiries must be fulfilled as quickly as possible (within 24 hours).
- Leads must be identified and tracked by sources.
- The database must generate communications in an ongoing and seamless fashion.
- The database must produce performance reports.

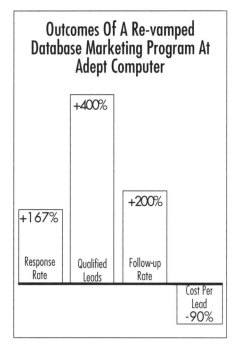

Outcomes Of A Re-vamped Database Marketing Program At Adept Computer

Second, Adept re-thought how its internal departments should work together to support the new database strategy. This meant getting the field and marketing departments to cooperate to improve the quality and quantity of leads.

Success Brings Acceptance

At first, the departments were skeptical and did not completely buy in, given the previous failure. The strategy became a game of small wins to build confidence among the various departments. But once this profound shift in the relationship between the field and marketing kicked in, the result was timely follow-up and closure which generated tremendous gains.

- Adept's response rate increased 167%, from 4.5% to 12%.
- Qualified leads increased 400%.
- The field responded to the improvement in the quality of leads by doubling their lead follow-up rate.
- Cost per lead plummeted up to 90%, from $150 to as little as $15.

CREATING A DATABASE PROGRAM THAT WORKS

The reason that databases of all sizes don't perform properly is because of a misdirected focus. At M\S Database Marketing, we believe in not being held hostage by a specific technology. We believe in being flexible and moving with the flow of technology. Our goal is to be smaller, faster, and less expensive.

Our experience has taught us eight simple rules to follow while developing the database technology to insure that a loyalty or database marketing program will work:

1 **Understand the customer.** Customers want to be appreciated and catered to. They understand that companies use database technologies and accept that these tech-

nologies will eventually lead to making their lives easier. Customers want the manufacturer to feed back information about their past purchases and consumption. They want to be "advised" about what products or services will be better for them in the future.

Demonstrate appreciation at the point of contact. Customers want to be recognized for their importance and status. The technology exists to accomplish this. Empower frontline employees to carry out this recognition at the appropriate time. This could include the ability to give spontaneous bonuses and to quickly correct a problem in order to keep a good customer.

2 **Keep your objectives straight.** Keep the system and architecture SIMPLE. A database that tries to do everything is either never going to be completed or is so complex that only a few stout-hearted people will ever embrace it. Remember why you wanted the system: to communicate customer information quickly. Every piece of information collected since time began is not needed in the database.

It is very important for marketing managers to plan carefully, write down their goals, and identify how many records will be accumulated after the next 12 months, 24 months, and 36 months.

Determine what critical data elements are essential, and determine what will be the outputs, reports, labels, communications, trend analysis, mail performance analysis, etc. Don't forget to budget revenue and expenses and measure the communications dollars performance. It's all trackable.

3 **Test the database and the process.** Management in general has not yet embraced the new database technology. Because it is new, in their minds it is untested. Most managers are aware of the benefits of the new technology and like the idea of being able to get to the market faster, reduce marketing expenses, and have more satisfied customers. But they have no experience with the database marketing process.

To begin a database program, start with off-the-shelf software and hardware. This provides a cost-effective environment that management will be comfortable investing in. At first, select only one market or customer segment. Generate as much support as possible inside the company by explaining what the goals of the database marketing program will be. Create both a financial and in-time goal and review it with management to get their buy-in. Develop a plan and budget for the expenses...don't forget the revenue.

4 **How to deal with a legacy system.** What if your company has had a computer system for years, which was originally designed as a financial system? It was built to keep general ledger and operations information, and to warehouse the addresses of buyers. The CFO is not going to quickly give up or fiddle with something if it's not broken.

This system is just not made to accommodate the needs of a marketing database. A separate system is recommended for the marketing database. Unless the customer records exceed 15 million, a large system is just not required. Through the use of mass storage and relational tables, tens of millions of records can be held in a lightweight computer.

5 **Be flexible.** The business environment is constantly changing. As marketers, we must change to meet the new demands on our companies, equipment, products or services. The architecture and construction of our database must be flexible. Increased flexibility equals relevance to the customer. Successful databases can easily change criteria and add or subtract fields. Advance identification of the critical data elements will keep the data integrity.

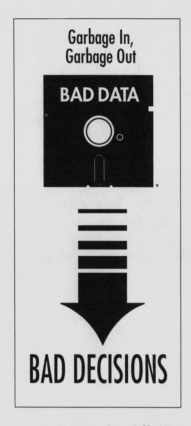

Garbage In,
Garbage Out

BAD DATA

BAD DECISIONS

6 **Limit bad data.** Industry averages say that business-to-business lists change 1% a week. This is even higher among consumer product companies. Moving, renaming, or going out of business is as high as 35% per year. Consumer moving, name changing, and leaving the face of the earth is 22% a year. Remember that your objective is to get the communications to the intended person. Even with the most well-maintained lists, the communications may not be reaching the "right" person.

Success is measured only by action, not by delivery of the mail. It is essential to commit to a data integrity program from the beginning in order to limit bad data from occurring.

7 **Determine internal responsibility.** The marketing database is a marketing tool and thus needs to be directed by the marketing department. It may be difficult to wrestle away from the Information Services department. However, marketing's needs are continually changing and marketing needs a system that is capable of delivering new information at a moment's notice.

8 **Get internal support.** Some marketing departments try to implement a loyalty database marketing initiative without getting the buy-in of other departments. Without the internal support of a company's various departments, especially those with direct customer contact, a database marketing program will come to an immediate halt.

Use your power of persuasion and personality to sell your critical counterparts on the loyalty database marketing program. Allow the field personnel to define the important characteristics which they feel must be met to have a successful program. Let the customer and the sales people make certain changes to the database such as name and address, phone, etc.

PUTTING IT ALL TOGETHER

When your loyalty marketing program is designed, begin to develop ways to measure the performance of the communications dollars and the long-term aspects of investment with the customer.

It has been found that the highest return on investment comes not from new business but from existing "best customers." Aggregate the customers into groups for the purpose of return on investment analysis.

This chapter provides you with initial information about how to make a loyalty program effective and how to set it up.

Your situation will be different from that of anyone else. However, if you understand some of the failures identified in this chapter and implement some of the success recommendations, you will be off to a great start. Remember, from that acorn a mighty oak can grow.

10 ACTION SECRETS

1 Make sure you can identify your most valuable customers.

2 Begin to improve the functionality of your customer database so that you can quickly measure their history with you.

3 Set up at least a pilot program to deal with your best customers on a customized one-to-one basis so that they feel special.

4 Set up customer advisory groups to both recognize good customers and gather ideas from them.

5 Use the profile of your best customers to begin to look for other groups like them.

6 Ask your customers to "nominate" people like them for a special offer.

7 Get input from your staff on how to connect with your best customers. Empower them to reward customers immediately in specific situations.

8 Calculate the lifetime value of a loyal customer.

9 Develop a series of custom rewards for good customers.

10 Develop a plan with a timetable on how you will continue to create more customer loyalty. Assign specific responsibility for the new program.

Chapter 15

TEN STEPS TO RAPPORT
How to Become the Emotional Twin of Your Prospect

Ray Leone

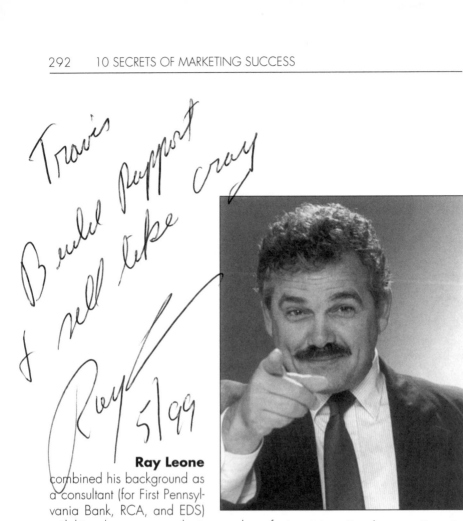

Travis
Build support
+ sell like crazy
Ray
5/99

Ray Leone
combined his background as
a consultant (for First Pennsyl-
vania Bank, RCA, and EDS)
with his sales success as the top producer for two international corporations, to
develop his highly-acclaimed Sales Funnel™ System. In addition to his Sales
Funnel™ seminars, Mr. Leone's "Logical Leadership," "How to Communicate
Like the Pros," "How to Develop a Sales Culture in Your Organization," and
"Blackbelt Service Excellence" programs are audience favorites. He is host of the
talk radio show "Winning the Game of Life" (heard Sunday mornings), and is
the author of the bestselling book *Success Secrets of the Sales Funnel*™.

Mr. Leone is president of The Leone Resource Group, and SSS Publishing.
He is a member of the National Speakers Association, American Management
Association, American Society for Training and Development, and the American
Society for Quality Control. He is on the faculty of The Peoples Network, the only
television network devoted entirely to personal development.

In addition, Mr. Leone holds a Captains and Masters license from the
United States Coast Guard, and was a professional tournament archer.
Experience in a variety of market areas gives him a unique understanding of the
challenges facing each of us.

Ray Leone, Leone Resource Group, Box 16039, Charleston, SC 29412; phone
(803) 795-9462; fax (803) 795-4113.

Chapter 15

TEN STEPS TO RAPPORT
How to Become the Emotional Twin of Your Prospect

Ray Leone

"All things being equal, people buy from people they like. All things not being so equal, people still buy from people they like."
—Mark McCormack, *What They Don't Teach You at Harvard Business School*

We can make our prospects feel comfortable by becoming more like them in as many ways as possible—in effect becoming their emotional twin. This builds rapport, the key ingredient to successful selling and communicating. It is important to note that this is not something you do *to* people; it is something you do *for* them.

The more alike we are, the fewer the barriers to communication. Clear communication of the message leads to a win-win relationship.

This includes nonverbal communication which can account for the majority of people's impressions of us.

Based on misreporting of studies by psychologist Albert Mehrabian, many popular authors and speakers claim that only 7% of our communication is in what we say, with 38% in tone and pace, and 55% in body language.

In fact, the emphasis on each channel depends on the circumstances and the person. However, the best current estimate is that, on average, about 35% of communication is based on what we say, and the rest on nonverbal factors.

DO THEY HEAR WHAT YOU MEAN?

During research for a speech I was preparing for a college fraternity, I asked the Director of Global Business Development for EDS, Tom Metz, what he thought was the most important principle for effective communication that I should share with these young adults. He advised, "Make sure they always receive confirmation of what they thought has been communicated—both as a sender and as a receiver."

Is it possible to misinterpret a conversation? Yes, it happens all the time.

Stephen Covey, in his book, *The 7 Habits of Highly Effective People,* explains how your beliefs and past experiences affect the way you interpret messages or events. Your paradigm is the lens through which you look at the world. For example, a white southerner whose grandfather died in the Civil War has a different definition of the Confederate flag than does a black American whose grandfather was a slave.

The more we mesh with another person's beliefs, paradigms, actions, and personality, the greater the rapport. The greater the rapport, the greater the likelihood of a doing business together.

You may be thinking, "Great Ray, I believe you. But how do we become people's emotional twins, especially if we have never met them before?"

I am glad you asked. Here are the ten ingredients to developing rapport:

Our paradigms are "the way we 'see' the world—not in terms of our visual sense of sight, but in terms of perceiving, understanding, interpreting."
—Stephen Covey, *The 7 Habits of Highly Effective People*

Because people are different and need different treatment, use the "Platinum Rule" not the Golden Rule. Treat them the way THEY want to be treated. There is nothing more unequal than the equal treatment of unequals.

—Ken Blanchard

1 **Personality profiles.** Many systems distinguish four dominant personality profiles. The Myers Briggs and DISC™ are the two most popular personality profiling instruments.

I find the DISC™ system easier to remember and apply to daily life. Personality differences are the basis of human behavior from which grow all other applications including how to sell, how to communicate, how to motivate, and how to manage. Using the DISC™ system, you identify personality profiles of individuals by the characteristics they display (see chart below).

Of course, most of us use different styles in different situations. Many of us also may combine two or more of the styles.

If you give a presentation without regard to personality differences, you will miss the mark 75% of the time! (For more information on DISC™ and its applications, please contact me.)

DISC™ Profiles

Dominant (D)
- Dominant
- Decision maker
- Do it now
- Results-oriented
- Impatient
- Appears insensitive
- Resists personal criticism

Steadfast (S)
- Team player
- Security-minded
- Resist sudden change
- Family-oriented
- Does things later

Interactive (I)
- Life of party
- Enthusiastic
- Do it now
- Disorganized
- Hates details
- Loves challenge
- Good verbal skills

Cautious (C)
- Do it later
- Reserved
- Critical thinker
- Conscientious
- Accurate

2 **Primary sensory mode.** All of us process information through a primary sensory mode—either *auditory, visual* or *kinesthetic*. If we present—communicate—in our prospect's dominant mode, they receive more of the message.

Conversely, when we communicate in a different mode than our prospect, then he or she is missing much of the message. For example, if you process information visually and I give a verbal presentation without visual aids, then I am not being as effective as I might.

If I were selling a car to a kinesthetic person, I would say, "Feel the leather. Notice how the seats hug your body, just like the car hugs the road."

To a visual, I would say, "Picture yourself driving down the road and the reaction of your friends when they see you in this car."

To an auditory, I would say, "Listen to the solid sound the door makes when you close it. The stereo wraps the music around you." You get the idea.

The clues to sensory mode are eye movement, rate of speech, and vocabulary.

Ask someone to remember their best sale or happiest day and watch their eyes.

Visuals look up to the right or left when trying to recall (picture) something. They generally speak fast and use phrases like, "I see what you mean."

Auditories look sideways when recalling information. Their speech is moderate and even. They use phrases like, "I hear what you are saying."

Tune In

Once identified, tune your communication style into the customer or prospect's station:

TO THE DOMINANT RECEIVER
- Be brief and to the point
- Display confidence
- Defend your position

TO THE INTERACTIVE RECEIVER
- Minimize details
- Be friendly and demonstrative
- Emphasize the positive
- Allow for interruption

TO THE STEADFAST RECEIVER
- Go slow and steady
- Be truthful and sincere

TO THE CAUTIOUS RECEIVER
- Respect their space
- Be specific and use facts
- Do not get personal

Presentation Tip: Start Multimodal

When presenting to a group or someone whose sensory mode is unknown to you, give a multisensory presentation. Use some visual, auditory, and kinesthetic cues and see how they respond.

Kinesthetics look down when recalling an event. Their speech is slow and deliberate. They use phrases like, "I feel I understand what you are saying."

3 **Rate, pace, and tone.** When I ask what Northerners think when they hear a Southerner speak, they reply that their first impressions are that Southerners are slow and stupid. When I ask Southerners what they think when they hear a Northerner speak, Southerners report that they perceive Northerners as shifty, pushy, and uncouth. What are these reactions based on? Rate of speech.

If you are an individual with a Northern accent selling to someone in the South, or vice versa, imagine how difficult it is to get past the perceptions.

To maximize the effectiveness of your communication, match the tone, pace, and rate of speech of your prospect. Notice how network news anchors are moderate in their pitch and tone. That is because they must appeal to a broad segment of the population and, more importantly, not alienate anyone because of their delivery.

4 **Life control.** I was very fortunate during the late 1970s to have sold a big-ticket item to Sheldon Glass, a prominent psychiatrist, educator, and author of the book *Life-Control.*

Not long after I met him, Dr. Glass gave me a copy of his book. I read it and was struck immediately by its relevance to selling, life, relationships—everything. Dr. Glass's theory was not designed specifically to relate to selling, but it is a perfect match. His theory is that every time we encounter

"I've found that every group (and its leaders and members) goes through an identifiable cycle, beginning with the moment it considers taking on a task to the time the goal is achieved."

—Sheldon Glass,
Life-Control

new ideas, experiences, or challenges, we go through four distinct phases.

Introductory phase. Dr. Glass: "This is a period during which new goals are worked out and agreed upon. This is a time of excitement, even euphoria. Interesting, promising new things are about to happen."

It is when Ray and Linda are first considering buying that new home.

Resistance-testing phase. Dr. Glass: "This is when the group reacts with anxiety to the change that the new goals require. It both resists that change and tests the leadership to see if it can handle the process. This is a time of uncertainty, disagreement, and general travail. The status quo has been shattered and replaced by something less comfortable."

Using the previous analogy, Ray and Linda experience concerns about moving to a new neighborhood and having to pay high interest rates. This phase if often marked by adjustments, conflicts, and arguments. In the buying cycle, it manifests itself as objections.

Productive phase. Dr. Glass: "This is when the group works to accomplish the task and meaningful change takes place. It's when the arguments subside and goal-directed work begins in earnest."

This is the "get-down-to-business" stage, when concerns and objections are resolved by Ray and Linda and they move toward the purchase of that new home.

Termination phase. Dr. Glass: "This is when the goal is accomplished, the group consolidates its knowledge, and the cycle comes to an end."

The cycle for Ray and Linda would end with the purchase of the home.

Not every member of a group may be in the same phase at the same time. This is the cause of most conflicts and disagreements. Ray may be ready to buy that new house, while Linda hasn't accepted the idea of moving to a new neighborhood.

There are many variations and angles to Dr. Glass's theory. Most of all, it helps you understand why people do what they do, especially as you learn to recognize and understand these patterns.

A Car-buying Example

Here's another example of applying the cycle model. As mentioned, the cycle can be applied to virtually any experience or progression in life, from buying a car to planning a vacation. Let me give a quick example of how simple the application of this theory can be. Suppose you and your spouse consider buying a new car. Let me break the typical scenario into components:

Introductory phase. You say, "We need a new car. Let's go look at them tonight." Your spouse says "Great! It will be fun."

Resistance-testing phase. After seeing various cars, a discussion ensues about trade-in value and having to pay the sales tax that dampens your enthusiasm. You even have difficulty deciding on a car both of you want.

Productive phase. After a short time, you not only come to grips (a kinesthetic phrase) with the sales tax and trade-in issue, but you also agree on a price range and make.

Termination phase. With all plans ironed out, you and your spouse go to the dealership that offers the vehicle you want.

The important point is to determine what phase your prospects are in when they appear before you. They could be in any of the four phases. You must recognize their phase and get in-phase with them before you can lead them along the road to rapport.

5 **Matching buying strategy.** We all do things for one of two reasons—desire for pleasure or avoidance of pain.

In my seminars when I say avoidance of pain is the stronger motivator, it creates lively discussion. I prove it by asking, "Isn't it true that if you own your own business, you have the potential to make more money than if you work for someone else?" Everyone agrees. "Then why doesn't everyone work for themselves?" Ah! Because the potential to fail and the risk of pain are greater.

Features And Benefits

Traditional sales presentations use features/benefits statements where the salesperson describes a feature and then bridges to the benefit with the phrase, "Which means to you...."

Example: Feature: Air bags in our cars. Benefit: Reduced chance of injury in the event of an accident.

Feature/benefit statement: "We equip all of our cars with air bags, which means to you, in the event of an accident, your chances of injury are greatly reduced."

Pain Avoidance

That is fine for those people who buy for the benefit or pleasure a product delivers. However, a large segment, maybe the majority of people, buy for pain avoidance.

You can determine their buying strategy by asking, "Mrs. Prospect, what will owning this copier mean to you?"

If she says, "It will give us increased capability. Our promotional brochures will have greater impact and we will be able to accomplish more in less time," then she is a person who buys for the benefits, also known as a move-toward person.

If she says, "I'm tired of the old copier always breaking down and my secretary complaining about how messy it is to change toner," then she is a person who buys to avoid pain, also known as a move-away person.

Everyone knows how to give a move-toward, feature-benefit presentation. To increase your sales success, learn to give a move-away presentation by emphasizing what they will lose by not buying.

A technique we use in our Sales Funnel™ system (described in my book *Success Secrets of the Sales Funnel*) is to create pain or discomfort in our prospect, and then provide the aspirin (the solution) that removes the pain.

Fifty percent of my income is the result of using this technique when sitting in the first-class section on an airplane. I will ask the CEO sitting next to me a series of questions that make her feel uncomfortable with her management team.

I'll ask a question like, "In terms of college semesters, how many semesters of leadership training, not management training, has your leadership team had?" The answer most often is "none." Then I say, "You wouldn't have a doctor without a medical degree, or an attorney without a law degree. Then why have a leadership team be in positions of responsibility where they have had no training for the job?" Big-time pain and deficit!

Match your message to the buying strategy of your prospects and watch your sales soar.

6 Trust and credibility. Before someone will listen to you, they must believe that you know what you are talking about. Are you credible? And they must believe that you care about them.

Notre Dame football coach Lou Holtz says there are three questions that must be answered affirmatively before anyone will follow you. They are:

- Can I trust you?
- Do you care about me?
- Are you committed to the goal?

Your prospects must believe these things about you if they are to make a decision based on what you say. To develop rapport with an audience of one or one thousand, they must know that you care and have earned the right to be called a professional salesperson.

As a speaker, I am proudest of the fact that my audiences think that I am from their industry. Whether it's bankers, insurance agents, car dealers, credit union managers, or national franchisees, they know that I care enough to have researched the problems and issues that are specific to them.

"No one cares how much you know until they know how much you care."
—Ken Blanchard, *The One Minute Manager*

The confidence that comes with preparation can not be achieved in any other way. Your prospects will know that you have earned the right to be there and will respond accordingly.

7 **Body language.** Remember, much of your in-person communication is body language. When you are in an airport, do you form opinions about the people around you— about whether they are successful, happy, sad, confident, or intelligent? I do. And it is all based on body language.

> ## Do Your Homework
>
> I have two simple rules for successful selling. (1) Never lie. If you never lie you don't have to remember what you said. (2) Be prepared. Know everything about your competition. Know everything about human behavior. Know everything about your product. Know everything about the psychology of selling and say as little as possible to make the sale.

When I owned a swimming pool company, I videotaped myself giving an actual sales presentation in a customer's home. What I learned about body language and myself was startling.

Here is what I saw on the video that I missed during the presentation. The husband leaned back on his chair whenever he got nervous. He was most receptive when we were both leaning forward. The husband and wife exchanged furtive glances while I was busy writing. They picked up the drawing of the pool which indicated to me that they had taken mental possession. Whenever we talked about fishing (the husband's favorite sport), his eyes would widen, he would lean forward and his body would relax. Whenever we talked about price, he would sit straight and constrain his movements. It was obvious that they wanted the pool.

By the way, I learned that I had a terrible habit of twirling my mustache. I looked like the villain in a silent movie. I wonder how many sales that habit cost me.

8 **Questions.** If you help raise someone's self-esteem, you will increase rapport with that person. Asking questions that uncover the true issues and concerns of prospects, allowing them to do most of the talking, raises their self-esteem.

By asking those questions, you are telling the customers that you care about what they think and feel, further increasing the bond (rapport) between you and them.

Ask Great Questions

I've compiled a list that will help you formulate good questions. When you develop a question, test it against my list. The more yes's you get, the more likely it is to be a great question.

- Does the question lower the comfort level of the client?
- Does it uncover pain?
- Does it invite the client to consider new information?
- Does the question focus on an idea that the client has not considered before?

- Does the question require careful thought before the client can formulate a response?
- Does the question increase your credibility?
- Does it reduce your competitor's credibility?
- Does the question move you further down the Sales Funnel™?

When selling swimming pools at an average price of over $20,000, I developed a powerful question that helped me earn over $1,000,000 in commissions. If I were coming to your home to sell you a pool, I would accompany you into the backyard and ask the following question, "Where have you decided to put your primary and secondary focal points?"

Test this question against my list. What happened to my credibility? What happened to my competitor's credibility when they did not ask that question? What happened to your belief that you knew everything you needed to know to make an intelligent decision? Did we create discomfort?

Create a list of several questions that have this impact and watch how differently (a visual phrase) your customers respond to you. You will position yourself as a problem solver, not a salesperson. Your customers will then treat you as a valued resource and not an adversary.

Key Questions

Here is a basic presentation based on just six questions that will lead you to a sale.

1. "Do you know we are the best or do I have to prove it to you?" This question establishes the tone for the entire presentation.

2. "What criteria are you going to use to choose a vendor?" (What is important to you?) Whatever criteria they select leads you to the next question. For example, if they say quality is their main criterion, then question 3 is......

3. "What is your definition of quality?" It is presumptuous of us to think that our definition of quality is the same as someone else's. We must make sure that we are addressing their criteria as they define them.

4. "Why is that important to you?" The answer to this question uncovers their dominant buying motive (DBM) or hot button. People buy on emotion and justify with logic. Too many presentations overlook the emotional side of the process.

5. "If I can meet the criteria you stated were important to you, will I be your vendor?"

> "When dealing with people, remember you are not dealing with creatures of logic, but with creatures of emotions— creatures bristling with prejudice, and motivated by pride and vanity."
>
> —Dale Carnegie

General Guidelines For Becoming A Sales Funnel™ Salesmaster

- The personality profile of the customer determines your strategy and demeanor.
- Ask for commitment prior to the presentation.
- Give the customer the right to disagree.
- Agreement must be obtained on every issue that you consider important or you must not continue down the Funnel.
- Ask questions that create a deficit in the comfort level of the customer.
- The WITY [What's Important To You] is a document that lists buying criteria, product features, and buying motives.

We have asked the customer to buy prior to the presentation. *This is one of the true secrets to sales success.*

Between questions 5 and 6, give your presentation based on the answers and then you are ready for the final question.

6. "What else do you need to know to be convinced that you have found the right _____ ?" (Fill in the blank with the appropriate appendage: builder, vacuum cleaner, car, banker, widget, etc.)

This is the perfect closing question because it can be answered in only two ways. One possible answer is nothing, which means they have bought. The other answer is a request for more information, which gives you permission to continue selling. Not wanting your product is not one of the answers.

9 **Balanced listening.** In Step 8, we asked the questions. In Step 9, we listen to the answers.

Have you ever been introduced to someone and ten seconds later forgotten his or her name? Why?

You weren't listening. Hearing and listening are not the same thing.

Isn't your best friend the one who listens to you without judgment. When we actively listen to prospects, we are telling them that what they say is important to us. When we take notes, that further underscores that we care about what they say.

A number of years ago, an auto manufacturer did an exit survey of people who did not buy a car. The number one reason given for not buying was,

"The salespeople did not listen to me. They gave their favorite presentation, not the one I wanted to hear."

Have you ever been thinking about what you were going to say while someone was talking to you? That is called a two-person monologue.

We can process between 800 and 1200 words per minute and speak at less than 200 words per minute. That leaves an enormous amount of idle time for our minds to occupy. Quite often, we use that time to daydream. Active listening requires a concentrated effort, but like most things, the result is worth the effort.

Just as we have different sensory modes and different personalities, we have different listening styles. Some of us listen more for facts, others listen more for the feelings behind the words.

Your goal should be to balance your listening style between fact and feelings so as to eliminate filters. There is a listening-style profile system put out by the Carlson Learning Company, similar to the DISC™ system, that identifies your listening style. The more we listen to the whole message being sent (verbal and non-verbal), the greater our understanding of our prospect and the greater the rapport.

"A leader who possesses the skill of adaptability is heaven sent."
—Sun Tzu - Ancient Chinese War Lord

10 **Adaptability.** Here's where you pull it all together. Once you can use the first nine variables of rapport, you are ready to become the emotional twin of any prospect. Because you can vary your style to match the person, others will be more comfortable with you.

When I first implemented this system, my confidence level soared. I was in total control of the process. I recall the CEO of a $6 billion corporation granting me a 15-minute appointment. Because I established true rapport, the appointment lasted two hours. He was enjoying himself and didn't want to end our conversation.

AN EXAMPLE

The most dramatic example of the power of rapport occurred when I was giving a presentation to the senior officers of a major financial institution. The CEO was a "High D," visual, move-toward person. The CFO was a "High C," move away-from, auditory person. The Vice President of Sales & Marketing was a "High I," visual, move-toward person. By changing my delivery, pace, style, and body language when addressing each of them, I was able to maximize the effectiveness of the presentation and control the entire process.

For the CEO, I summarized key points and gave them to him in rapid fashion. I arranged to meet with the CFO one hour early because I knew that he would want to go over every detail. I praised him on his ability to uncover ambiguities. I pointed out how our system would prevent mistakes. I gave him reports to substantiate our conclusions. For the VP of Sales, I joked with her and described how other institutions would envy the marketing plan that would support the new services.

Because I adapted to each person and presented the way they preferred, the deal went through. It is still one of the biggest deals of my career.

How will our marketing plan compare?

Other companies will be envious of your marketing plan.

SUMMARY

Learning to use the techniques discussed will do two things for you. First, it will make you more comfortable because you have a way to read people and adapt to each situation. You have a system to apply. Second, you will make others more comfortable with you. When they are comfortable, they will be more open to your message of how you can help them.

FULL SPEED AHEAD

10 ACTION SECRETS

1 Adjust your approach to match the personalities of your prospects and to put them at ease.

2 Present in your prospects' primary sensory modes. Convey your message the way they prefer.

3 Match your rate and tone of speech with theirs.

4 Ask questions that elicit their strategies. Understand what they want.

5 Mirror their body language and observe what their body is saying. Become "literate" nonverbally.

6 Be aware that different people can be in different stages of the buying cycle. Bring all parties into the same phase of the buying cycle.

7 Establish trust and credibility by being totally prepared. Do your homework about their industry and situation.

8 Your questions show that you are a professional. Ask questions that let the prospects know that you are there to solve their problem and want to do the best possible job for them.

9 Actively listen. Eliminate your natural filters by balancing your listening between fact and feeling.

10 Take what you have learned in steps 1 through 9 and adjust your presentation and delivery to best match your prospect in every way. Become your prospect's emotional twin and everyone wins.

Good luck and good selling!

Part Four

TECHNIQUES TO BOOST RESULTS

How To Create An Effective Sales Brochure
John M. Mora

15 Rules For Successful Selling By Phone
Margie Seyfer

Trade Show Marketing
Mim Goldberg

Special Event Marketing
Dedie Leahy

Secrets of Network Marketers That Could
Make You Wealthy InAny Business
David Klaybor

Chapter 16

HOW TO CREATE AN EFFECTIVE SALES BROCHURE

John M. Mora

John M. Mora is owner of Creative CopyWriting, a business specializing in providing copy-writing and marketing consulting services to clients nationwide. He provides copy for brochures, catalogs, and other written communication to both *Fortune* 500 corporations and individual professionals. Some of his corporate clients include Quaker Oats (Gatorade), Life Fitness, FMC, NutraSweet, Nissan, Platinum Technology, Abbot Laboratories, and Reynolds Metals.

Mr. Mora is an accomplished business writer and editor of *The Creative CopyWriting Newsletter.* His byline has appeared in many consumer and trade magazines including *Nation's Business, Construction Marketing Today,* and *Securities Technology.* Article topics he's written about include creating better brochures, increasing direct mail response rates and writing better Internet site copy, Other topics of expertise include health & fitness, nutrition and medicine. Mr. Mora invites readers to call or fax to receive a free information kit or to get a free subscription to *The Creative CopyWriting Newsletter.*

Born in Chicago, Illinois, Mr. Mora competes in triathlons and marathons in his spare time. He has competed in eight marathons, fifty running and cycling events, and sixty triathlons of various distances.

John Mora, Creative CopyWriting, 4300 Glenlow Drive, Plainfield, IL 60544; phone (815) 439-9160; fax (815) 439-9158.

Chapter 16

HOW TO CREATE AN EFFECTIVE SALES BROCHURE

John M. Mora

"Write the way an architect builds, who first drafts his plan and designs every detail."
—Schopenhauer

When Kent Carlson sat down to face the challenge of writing a product brochure for his bicycle parts company, he was frustrated.

His products—high-end lightweight bicycle stems and cranksets—were targeted for the serious bicycle racer and pro shop. His brochure had to speak their language, and distinguish his parts from the competition in a crowded marketplace.

"The goal of our brochure was to show that our products are radically different from anything out there," says Carlson, owner of California-based Sweet Parts. "We also had to convey some very technical information in understandable terms. Frankly, I didn't know where to begin."

WHERE TO START?

Every business owner or marketing director can identify with this problem. No matter what industry you're in, communicating information and creating a distinctive image for your company is a difficult task.

And even if you can convey the information successfully, will the brochure help accomplish the ultimate goal of selling?

It Starts With Great Design

Design is probably the single biggest factor in the success or failure of a brochure (and this is coming from a copywriter, so don't take that statement lightly).

People form an impression visually before they ever read a single word. The right look is critical for an attractive, compelling brochure.

BROCHURES, PAGE-BY-PAGE

Every brochure is unique, but here are some guidelines that you can use when putting together your brochure.

The Cover: Visual & Headline

The cover is the most important page on a brochure. It catches the attention of the reader (hopefully) and entices him or her to open to the inside of the brochure and read on. Don't use a graphic alone; include at least one powerful selling sentence.

A great cover immediately sends a message to prospects that your company is smart, sophisticated, and "a player." A poor cover has the opposite effect, making your business seem like a small-time outfit.

Your brochure cover is like a full-page ad. It should have as much pulling power and creative

YOUR COVER IS READ
"The cover of a brochure works like the headline of a print advertisement. *Four out of five people never get beyond it!* If you depend on the inside pages to make the sale, you are wasting 80% of your money."
—Jane Maas,
*Better Brochures,
Catalogs and Mailing
Pieces*

thinking behind it as any advertising campaign. And if you look at the components of a successful ad, you can apply those same components to come up with a striking brochure cover.

Ads often feature a visual of some sort—a funny photograph, or a creative illustration...anything that catches your eye.

Alongside the visual, ads usually have a headline or brief copy. This describes the product, or creates enough curiosity to want to learn more about the product or service. Although there are many ads that have only one of these components, I believe the best brochure covers include a creative use of both a headline and a visual. (See one of my client's brochures in the example below.)

Before

Universal Triathlon Alliance

UNIVERSAL TRIATHLON ALLIANCE
—bringing multi-sport athletes the benefits and values they deserve.

This brochure has a large graphic and tells you the name of the organization, but what's in it for you? There is no reason to open this brochure.

After

You Train Hard.
You Race Hard.

Why Not Join a
Multi-Sport
Organization
That Works Hard
for You?

Universal Triathlon Alliance

—bringing multi-sport athletes the benefits and values they deserve.

Here the focus is on you. The ad copy alludes to potential benefits. The question creates the motivation to open the brochure.

Brochure Headlines

The right headline can make a big difference. What are the characteristics of a great headline? Headlines can vary widely, depending on the nature of the business, the goal of the brochure, and the cover design. However, there are some commonalities. The best headlines are:

Short and to-the-point. Be concise. Don't be afraid to use sentence fragments or break rules of grammar to create interest or put a new twist on a common phrase or word.

Questions. Many very good headlines start with a question. A question naturally arouses curiosity and demands an answer (one that's in *your* favor!).

Relevant. Don't use a cover headline that has nothing to do with your company or product. And avoid gimmicky or "cute" headlines that aren't relevant. You may get more prospects to open your brochure, but they will be put off when they realize they've been duped.

Simple. Use simple words and phrases. Avoid any kind of technical jargon or terminology that may be confusing.

Consistent. Your headline should be consistent with the rest of the copy. It should lay a foundation. The main brochure copy should follow that theme as well.

Page 1-2: Benefits, Benefits, Benefits

Coming off the strength of a great cover, use benefits to transition into the body of the brochure.

Benefits Copy Starts Here

(Back of front panel)

The first sentence and paragraph are particularly important. They quickly give the reader a sense of what the rest of the brochure is about.

What's In It For Them? The best way to keep readers' attention is to quickly answer the most pressing question on their minds. Of course, that question is "What's in it for me?" The

Use Your Brochure To Highlight Your FAB-ulous Benefits

Here's a way to remember the feature-benefit distinction. Your product or service has:

Features that have
Advantages that provide
Benefits for your customers.

very best way to answer this primary concern is to write about the benefits of your product or service.

You want to get right to all the wonderful things your wares can do for your prospects. Everything else is just icing on the sales cake.

Benefits are often confused with features. Simply put, features are the capabilities of a product or service provider. Benefits are the tangible, practical, positive results of that feature.

See the box below for an example of how typical features translate into benefits for a treadmill.

Features And Benefits Of A Treadmill

Feature	Benefit
LCD console displays workout information like distance, time, calories burned, and speed.	Gives you everything you need to know about your workout at-a-glance and takes the guesswork out of fitness.
Power incline feature goes from 1% to 10% grade.	Get fit fast and increase your workout intensity with a simulated hill run. Also works different leg muscles for total fitness.
Heart rate feature monitors your beats per minute.	Burn calories faster by staying in your heart rate "fat burning" zone.
Extra wide, long running deck.	Provides a safer, more comfortable running surface.
Heavy-duty motor.	Enjoy years of maintenance-free, dependable running or walking.

You get the idea. Sometimes it's difficult to translate a feature into a benefit. Put yourself into your customer's shoes and you will find the task easier.

Page Three And Beyond: Stick To What's Important And Progress Logically

Once you've covered the benefits, there are many different options for organizing the content of the rest of your brochure. Some of the items you may want to include in the body of your brochure are:

- Company history
- Mission statement
- Testimonials
- Case studies
- Client list
- Features
- Technical information

There are many other types of information you can have in your brochure. However, keep in mind that the purpose of a brochure is usually to be a marketing or selling tool. Try to limit your choices to the most vital elements of your sales message.

Whatever topics you decide to cover, organize them in an orderly fashion so they make sense to the prospect. If you're selling a line of products, you may want to start with the entry-level model and progress onward. If you're selling the image of your company, divide up the remaining pages into the main strengths of your company.

The Last Page Or Back Cover

Make sure you give your prospect all the information he or she needs in order for you to make the sale. Include names, addresses, phone, fax, e-mail, and whatever is needed for them to have a clear understanding of the action they should take.

BROCHURE FORMATS

There are many different formats you can choose for your brochure. Each has its own strengths and weaknesses. The trick is to choose a format that caters to your target audience, creates the right impression, and fits your budget.

Here are some typical formats with some thoughts on what they are best used for.

The "Slim Jim" (3-fold)

This is a very popular, cost-effective brochure used by many small business owners. Sometimes referred to as a "tri-fold," this is merely an 8½" x 11" page folded twice to create three panels. When printed on both sides, the brochure has a total of six panels. Another variation is to use legal-size paper (8½" x 14") folded three times to create an eight-panel brochure.

The slim jim can be mailed in a #10 (business size) envelope as part of a direct mail package, or it can be designed to be self-mailing by using one of the flaps for the address label and postage. It also makes an excellent handout or in-store display sales piece.

Advantages: Since it is a relatively small size, printing and paper costs are low (compared to larger formats). It's also one of the easier formats to put together, since it involves a relatively small amount of copy and design.

Drawback #1: Despite all the advantages of a slim jim format, it's not one I would recommend for a large product line with a more detailed marketing message. There's just not much room with this format for more than 500 words of copy and even less room for photos or graphics.

Drawback #2: If your ideal customer represents a significant amount of revenue, or if your product or service caters to a sophisticated market, the small size of a slim jim may work against you. It's better to go with something bigger and more substantial.

Drawback #3: Since most brochures look like this, you lose distinctiveness.

Four-page Format

This is another popular brochure format which consists of one 11" x 17" page folded once in the middle to create four separate pages. This is generally on a heavy paper stock. Here you have the advantage of having four full 8½" x 11" pages to convey your marketing message, so it's easier to design something with greater substance. It's also an easy format to attach a cover letter to and send in a manila envelope.

Another consideration in terms of format is worth noting here. Although, ideally, you want your reader to act immediately, circumstances don't always permit a fast sale. So hopefully, they'll file your marketing literature instead of tossing it in the trash can. A four-page format easily fits in a hanging file folder or— when pre-punched with holes— fits snugly in a three-ring binder.

The four-page format is great

Pros And Cons Of Preprinted Paper Stock

Preprinted paper stock specifically designed for the slim jim format is available through several mail order companies and large stationery stores. (See disk.)

Pros: Preprinted paper has design elements and color schemes to give your slim jim brochure a more sophisticated, expensive look. The same design is often available in business card, letterhead, and envelope stock. You can print small quantities at minimal cost.

Cons: It can get costly and time-consuming to produce larger quantities. Additionally, as preprinted papers are becoming more popular, they might be recognized by your clients as a cheap way to obtain an expensive look. You may even see a competitor using your same paper! Another drawback is that if the manufacturer discontinues your line of paper, you lose the identity you worked so hard to create.

for conveying a marketing message in a relatively small package. In fact, many companies use this format for a single product line, or for corporate identity brochures that convey the nature and philosophy of the company in a nutshell.

Six-Page (or more) Format

The sky's the limit on the size of multiple-page brochures, which are usually saddle-stitched (stapled) or bound at the seam like a small booklet. Page length can range from six all the way up to 12 pages and beyond. This format is ideal for larger product lines or complex marketing literature that involves a variety of components.

One warning: Don't go nuts on the number of pages. Keep in mind that marketing literature has to be concise. Once you get into double-digit pages, the literature is coming perilously close to losing the reader's interest simply by the length of the piece.

Your best bet is to stick to a length that says all you need to say in as little space as possible. Usually no matter how complex your business or product, that can be done in 12 or fewer pages.

Folder Brochures

A flexible format that some people like is the presentation folder. Custom printing on folders is costly. But you can also use generic folders from the stationery store and put a nice label on them.

The real flexibility in this format is that you can vary what's inside. The contents are also inexpensive and easily updated. For instance, you can build a custom brochure for each prospect by putting just what they want to know in the folder.

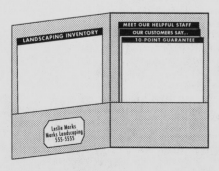

When you get new information, like a new testimonial letter, you can easily add it to the folder. When a piece goes out of date, you can change it and reproduce just the number you need on your copy machine.

USING COLOR

We've already discussed pre-printed paper that brings color, or even quality photography, to a brochure. But what about the use of color for brochures that are offset printed?

A second color on a brochure is almost required for even a simple professional look. You'd generally use the second color for borders, headlines and subheads. Often, a second color only adds about 25% to your printing costs.

Of course, a four-color brochure is the most expensive, but it presents the most striking image, and gives you the greatest range when it comes to visual elements. Four-color "process" actually gives you thousands of colors. This is the only way you can print full-color photographs.

If you get a quote from a designer or printer on a two-color job, why not see how much more it would be for full color? Although the price may jump considerably, at least you'll have all the options in front of you. Four color might cost about twice what a two-color brochure would.

PROSPECT EXPECTATIONS
Your brochure needs to meet your prospects' expectations for quality. If they expect before-and-after pictures in a four-color format, that's what you need to do.

TEN TIPS FOR WRITING BETTER BROCHURES

I've found that there are some basic factors that dramatically affect the success or failure of marketing literature. Without a careful examination of these variables, you risk spending a lot of money on a sales brochure that just doesn't do the job.

I've condensed these factors into ten tips. Use these to write copy that's on-target. Or if you've hired someone else to write your brochure, you can use these tips to check the quality of the work.

1 **Know your target reader.** Whether you're preparing for a visual presentation or a phone call, the key to any sale is to know the prospect. Writing effective copy for a brochure is no different.

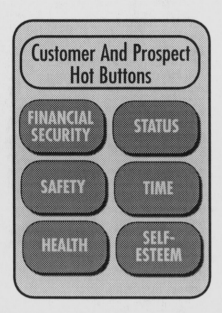

Knowing your reader means finding your prospects' "hot buttons," their unique needs and wants. Before you touch a pen or keyboard, ask yourself the following questions:

- Who is my target reader? What are his or her needs, concerns, and wants?
- What is it about my product or service that will benefit the reader most?
- What is it about my product or service that is different or better than the competition?
- How, exactly, will it benefit my reader?

2 **Identify your brochure's role and function.** Will the brochure be used as part of an in-store display, a direct mail package, a selling tool for sales reps or the centerpiece of a fulfillment package?

If you don't have a clear understanding of its role and function, your brochure may suffer from one or all three of these afflictions: lack of focus, irrelevancy, or excessive length.

To get more for their money, many companies opt for a "one-size-fits-all" approach. Although it's possible to create an all-purpose brochure, writing the copy is much more difficult than a more tightly focused piece. In addition, the brochure's impact for each specific audience is reduced. If your budget allows, you may want to consider creating different pieces for different roles and functions.

3 **Use an outline.** If you're having a hard time deciding on your brochure's content, an outline is a great way to narrow your options and organize your thoughts. See the box for an example of a basic outline for a product brochure.

Other categories you might consider are lab performance tests or comparison charts (if available) and a selection guide (if applicable). A price list is another option, although you may prefer to use a separate sheet or insert. That way you won't have to revamp your entire brochure should your prices change.

> ## Outline For Product Brochure
> I. Lead (Headline)
> II. Benefits
> III. Features
> IV. Applications
> V. Availability and options
> VI. Technical specifications
> VII. Background on company
> VIII. Support and service
> IX. Ordering information

4 **Grab their attention.** Graphics and design play a large part in creating interest in a brochure. Then cover copy and the first few inside paragraphs need to entice your prospects into continuing to read. An effective way of doing this is to address an urgent and immediate concern.

"We knew that our brochure had to capture the attention of people who need their packages delivered yesterday," says Qusai Mahmud, owner (with wife Denise) of Apex Courier, Ltd. in Chicago.

Two years ago, Qusai Mahmud quit his job as a downtown bike messenger to start his own courier business when he saw a need for a 15-minute service. Mahmud hired a local freelance copywriter to write his brochure. It included a dialogue on the cover written from the point of view of a secretary worried about losing her job because of a late package.

This lead related to the immediate concerns of the buyer. During the first few months of business, Apex received several comments from new customers who said they could identify with the

An Easy Lead

Think of the cover copy, opening sentence and the first few paragraphs of your brochure as the first five minutes of a sales presentation. Here are a few ways to grab attention.

- Start with a short sentence or phrase. Make the first few blocks of copy the easiest to read.
- Get right to the point. Avoid unnecessary phrases like "Getting to the point." Practice getting to the point without having to say it.
- Try several different leads. Write five or six different leads, then try them out on co-workers or your boss, and on family and friends.

situation the brochure cover copy conveyed.

5 Emphasize benefits. Most advertising and marketing experts agree that benefits sell.

Does that mean you should leave features out? Not at all. Your customers need all relevant facts and information to make intelligent buying decisions.

Hard, cold facts are essential. Put the spotlight on benefits first. Prospects who have an interest will tend to read on for information on features.

6 Make it quick and easy to read. Think back to the last time you had a pile of literature to read. If you're like most busy people, you probably went into "scan mode" and skimmed through several brochures, flyers, and booklets.

When writing your copy, leave your ego at the cleaners and realize that not everybody will read every word you write.

That's why it's important to divide text into short blocks of copy and use descriptive subheads (much as this book does!). For example, in the benefits section, you can use a short descriptive phrase as a subhead for each point, followed by a more detailed explanation. (See the box on the next page for an example from the Universal Triathlon Alliance [UTA] brochure pictured earlier.)

Using a short list or two with eye-catching bullets (dots, check marks, boxes) is an effective "scan mode" strategy as well. It makes it easy for readers to pick up on vital information quickly. This combines well with the descriptive subhead above. For instance:

Benefits of a Good Brochure:
- increase sales
- establish your credibility
- pictures convey complex information

7 Make your brochure a "keeper." Are there valuable facts related to your product, service or industry that are worth keeping on file? If so, create a check list, chart, graph, or illustration that prospects will refer to again and again.

Apex Courier saved the back page of their brochure for their rate chart, something they know their customers keep: "We frequently get calls from customers who haven't used us in a while and want to know if the rate chart has changed," says Qusai Mahmud. "That's a pretty good indication that the chart helps keep our brochure from being thrown in the garbage."

8 Keep it brief. Nathaniel Hawthorne once said, "Easy reading is damn hard writing." Although the literary content of your brochure may be far from *The Scarlet Letter*, (I'm no Nathaniel Hawthorne either), your literature will convey a sales message more effectively if you keep it brief.

A sentence of more than 30 words usually suggests a need for a "brevity-check." First, look for any unnecessary words that don't add anything to the thought you're conveying. Then check for redundancy. If all else fails, try rewriting to

---

Sample Brochure Text With Subheads

When You Join UTA, your membership will include:

- **The Official UTA Guidebook to Triathlons/Duathlons**
This unique triathlon/duathlon guidebook will be mailed at the end of each racing season. This handy racing reference tool will be available to members only and will give you...

- **World Wide Web Site**
UTA provides a World Wide Web site solely dedicated to multi-sport athletics. Through the postings on the UTA site, you will have instant updates concerning...

- **Race Application Service**
Forget all your race paperwork and let UTA simplify your life. As a UTA member, you can request all of your race applications through our 800 service line...

- **National Ranking System**
The UTA National Ranking System will be...updated weekly...As a UTA member, you will be provided the criteria for being ranked...

Keep It Simple

Is your copy littered with big and fancy words? If so, carefully read your draft and replace big words that may have a better synonym. Here are a few examples....

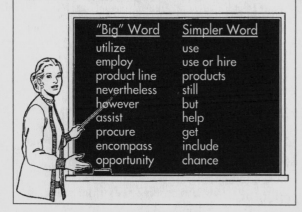

"Big" Word	Simpler Word
utilize	use
employ	use or hire
product line	products
nevertheless	still
however	but
assist	help
procure	get
encompass	include
opportunity	chance

form two separate sentences.

9 Be creative.

Yes, brochure writing can be creative. The secret is finding interesting ways to convey some of your passion and excitement about your company and what it does.

"You cannot bore people into buying your product," said David Ogilvy in his book *Ogilvy On Advertising.* "You can only interest them in buying it."

The best way to interest readers is to write copy that not only informs, but keeps them reading with crisp, creative writing.

Here are some suggestions for writing creative copy:

- **Tell a story.** A great way to do this is by using case histories—stories about past clients and how your product or service helped solve a problem or created profits.
- **Be personable.** Don't write "encyclopedia copy." Put the reference books away and try to write much like you speak. If a personable style is not appropriate for your target audience, at least try to avoid getting too technical and wordy.
- **Write first, edit later.** Don't write and edit at the same time. If your

deadline permits, walk away for a few days before you come back to the rough draft. With this fresh perspective, you can catch errors and easily plug in stats, facts and numbers.

10 **If you need to, get help.** If you've followed the previous nine tips and you're still experiencing "writer's block," or if a deadline has crept up on you and your staff, don't be afraid to use outside help.

Kent Carlson of Sweet Parts chose to hire a freelance copy-writer (me.) "I just kept putting it off and I had to have a brochure for an upcoming trade show," says Carlson. "Being a small shop focused mainly on just getting a product out there, I chose to hire outside help to get the brochure done. I'm glad that I did. I just couldn't have done as good a job, even if I had the time." Or, if you have a tight budget, for a small fee an expert can look at your draft and give you suggestions for improvement.

More Tips For Effective Brochures

Use photo captions. Photo captions are the second most frequently read brochure copy (after the headline). Yet many photos aren't captioned at all. Don't limit yourself to a few descriptive words—use the caption as another opportunity to point out your benefits.

Be honest. If a product or service isn't for everyone, say so. It will *steer* people to more appropriate products, and give your other statements credibility.

Use testimonials from satisfied users. Brochures represent individuals or companies touting their own products or services. Testimonials make your words believable.

Use your resources wisely. Your brochure represents your product or service. It's better to have a smaller, nicely designed brochure on quality paper than a larger one on inferior paper. Get at least three quotes from printers. Printing bids can vary by more than 100%.

THE LAST WORD

For most people, I recommend that they hire professional help on their brochures whether it's for copy, design, or both. (See the disk for details on different sources of help.) But whether you are doing it yourself, or working with experts, use the tips I've given you as a guide.

The right brochure can increase sales and bring in profits. That's what any great marketing tool should do.

TEN ACTION SECRETS

1 If you want a brochure done, set a date for completion now and get started.

2 Be clear on who your brochure is "aimed" at.

3 Collect testimonials that can brag for you in your brochure.

4 Develop an outline of the sections you want to have and then start filling the outline in.

5 The cover needs more than a graphic. Test different headlines to develop a "grabber."

6 Focus on benefits, not features.

7 Make it easy to scan and easy to read. Use short words, short sentences, and short paragraphs. Use lots of subheads and bullets.

8 Include industry information that people will want to save, like rates.

9 Be very clear about who you are and what you do that is different from others. Emphasize your uniqueness.

10 Get professional design and copywriting help if you need it.

Chapter 17

15 RULES FOR SUCCESSFUL SELLING BY PHONE

Margie Seyfer

Margie Seyfer
of Impact Presentations has been a professional speaker since 1985. Her high energy, interactive topics include "Lip Service" (first-class telephone and listening skills; correcting offensive vocabulary; handling irate customers; and attitude awareness); "Telephones Don't Snap—Turtles Do" (telemarketing techniques that incorporate voice mail as a sales tool); and "Attitudes Are Infectious! What Kind Are You Spreading?" She leaves her participants with value packed ideas and information. Her clients include banks, airlines, insurance, medical, securities, automotive, real estate, restaurant, telecommunications, and environmental agencies

Margie Seyfer, Impact Presentations, 3405 Ward Road, Wheat Ridge, Co. 80033; phone (303) 233-0836; fax (303) 237-3542; e-mail SeyferMarg@aol.com.

Chapter 17

15 RULES FOR SUCCESSFUL SELLING BY PHONE

Margie Seyfer

"Telemarketing is a growing $48.9 billion consumer market and $56.3 billion business-to-business market."
—Direct Marketing Association

With all the new technologies available, the telephone may still be your most cost effective tool—IF you use it well. With a systematic program of regular telemarketing, you can make big things happen for your business.

WHEN SHOULD YOU CALL?

It's been well documented that the most productive business days are Tuesday, Wednesday, and Thursday.

So which days are best for you to call prospects? When others aren't calling! Make Mondays and Fridays your big telemarketing days. There are three profitable reasons for this strategy:

- You'll start and end your week with positive activity. Momentum is the key in telemarketing—or any marketing program.

- Monday calls give your prospects an opportunity to check their calendars for the rest of the week for open appointment times. Many salespeople delay calling on Monday, believing everyone is in staff meetings. Not true!

> ## The Magic Hours
>
> The best hours to call prospects are early in the day. Depending on your industry, 8-10 am reaches people before they're tied up in meetings or out in the field. It also gets your day off to a strong start when you connect with people early.

- On Friday, you have no competion from salespeople who started their weekends at noon. Your product or service could become a hot topic at a Monday morning staff meeting. Friday is also a good day to make appointments for the next week. If you reach your prospects' voice mail Friday afternoon, simply let them know you will call again on Monday.

And obviously the other best days to make your calls are Tuesday, Wednesday and Thursday. But you already knew that!

DEALING WITH GATEKEEPERS

When trying to reach decision makers, you'll have to deal with gatekeepers.

Don't attempt to manipulate them. Make an ally of the support staff. Often receptionists and administrative assistants know more about what's going on in the office than the boss. Win over the support staff and you'll eventually get to the boss. Ruffle the support staff and you're dead in the water!

Respect and make friends of administrative assistants. Tell them why you're calling. Ask for their assistance. Remember they want to look good to their supervisors. They will listen and deliver a message if they see the benefit. Don't underestimate their power. Win over administrative assistants and you'll win the prospects.

15 WINNING RULES

RULE #1. Always Sell The Worth (Value) Before The Work (Price)

Inevitably, when you've finished your "script," the potential customer will ask, "How much does that cost?" Don't stutter or spill the beans. The question can be a buying signal.

Try this instead: Say, "Seriously, would you hire someone to train your people or buy a product based on a price given over the phone?"

They laugh and say, "Probably not. But I just want to know if we can afford it." (As salespeople, we know they can afford whatever they choose to afford.)

Then say, "I understand. We're competitively priced. I'm sure we can agree on an amount that works for both of us if you decide that what I have to offer will work for you."

Handling The "Send Me Some Information" Stall. Have you ever had prospects stall the face to face appointment by asking you to send information so they can look it over first?

Take it for the stall it is. Be gentle yet direct. Try saying this, "Whenever people ask to see information first, I often discover that they are really not interested in my service but feel uncomfortable in saying 'No.' Is that the case here?"

They often will respond with, "No. I really am interested." But

---

In Person Is Better

You may have a strong desire to mail or fax your monthly special or product brochure. Don't do it. Take it in person. If your brochure can sell your product, why does your company need you?

if they admit they're just trying to get rid of you, you've saved yourself time with your frankness.

RULE #2. The Majority Of The Time Prospects Will Not Call You

Some will. Most won't. If you want to become a member of the shopping cart pushers or "I'll work for food" sign carriers, you can sit and wait for prospects to call you!

It's amazing how many people prefer to avoid calling on the phone or in person to avoid rejection. Less personal methods don't work as well. And you don't get the useful feedback that allows you to improve, or even change, your product or service.

RULE #3. When They Don't Return Your Call It Doesn't Mean They Aren't Interested

Successful sales veterans know that a call not returned doesn't necessarily indicate a lack of interest. It most often indicates a lack of time or attention.

It's a zoo out there. Companies are short-staffed and right-sized to the point where every employee is buried with barely enough time to get all their work done. With current technology in the form of voice mail and pagers, it takes more than the old proverbial five calls to make a sale. Double that number for a more realistic picture.

Some salespeople would prefer to do "business drop-ins" than make a phone call. Good telemarketing is far less stressful, and more polite than arriving at a small business or receptionist desk without an appointment.

When to take 'no' for an answer. As salespeople, we don't

Respect Your Prospects' Time

When you're at appointments, ask them how much time they have allotted for your time together. Very few salespeople ever show this kind of consideration for their prospects' time. If your prospect tells you 15 minutes, you know how much time you have for your presentation. Stick to it.

get much pleasure out of rejection. When customers like you and don't want to hurt your feelings, they have a hundred indirect ways of telling you no.

If clients say, "It's best if I call you," ask a couple of qualifying questions to see if you can call them on a specific date about their decision. However, at this point, if they prefer to call you, it is important to know that they have just told you "No" and let it go.

People with certain personality styles avoid confrontation and disappointing others to the point that they never say "No." They just hope to wear the salesperson down. Since most salespeople give up after the third call, wearing them down is usually pretty easy. (See Chapters 7 and 15 for more on personality styles.)

Success in telemarketing means being tenacious. However, even sharks need to know when to let go and move on. Never show any disappoint-

ment or frustration when prospects tell you they will call you. Remind them to keep your information and that you appreciate all their efforts in getting your service or product approved. Then when you get back to your office, do something really out of the ordinary—send them a thank-you note. Yes, send a thank-you to the one that got away. The door is always open.

Leaving Effective Messages

You've just called a prospect. You get their voice mail. Now what? Do you hang up and call later or do you tell them who you are? Let's explore modern-day selling.

The so-called gatekeeper is happy to place us in the decision maker's voice mail where we can be erased by pressing 7. But what if there were a way to get their attention on voice mail? What if they did call you back because you peaked their interest in your product or service? Read on.

RULE #4. If You Dial The Number And Get Voicemail, You *Will* Leave A Message

- Your message will be a prepared commercial which will address one pain and one gain (see next page).
- Your commercial will be spoken at a cadence that will make your message easy to comprehend.
- You will request that the prospect return your call.

RULE #5. Know The Purpose Of Your Call

The following teledirecting method is not foolproof. It will not get you 100% return from calls to prospects. However, it will increase the number of people who do call you back.

When prospects return calls, they feel that they are in control of the sales process—it's the opposite of a salesperson trying to get into their office. Our responsibility is to have researched our prospects' needs to trigger their famous "hot buttons."

Identify the purpose of your call. Is it to:
- establish rapport,
- set an appointment, or
- make a sale?

Your purpose will determine the "pain and the gain" you use in your message.

Developing your pain-and-gain script. How much have you researched your prospect? The more industry-specific the pain, the more powerful will be the gain.

The following exercise is very helpful in determining the pain

Sample Pains and Gains

PAINS	GAINS
• missing sales opportunities	• more profits
• not giving customers the best	• lower expenses
• unhappy employees	• more time
	• less distraction

and gain. Sarah Reeves, a former professional actress and now a speaker's coach based in Newport Beach, California, teaches the following formula in her business training programs. Use the message template "You know how...Well, what I do is..."

Here is an example of how to put it into practice:

> "You know how your people sometimes feel inadequate in handling irate customers? Well, what I do is teach people a six-step strategy to control their emotions with unhappy customers."

Another example:

> "You know how when you're placing postage stamps on an envelope and you are unsure whether you should add that extra stamp? Well, what I do is help companies stop the guessing and reduce their annual postage costs by over 25%."

Identify what is hurting your prospect's company by not using your service or product. Also identify what the company will gain by using your service/product.

PAIN #1: _____

GAIN #1: _____

Decide on three pairs of pains and gains that work together. These three pains and gains will take some conscious preparation on your part. Your example should paint a vivid picture of the pain. Now write it out and practice it several times before you place your first call.

For example, if you are an accounting firm, a pain your prospects feel could be the IRS after them, or job cost data too slow to help them make decisions. A gain you offer might be helping people understand their product line profits and expenses better, or avoiding the hassle of thinking about taxes.

If you sell hand cream, a pain your prospects feel might be dry skin that makes them look old. A gain might be softer hands for romantic touching.

RULE # 6. Offer Something Free In Your Telemarketing Commercial

Tom Foy of CBT International, a computer training group based in Bountiful, Utah, finds that telemarketing results far exceed the results of magazine, radio, or newspaper advertising campaigns they have conducted in the past. He uses a 27-word script. "Hello! I'm calling to see if your office could ever use computer training and would like a free class. Call Tom at 1-800-293-5550. Thank you very much."

When you return his call, his greeting indicates that he is automatically being paged and will return your call. In their ten years of business cold calls, they've averaged about 9% who say yes they can use computer training—and 2% actually become customers. This 2% keeps CBT busy training hundreds of new customers every year!

RULE #7. Start Leaving Messages That Don't Sound Like A Salesperson's

There is an easy three-step process to leaving a message that will get attention:

Step 1. State your name, your company's name, and phone number. Speak clearly and give the information at writing speed, not speaking speed. Say who referred you.

This information is given before your prospects even know why you are calling. This makes it likely that they will jot the information down. You are placing so much emphasis on basic information that prospects assume the call must be important. Think of this as teledirecting. You are controlling the first phase of the sales process from afar.

Step 2. Use your pain and gain script (for instance, "If you have a problem with ___, we can help you achieve ___").

Breaking Out Of Voicemail Greetings

Here's what to do when you call a customer or prospect and get that familiar and routine greeting, "I'm sorry I can't take your call. If this is regular business hours, I'm either...." Simply press the # sign on your telephone and you will immediately exit the greeting, receive the beep tone, and be able to leave your message. This is a big time-saver for telemarketers— and others.

Step 3. Finally, close by asking them to call you for an appointment to explore your product or service with them. Leave your name and your phone number again, at writing speed.

Make at least three calls, leaving messages, to each prospect.

RULE # 8. Leave Your Three Different Commercial Messages At 5-7 Day Intervals

RULE #9. Remember, A Call Is A Performance

You are an actor. You're not boring or overbearing. Both are deadly in a salesperson.

RULE #10. Keep Your Energy High, Your Speed Low

You are going to increase the energy level of your voice and at the same time decrease your pace.

Fast does not equal energy. Try taking two or three deep breaths before you call.

RULE #11. Be Prepared To Talk To Your Prospect

Be ready to deliver your full script—you do have one, don't you?—in case you get to talk to the prospect in person.

RULE #12. Use Your Voicemail To Advertise What You Do Best

Give a specific feature-and-benefit description of products, services, and guarantees in your voice mail greeting. Be creative! Write several different scripts to advertise what you do and change them from time to time.

What callers should hear when they return the call and get your voicemail. You're out of your office and your prospects return your calls and get your voice mail. Does your message say something like the following?

> "This is Susie Swell with ABD Company. I'm sorry I can't take your call right now. I'm either away from my desk or on another line. Please leave a message and I'll return your call. Thank you."

If your voice mail message is anything like this, you have just missed a big opportunity to further educate or excite a prospect about your product or service.

Let's write your script! You want your message to be upbeat and informative. Use the opportunity to educate the caller on a little-known feature or benefit of your product or service.

As an example, this is my current voice mail message:

> "Thanks for calling Impact Presentations. This is Margie. At any time during this message you may press pound...[planned pause]... and immediately leave a message which I will be most happy [delighted] to return.
>
> "Impact Presentations offers Lip Service...an advanced business telephone skills and customer retention workshop. Are your people making any of these statements to your customers? 'She's not in. He's at lunch. She's in a meeting?' Did you know these kinds of statements can increase your company call load by one fourth? Our training guarantees techniques that will get

Voicemail Messages Can Be Used to Test Market New Products or Services

Recently, when I developed a new training topic, I placed a description of it on my voice mail greeting. I knew I had a winner when, in one week's time, five companies who were returning calls about an entirely different subject specifically asked for information on my new topic.

We have never sent a direct mailing piece making an announcement about a new training topic. As old clients come up in our ACT! database, I simply leave a descriptive, exciting voice mail message. I give them information about new topics and how the training can help them, along with an invitation to call for more information and they return the call. What a concept!

Five Steps To A Super Script

1 Thank them for calling and give the by-pass instruction—total time 15 seconds.

2 Introduce the name of your company, the product/service and what it is.

3 Ask one or two pain questions.

4 Make the gain statement of what you and your product or service will do.

5 Close by thanking them—total time—steps 2-5—thirty to forty-five seconds.

your people into the '90s both in the way they are handling your phones and your customers.

"Thank you for your call."

RULE #13. Keep Your Commercial To 60 Seconds Or Less

The above script is 111 words and lasts approximately 50 seconds. This is why it is important for your customers to be able to utilize the by-pass feature on your voice mail service or answering machine. You may wish to make your message longer but first consider making it shorter and changing it more often. One minute is the attention maximum.

RULE #14. Choose Your Words Carefully To Power Your Message

A good salesperson emphasizes the words "you" and "your" rather than "me" and "I." Review the sample script again. The words "you" and "your" are used nine times. The word "I" is used once.

RULE #15. Answer Your Phone In A Way That Will Make The Customer Say "WOW!"

When you are in your office, answer your phone personally.

Most of us have had no formal telephone training. We simply copy what everyone else does without giving a whole lot of thought to that important first impression.

Are you answering your business phone like this?

"Green Mountain Tree Service. Tom speaking."

Tape record about fifteen minutes of you or a co-worker answering the phone now and play it back in your car's tape deck when you drive home or go to meet a client. It can be very enlightening.

Let's analyze what we can do better than this common way most firms answer their phone.

Start with a greeting. Whether it is "good morning," "good afternoon," or "thanks for calling," it gives the caller's brain a chance to connect with where they are calling.

Use "Thank you for calling" as an opener and you won't have to think about what time of day it is and can concentrate on thanking the customer for choosing to call your business. ("Good morning/good afternoon" greetings aren't good for people outside your time zone either.)

Next say your company's name at a cadence that can be understood. When you sound rushed, it says to the customer that they are interrupting you and you have better things to do. They hear it and get the message.

Recommended Telephone Greeting

"Thanks for calling Mile High Comics. This is Susie. I can help you!"

Now introduce yourself. Just your first name, please. That's all the caller can mentally connect with. You identify yourself to establish an emotional connection and so that the caller can immediately call you by name. And you can drop the "speaking" part—it is obvious that you are speaking. "Speaking" is a wasted word.

Here's how you can get a WOW! With energy make this statement, "I can help you!" or "We can help you!"

Here's the kind of responses you will get: Laughing, the caller responds "Well, I'm sure you can!"

URGENCY + PERSISTENCE = SUCCESS!

What will make you successful at telemarketing? A sense of urgency plus persistence.

When I began training as a new salesperson, my manager suggested that to be successful I spend at least two straight hours every day telemarketing. Every day. Day in and day out!

Be Consistent

Take this rule to heart. What new salespeople discover is that you can actually spend a lot more than two hours a day telemarketing. Count the calls and you can count the sales.

Does this mean you can never goof off? Of course not. Make those times an intentional celebration of a goal you have accomplished.

Here's the payoff for developing the two-hour habit. You will find that after two straight hours of presenting your script, you will get on a roll and your effectiveness and enthusiasm will increase.

I have actually bounced off the walls in my office when I have landed an important appointment or have been selected to present to a large group. Exciting messages on my voice mail have brought me to my knees. There are true moments of joy in telemarketing. Pick up your phone. There are people out there waiting to hear from you!

SELF-TALK, PERSONAL GOALS, AND A LOVE OF SALES WILL MOTIVATE YOU TO BE SUCCESSFUL IN TELEMARKETING AND IN LIFE!

New ways of doing things make our jobs more exciting. When we have more success, it becomes more fun. Here are some ways of motivating yourself to get on the phone.

• **Use instant replay.** If you have spoken to the prospect before, relive in your mind everything about the previous conversation or meeting. Remember the friendliness of the person. Analyze how else you can help this prospect that you failed to mention the last time you called.

- **Build on past successes.** Read aloud to yourself a testimonial letter you received from a client.

- **Picture a group of people discussing how to find a new vendor to provide the kind of service you offer.** The person assigned to the task of finding this new vendor is in your prospect file. They are just too busy to try to find us. Sometimes sales can be equated to finding that proverbial needle in the haystack. But they are out there and it is up to us to find them.

- **Repeat your script three times out loud before you make the first call.** Add more enthusiasm to your script each time you repeat it. This is your one-person sales meeting. It may sound goofy but it works.

- **Celebrate successes with tangible rewards.** Whenever you have a success that makes you shout with excitement, buy yourself something that will remind you of the success every time you wear it, carry it, or see it. For me, it has been a rolling catalog case, a new watch, new clothing, and recently a new pen.

These tangible rewards trigger memories of big accounts landed, the biggest check received, and the most money received in a week or a month. (Being invited to contribute to this book now merits a success trigger the day the book is available in book stores.)

Set goals for yourself. When you attain them, reward yourself and set higher goals.

TEN ACTION SECRETS

1 Make calls every day on a regular schedule, starting early in the morning.

2 Develop an appreciation of gatekeepers and show it. They can help you get to the decision makers.

3 Sell value before you discuss price.

4 When people stall you by asking for information, ask them frankly if they are just trying to get rid of you. You win either way. Your honesty will help break through to the person, or save you time.

5 Don't be discouraged when people don't return your calls. It doesn't always mean they aren't interested.

6 Follow up successes AND failures with thank-you cards.

7 Use a prepared script when you speak to people.

8 Develop specific message commercials to leave on voice mail that will motivate people to return your calls. Include a specific pain they feel and how you can or will solve the problem.

9 Use your own voice mail to leave a commercial for your services and products.

10 Answer your phone better by using the formula: greeting, company name, your name, and that you CAN help them.

BONUS TIP: Make a real commitment to calling and be persistent.

Chapter 19

TRADE SHOW MARKETING

Mim Goldberg

Mim Goldberg
has been with Marketech since
its inception 11 years ago. Six
years ago, she assumed the role of vice president of training, and in 1995
became president.

Ms. Goldberg is rated as one of the best trainers at conferences and seminar
programs across the country. Her clients include for-profit and nonprofit organizations, show management, and professional and trade associations. They
range from *Fortune* 100 corporations to small entrepreneurial novices in the
exhibit market. Some of her most recent clients include *Instrument Society of
America, Newport Yachting Center, Hewlett Packard, Mylex, Quebecor,
SEMA, US Robotics, and Educational Testing Service.*

Many of the concepts and skills communicated through live presentations
have been captured in Marketech's *Exhibit Manager's Companion Series* of
exhibitor educational materials which include ten different products (print, video
and cassette), for use by both the exhibit manager and show management.

Ms. Goldberg is widely published in publications such as *Exhibitor
Magazine, Trade Show and Exhibitor, Creative Exhibiting Techniques, Tradeshow
Week, Nations Business and Sales,* and *Marketing News and Strategies.*

Mim Goldberg, Marketech, 19 Powder Hill Way, Westboro, MA 01581; phone
(508) 836-2633; fax (508) 836-2633.

Chapter 19

TRADE SHOW MARKETING

Mim Goldberg

"It costs 62% less to close a lead generated from a show than one originated in the field."
—Center for Exhibit Industry Research

Trade shows are big business. But just how big?

Currently $81 billion is being spent each year on some 10,000 shows within the US. By the year 2000, that figure will approach $100 billion dollars.

In a 1996 study sponsored by the Center for Exhibit Industry Research, trade shows ranked 22nd in contribution to the GNP. On any given day, 50 shows are taking place in the US and some 50,000 exhibit staffers are on the show floor.

Trade shows are a highly effective selling tool. Yet they are also a very misunderstood medium. Trade shows are often not as effective as they might be because they are not handled well and not treated as an integrated part of the marketing mix.

THE MARKETING MIX

What is the marketing mix? It is a blend of strategies and programs that allow an organization to maximize its strengths and minimize its weaknesses to achieve its marketing objectives.

You must understand your overall marketing strategy before serious consideration can be given to what your exhibit should look like, what your graphics should say, and what kinds of giveaways should be employed.

THE BENEFITS OF EXHIBITS

Exhibiting lets you to meet face-to-face with prequalified prospects. Where else in such a short amount of time—two to four days—can you come in contact with 2,000–100,000 potential prospects?

Exhibiting provides you a three-dimensional stage upon which you can determine needs and qualify prospects.

Exhibiting is an integrated selling tool that allows you to bring together all the resources in your arsenal to meet visitor needs. Trade shows give you the opportunity to sell to existing customers, show them what's new, and further your relationship.

Here are things you can obtain from a good trade show that delivers your audience:

Generate qualified leads. Eighty-five percent of all exhibitors list this as the primary reason for exhibiting.

Build rapport. Enhance relationships with your current customers and begin to establish relationships with new prospects.

How Do Trade Shows Fit Into Your Marketing Mix?

To answer this question, you must ask yourself these four questions:

1. What function do trade shows play within your marketing mix? The mix may also include direct mail, telemarketing, advertising, and press releases. What are their respective roles and what can exhibiting do to help achieve your overall objectives?

2. Who is the target audience? Is this the right audience?

3. How do trade shows fit in the economic mix? Your marketing dollars are finite, therefore careful consideration must be given to their role and the expected outcome.

4. How will success be measured? Will it be the number of qualified leads? Or will measurement be the number of demonstrations performed with a post show survey of memorability and recall?

Gather market intelligence. See what is going on within your industry and see what the competition is doing.

Introduce new products. You'll get your products into the hands of those most interested, and receive immediate feedback.

Network. Meet and talk with your peers.

Increase name awareness. Let a greater number of people know who you are, what you do, and how you can help them meet their needs.

Penetrate new markets. In a short amount of time, you can communicate a different aspect of your company to a prequalified group of people.

Plant seeds. Encourage existing customers to think of you in a different manner, and provide new prospects with reasons to consider you.

Restate your image. With so many companies downsizing and restructuring, shows are an excellent means of getting out your message.

Change your positioning. Many companies undergoing great change use exhibiting to clarify their current situation.

Teach and learn. Every time you communicate with a prospect, you are teaching. Every time you walk the show floor, you are learning.

Contact suppliers. Often they are also exhibiting or are attendees. This is an excellent chance to communicate.

Recruit personnel. You have the right pool of people who can see you personally, and who you can often see in action at the show.

Shows = Good Prospects

Did you know that:

91% of decision-making attendees consider trade shows as an extremely useful source of purchasing information.

80% of attendees are decision makers or influencers.

90% of the attendees have not been seen by your sales force within the last year.

90% plan on making a purchase within the next 12 months.

30% have a definite interest in your product or service.

It costs **33%** less to generate a lead at a trade show.

It costs **62%** less to close a lead generated from a show than one originated in the field.

Center for Exhibit Industry Research

11 KEYS TO TRADE SHOW SUCCESS

Question: How can you assure that your exhibit program will succeed?

Answer: Create an effective plan and budget; execute aggressively; follow-up thoroughly.

Key #1. Create A Plan

Include sales, customer service, project management, and technical personnel along with marketing so that your exhibit plan is truly representative of your "internal customers" and meets the needs of the units represented. This will help overcome any resistance, improve understanding of the medium, and get everyone on board.

Identify your target audience. What differentiates them from the remainder of the show's audience?

Consider what attendees will want to do and see when they visit your booth as well as how you want to interact with them. What do you anticipate from your competition? These and other broad-based exhibit marketing issues will form the basis for your trade show plan.

What other marketing communication vehicles will you use to communicate your message? What preshow promotion can you do such as direct mail, telemarketing, personal phone calls, faxes, or the World Wide Web from your sales staff to hot prospects and current customers?

Other preshow planning should concern booth graphics, show directory advertising, sponsorships, press releases, collateral materials at the show (like literature and giveaways), and live presentations.

Virtual Trade Shows

The first "virtual" trade show happened online in 1996 (InterAct '96). Speakers presented, exhibitors gathered leads, and attendees found out about new products. Virtual shows won't replace the value of face-to-face contact, but they will be an increasing presence.

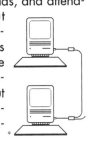

ALICE LEARNED HER LESSON
"If you don't know where you're going, any path will take you there."
— The Cheshire Cat in *Alice in Wonderland*

Key #2. Have Specific Objectives

With substantial dollars at stake, it seems amazing that so many exhibitors just show up without a plan. In fact, 50% of all exhibitors never set objectives.

What do you want to accomplish at the show? Determine your objectives for exhibiting. These can include generating leads, introducing a new product, getting feedback from attendees, increasing name awareness in a new market segment, or conducting demonstrations.

Any or all of these may be viable objectives. The key is to set quantifiable numbers so that you are able to measure their success for you. How many qualified leads do youwant to generate? How many demonstrations can youconduct?

Set measurable objectives by drawing upon past experience at the show,and taking into consideration your booth size, the number of staff, the number of show selling hours, whether there are concurrent sessions taking place, and the expected number of attendees.

Key #3. Focus Your Message

Cost Rule Of Thumb

Space costs equal approximately 25% of your budget. Therefore if you know how much your space rental is, then multiply that rental by four and you will have a rough estimate of your total budget (not including personnel costs). Other costs include transportation, drayage (moving your goods from the receiving dock at the show hall to your designated space), installation and dismantle, ad specialties, preshow promotions, and special events or activities.

Decide what message you want the staff to communicate. What two or three key points are of particular importance at this show? What do youwant the attendees to remember about your company's product or service after the show? The less complex your main message, the greater the chance it will be retained.

Key #4. Create A Budget

Often your exhibit can account for between a quarter to a third of your company's marketing budget. Setting a realistic budget is critical.

Key #5. Supplement The Exhibit Function If Necessary

Too many marketing dollars are at stake to shortchange your exhibit preparation. Often your exhibit manager is one person who wears a variety of hats

Outsourcing of particular functions assures all aspects of your plan are met. Supplementing your staff can be through specific functions, such as development of collateral material, hiring local "meeters and greeters" for your booth, or hiring an exhibit coordinator.

Key #6. View Exhibiting As A Total Marketing Communications Tool

Exhibiting is unique because it is an integrated marketing communication tool. Trade shows are three dimensional and offer the attendee the opportunity to see your products in operation, to touch them, and sometimes even to try them.

Trade shows are far more than a marketing function. They are events chosen by attendees who have interests or needs in a market area. They have come to see what is new, to get answers to their questions, to meet with technical experts, and to make buying decisions.

Exhibitor First Aid Kit

Murphy's Law reigns at trade shows—what can go wrong will—so be prepared and bring along the following items.

- Hammer, selection of nails, nail puller
- Pliers and wire cutter
- Screwdriver assortment
- Tapes: rug, strapping, masking, double-sided, and Velcro loop, indelible marking pens and chalk
- Staple gun and staples
- Tape measure (25 ft.)
- Shims for leveling
- Fire extinguisher
- First aid kit
- Electrical supplies: 25ft. industrial extension cord, 4-way box, hot-wire tester, spare bulbs
- Touch up paint
- Cleaning and repair solutions: lighter fluid, glass cleaner, fabric spot remover, plexiglass repair kit and polish
- Portable vacuum cleaner
- Flashlight
- Plastic sheet to cover carpet during setup
- Wire bailing and rope

Preshow Promotion Tips

- Identify and contact targeted prospects
- Invite your existing customers, hot prospects, and other prospects
- Use show supplied invitations
- Print your own personalized invitations
- Use a post card—oversized is better
- Send a personal letter
- Follow up the letter with a phone call
- Use telemarketing or fax

Tips For Preshow Direct Mail

- Tie your booth theme into your preshow promotion
- Use a colored envelope to get attention
- Handwrite or type the address on the envelope
- Use a postage stamp instead of a meter indicia—it's more personal
- Use some type of verbal teaser on the envelope
- Identify the name of the show on the envelope
- Be certain to include your booth number

Trade shows are a condensed selling situation. In a very short amount of time, you can discover who a visitor is, who they work for, what they do, why they have come to the show, and what their needs are. You can find out their roles and their economic buying power.

Trade shows bring the decision makers and influencers—the people who drive the buying decisions. There aren't many better opportunities to be able to meet with the right individuals.

Key #7. Preshow Promotion—It's A Call For Action

In today's environment, 75% of all attendees have preset agendas: They know who they want to see, who they have time to see, and how much time they can spend in the exhibit hall.

Exhibitors can no longer take the attitude, "I'm here, they'll find me." Invite attendees to visit your booth through a preshow promotional program. Use some of the added-value tools that trade-show management provides such as direct mail lists, show logos, VIP passes, free floor admissions, etc.

Remember, no one knows you are at a show unless you tell them.

Key #8. Use Giveaways Effectively

Beware—those attention-getting devices can be over-attracting and nonselective.

Remember why trade shows are called TRADE shows. You are there to trade something for information that will allow you to accelerate your selling cycle. Each time you use a giveaway, or entertain attendees with a live presentation, you should expect a return.

There is an art to selecting effective giveaways. Determine what you want your giveaway to accomplish. Your giveaway can:

- **communicate** a message about your company or your product
- **reinforce** a message
- **motivate** the attendee to come and see you
- **reward** the attendee—a thank you for taking the time to stop

Seven Rules For Using Giveaways

1. Make the gift specific to your business
2. Be selective to avoid "hit and run" attendees collecting "stuff"
3. Keep the premiums out of sight
4. An effective giveaway should have high perceived value
5. Useful gifts are retained
6. Unique is better than expensive
7. On-the-desk items are in better than in-the-desk items

Key #9. Give Out Literature Selectively

Use your literature selectively. Studies show that 90% of all literature never leaves the show city (and much of the rest gets thrown away at home!). Note the attendee's interest and needs, and send the literature *after* the show.

This is a double benefit. It assures that the requested information reaches the desk of the prospect, and it gives your sales staff another reason to make contact with that individual.

Key #10. Make Your Live Presentations Work Smarter

Those entertaining performers, those magicians, can be an excellent means of gathering an

audience and communicating your message. But they can also be a waste of money if, after their performance, everyone gets up and leaves your booth.

How do you keep those interested visitors in the booth, to see more, to talk to staff, have demonstrations, etc.?

Position staff around the perimeter of the entertainment, so that they can engage the visitors when the show ends. Have your entertainer use some qualifying questions to the audience to identify various needs so the staff can key in on these people after the show.

Be certain your staff does not become the audience. They have an important role to play to make the entertainment work for you. If there is no personal interaction after the presentation, if the attendee came only to receive the free t-shirt or water bottle, if they did not complete any type of lead form—then you traded something for nothing.

Key #11. Use Staff Effectively

Your booth, your giveaways, your live presentations, and collateral material are all only support. Yet too often the booth becomes all important. All the resources go into creating a magnificent edifice, but when it comes right down to it, only your staff can sell.

Eighty-five percent of your show success depends upon staff. Only 20% of those companies which set objectives for their booths ever communicate them to their staff.

Your company needs to stress the importance of obtaining results. Staff must understand the reasons for exhibiting and what they are expected to accomplish at the

Watch Out For Managers?

According to the Trade Show Exhibitors Association, your *senior managers* often clutter your booth and distract efficient staff! Make sure to give them specific jobs, or restrict their time in the booth!

show. Otherwise, they may resent the time they are asked to spend at the show. They may show up grudgingly. They may talk among themselves rather than to attendees.

STAFFING UP: SELECTING AND TRAINING

The best staffers for a trade show booth have a good appearance, and are open and friendly—and project that feeling. Personnel need to have good product knowledge and be able to solve problems that the attendees may bring.

Prepare your exhibit staff using either an internal person or hire a trainer to help them transition their daily skills effectively to the show floor. Conduct a preshow meeting, provide cross-product training, and build a team approach.

Nine Attributes Of A Successful Staffer

1. Has a "can do" attitude
2. Conquers fear of rejection
3. Knows the product/service and is confident
4. Understands that time is money
5. Remembers the process: get information, give information, get commitment
6. Listens more than talks
7. Establishes rapport by being consultative
8. Remembers to close on a commitment
9. Knows that sales result from lead follow-up

Why Should You Train Your Staff?

There are several good reasons to develop a show training program.

- Direct selling and exhibit selling are different because of the impact of time and location.
- Many non-sales staff may be there, such as technical support.
- You may have hired local, temporary staff who don't know your company.

The staff need to understand how to communicate in different modes with less time and more focus. They need to be armed with skills and techniques that will allow them to be effective on the floor.

Conducting A Preshow Meeting

A 45- to 90-minute meeting, along with a preshow briefing document, will assure that all staff know the show objectives. This includes the key messages and theme of your booth.

Staff need to understand what qualifies a prospect at this show. They need familiarization with the visitor IDs, to know how to use attention getting devices, and how often the demonstrations or live presentations will be conducted. You must familiarize them with the type of lead form being used and what kind of information to capture.

Cross-Product Training Pulls It Together

There is nothing worse than having a staff person say "Oh, I don't know that product," or "I have no idea where that area is in the booth." This leaves the visitor wanting a higher level of product knowledge and staff skill.

Prior to the show, you have a number of options. You can utilize a preshow briefing document, e-mail, or a newsletter in conjunction with a preshow meeting. At the show, you can include cross-training in the booth orientation by having each staffer train others in his or her area.

You need to include a product overview, target market, several key message points, several competitive advantages, the benefits in using the products, and several of the most often asked questions.

Creating A Thinking Team: The Whole Is Greater Than The Parts

Creating a team is sometimes very difficult at a show.

Cross-Product Training Checklist

- Product Overview
- Target Market
- Key Questions
- Pricing
- Features
- Availability
- Benefits
- Competitive Advantages
- Demonstration Information: How to involve the attendees

There can be multiple divisions in one booth, with various products sometimes in competition with one another.

The preshow meeting should work to create a functioning team. Familiarize staff with one another, the booth layout, and the company objectives and messages. This will go a long way in making staff feel they can direct or redirect an attendee with ease, as well as making attendees feel a sense of unity among staff.

Help Your Technical Staff Feel Comfortable In This Face-To-Face Environment

The technical staff who are accustomed to working with *things* rather than people are in an uncomfortable situation at shows. They need to be provided with skills to deal with these issues.

Technical staff discomfort manifests itself in procrastination (facing inward and fine tuning the equipment) and limited face-to-face communication. Visitors to a booth sense this and are turned off. Attendees often look forward to talking to technical experts, rather than "sales-types." Visitors want to find out what is new, and to get answers to their technical problems and find solutions.

Help technical staff understand that they don't have to become traditional salespeople to succeed. If they smile, face the aisle when not engaged, appear approachable, avoid speaking in technical jargon, and ask open ended questions, they will then be able to meet the needs of the

What To Wear?

Dress too formally and you run the risk of looking unapproachable. Dress too informally and you don't look like a professional. What's an exhibit booth worker to wear?

According to the International Association of Exposition Management, the best apparel depends on what the attendees are wearing. Dress slightly more formally than the attendees to look professional and approachable.

attendees. And as a bonus, they may get some interesting questions that give them ideas.

WORKING THE SHOW: ENGAGEMENT, QUALIFICATION, COMMUNICATION, DISENGAGEMENT

Engagement

Frequently, the most difficult thing for the staffer to do is to begin a conversation.

What do you say to someone you don't know that will begin a dialogue? "Can I help you?" doesn't work at all. The response to this question is usually, "No thank you, just looking."

Train for open-ended questions that will provide some information. Then the dialog can move forward without seeming like an interrogation. Openers like:

"Tell me a little bit about what you do, what brought you to the show, what you are looking for, etc." are most helpful.

Remember that the attendees are just as uncomfortable as you are. They are concerned you will try to strong-arm them and put on the hard sell.

"Seek first to understand, or diagnose before you prescribe.... It's the mark of all true professionals."
—Stephen Covey, *The 7 Habits of Highly Effective People*

Qualifying

Be certain the staff understands how to qualify. In other words, what makes someone a viable prospect for you? Using probes will clarify who is a prospect and who is not.

Probes can include: Are they the decision maker or influencer? Do they have a project, do they have a budget, and what is their time frame?

Communicating

Before communicating your message, the staff first needs to let the attendee set the agenda.

Far too often, staff jump in and say, "Let me tell you about our product" before they know or understand the prospect's needs.

You have to get information before giving information. If you give too much information too fast, you will be "information dumping." You may be wasting the attendee's time—and yours.

In exhibiting, it is more important to be a good listener than a great speaker. Listening skills are critical on the show floor, where there are so many distractions.

Effective staff should listen at least 60% of the time and talk no more than 40%. Listen with the intent to understand the prospect's issues, problems, and needs, rather than with the intent to reply. Listening this way shows the attendee that you really heard them and that you—or the staff—valued what they said.

> The old sales advice is good at exhibits too. Your have two ears and one mouth—use them in that proportion.

Once you understand their needs, communicate your messages clearly and succinctly using examples, supporting data, and stories about people who have used your product. Summarize periodically to reinforce the message and always use positive language. Remember—you only have one chance to make a good first impression.

Disengagement

Be sure to "close on a commitment" as you disengage. What do you want to have happen after the show? Do you need to take an action, such as send key literature or arrange an in-house demonstration? Or do you want a reaction—"What did you think?" or How do you feel about what you saw?"

Be certain to capture this information on your lead form. Your leads are the bridge to accelerating sales.

LEAD MANAGEMENT: CLOSE THE LOOP

Do you want to make your exhibits 400% more effective? All you have to do is follow up effectively!

If you follow up your leads generated from shows, you will be four times more effective than the average company. In fact, a whopping 80% of leads are never followed-up *at all* according to the Center for Exhibit Industry Research!

Many times leads are nothing more than contacts or lists—containing name, address, and phone number. For the lead to be worth anything, it must be qualified. That's why your well-designed lead form is so important to capture the right information.

Your sales staff have enough cold calls of their own already, without adding to their list of unqualified leads. Show leads must match a profile so that they can eventually become sales.

The work just begins when the show closes. That is when the sales staff follows up the leads generated at the show. Once the show is over, you need to have a system in place so that follow-up is automatic.

Lead Tracking Form

Name_____

Address_____

Phone_____ Fax_____

e-mail_____

Specific interests _____

Time frame _____

Authority _____

Concerns (price, availability, etc.)
_____

Trade Show Reports

Lead summary. Tracks leads by territory, by quality, or by sales generated.

Sales tracking system. Tracks by the show, by the customer or product, by the value, by the date and by whom.

Cost per lead system. Tracks the total number of leads by show, the actual cost of participation, and the cost per lead.

Show comparison report. Compares from show to show the number of leads, quality of leads, and sales generated.

Remember, it doesn't matter what you use as long as you use something!

A closed-loop management system with accountability is needed if you want a return on your exhibit investment. This means capturing the lead, fulfilling the request for information, tracking the lead, and then creating some type of reporting function.

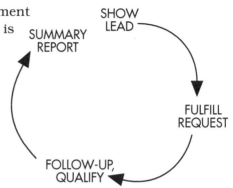

SHOW LEAD

SUMMARY REPORT

FULFILL REQUEST

FOLLOW-UP, QUALIFY

CONCLUSION

Exhibiting is an economic event that should generate a return on your investment. Rather than being a lot of work that interrupts your regular routine, it can be an economical way to gather information and many qualified leads at one time. To make shows work for you, plan well, execute aggressively, and follow up completely.

Practice what you learn. What you learn becomes your habits. Your habits become your results. Let successful trade shows become a habit. When you work them right, they'll work for you!

10 ACTION SECRETS

FULL SPEED AHEAD

1 Decide how trade shows fit in your overall marketing mix. For instance, are they a prime source of new leads or a way to stay in front of existing customers?

2 Create a plan to appeal to your target audience at each show. Develop measurable objectives for each show.

3 Prepare your staff ahead of time on how to "work the booth." The difference between an active staff who reaches out and greets passers-by and one that hangs back and doesn't initiate contact can be 5 to 1 in results.

4 Realize that up to 90% of your booth's effectiveness can come from preshow promotions. Do preshow publicity releases. Invite key contacts ahead of time. Send them part of a giveaway that they have to come to the booth to complete, etc.

5 Create a team environment at the booth. Consider offering incentives for total team performance to encourage staff to cross-train each other and handle visitors together.

6 Let technical staff know that their job is to be resources and consultants for visitors, not "hard sell" salespeople.

7 Focus on qualifying visitors and recording information for later follow-up. Don't be among the 80% of companies who waste their show leads.

8 Don't use attention-getting devices that distribute a lot of free "T-shirts" but don't let you qualify attenders.

9 Try to avoid giving out literature to those who show only a casual interest. Most will be overwhelmed with a mass of show literature, and discard it before reading it. It's better to collect their names and contact information, and follow up after the show. Then you can follow up with the 90% of attendees who throw away literature.

10 Don't forget to make those little extra efforts that can mean more exposure at the show. These can include developing leads among other exhibitors, and personally inviting press people from the press room to come to your booth. This is easy to do when you take your press releases in there and then check back to keep the supply full!

Chapter 19

SPECIAL EVENT MARKETING

Dedie Leahy

Dedie Leahy has an extensive background in marketing, public relations, graphic design, fashion, public speaking, and literary representation. With this background, combined with her experience as a newspaper columnist and in television, Ms. Leahy is uniquely prepared to help clients bring out the best in themselves and their companies.

Ms. Leahy is a creative strategist with a cost-efficient approach to communications. With a keen eye for detail, and sense of purpose in design and production, she bridges the gap between creating the appropriate message and sending it effectively.

Serving as an "executive coach," Ms. Leahy also conducts seminars and workshops for companies, conventions, and nonprofit organizations. Topics include: "Creating Effective Marketing Strategies," "Seven Keys to Effective Media Relations™," "Customer-Winning-and-Keeping Communications™," and "Business Etiquette and Corporate Entertaining." Dedie Leahy & Company provides marketing and creative direction as well as Solution-Focused™ Motivational Training on a consultancy basis.

Dedie Leahy, Dedie Leahy & Company, 3883 Turtle Creek Boulevard, Suite 1704, Dallas, TX 75219; phone (214) 521-9577; fax (214) 521-9578.

Chapter 19

SPECIAL EVENT MARKETING

Dedie Leahy

"You can get more free publicity from a
great event than by winning a Nobel prize!"
—An anonymous editor

Event marketing—hosting a special event such
as a gala benefit, corporate reception, or a 10K run
for charity—can *magnify* your organization's value
significantly. It can motivate your customers, patrons, and community to think of you as a preferred
supplier. It can create reasons to merit media coverage. The right event, thoughtfully and creatively
produced, can enhance your organization's credibility and increase the understanding and positive
awareness of your mission, goals, and services.

A MARKETING CHALLENGE IS AN EVENT OPPORTUNITY

The phone rang. "Dedie," the caller said with a
smile in his voice, "I know you like a challenge." Ed
Frazier is one of my all-time favorite clients. He is a
smart, honest Texan with an easy, down-to-earth
charm. He was making successful megadeals around
the country then. Today, it's around the world.

At the time, he served on the executive committee of the board of the USA Film Festival.
Because of an unforeseen situation, the organization found itself in a predicament. They had
announced a date for the "Master Screen Artist
Award and Gala." But they had no star to receive
the award, no place for the elegant event to occur,
no host committee, no theme, no invitation, no
music, no menu, and no publicity plan.

And the date was only 45 days away!

This was the organization's major annual
fundraiser as well as its primary marketing effort
with the community. I said yes to the challenge of
making it happen *as scheduled.*

PULL OUT ALL THE STOPS

When you absolutely have to make something
work at a quality level, you must commit 110%. If
you're even a bit tentative, other people won't come
on board. Genuine enthusiasm, however, is conta-
gious.

My first mission was to locate a star. He/she
had to be very famous, deserving of the USA Film
Festival's highest honor, approved by the board of
directors—and available on that date.

By the grace of God, after brainstorming and
working closely with the board, as well as calling on
friends and acquaintances connected with the entertainment business coast-to-coast, I reached
Robert Duvall's manager. He said that he thought
Duvall, the Academy Award-winning and exceed-
ingly deserving actor, would be available and
delighted. In fact, he was.

> "Nothing great was ever achieved without enthusiasm."
> —Ralph Waldo Emerson

DO YOUR HOMEWORK

What makes a special event successful is the
foundation upon which it is built. My philosophy

is that the concept, basis, and positioning must be *meaningful*. When you build your event with a solid foundation and do your homework, it works.

I rented seven of Robert Duvall's films and watched them all in one weekend. By researching the star's background, film career, and his likes and dislikes, we built an event that was *interesting* to the community. It was fascinating—in fact, it *merited* megapublicity coverage and, importantly, it was fun for the star himself. When it's fun for the star, it's more fun for the audience.

We built a committee—who now had something to be excited about—and the process took off.

THE THEME SETS THE TONE

Once we had the star, the wheels started turning as we built the theme and all of the details of the evening around the down-to-earth, yet exciting image of Robert Duvall. Research revealed that he loves "kicker dancing," better known as the Texas two step. That gave us a Western basis for the theme.

THE CREATIVE PROCESS MAKES IT HAPPEN

From a publicity photo taken for his role in *Tender Mercies*, I commissioned a wonderful artist, Louis Daniel, to sketch an illustration of the close-up shot of Robert Duvall wearing his cowboy hat. It was one of Duvall's favorite photographs and an extremely expressive one, made more dramatic as an illustration.

That great piece of art became the invitation cover, the program cover, and the first thing guests saw when they entered the ballroom of the Fairmont

Hotel in downtown Dallas. It was projected on the screen above the stage and was the open and close of the video tribute to Robert Duvall at the event.

Duvall loved it. And, so did the guests who filled the ballroom for the black tie, star-studded evening of film clips, dinner, dancing, a casino, the award tribute, and a whole lot of fun.

THAT EXTRA SPECIAL TOUCH

After the engraved crystal Master Screen Artist Award was presented to the star, we surprised him with the framed original illustration. His response was a genuine and emotional expression of thanks that endeared him even more to the guests.

MERIT PUBLICITY

From the minute we knew Robert Duvall would be the recipient, we kept the media abreast of the various plans and behind-the-scenes preparations for the event. We customized many items and never gave the same column item to more than one columnist. Media coverage in the arts, society, business, and entertainment newspaper pages, as well as on radio, was frequent and excellent.

GUESTS MUST BE WON

The excitement generated by the media coverage, as well as the style and elegance of the invitation, enticed invited guests to buy those tickets.

The invitation featured the influential and prestigious committee listed prominently on a sheer paper stock insert. In a short time frame, we had a good response and a "successful, memorable" special event!

7 SECRETS TO PRODUCING VERY EFFECTIVE, SPECIAL EVENTS

The opening case study illustrates many things that can make a special event successful. Here are seven points from a more analytical perspective.

1. Analyze and create a unique position.
2. Make it meaningful.
3. Build an interested team.
4. Walk the event from the audience's side.
5. Be creative and cost efficient.
6. Publicity is powerful.
7. Make a punch" list of details.

1 Analyze and create a unique position. Be sure to position your event with the big picture in mind.

Consider carefully the *past, present* and *future* perspectives of your organization in order to generate positive public awareness and lasting results. In other words, the past must be respected and the present successful in order to make a difference in the future.

For example, analyze the *history* of the organization, any previous functions, the leadership and any sensitive issues. Determine if there is a leader, constituent, donor, officer, or others who should be given special recognition in some way at the event.

The *present* planning and preparation should be orchestrated with the perspective of the attendee in mind rather than just the goal of the sponsoring organization. If those two perspectives (which often are not part of the planning focus) are recognized in each phase, then the results will have a 1,000% better chance of being a smashing success and achieving the desired *future* results.

2 Make it meaningful. The Palm restaurant, founded and owned by the Bozzi and Ganzi

> "Positioning is not what you do to a product. Positioning is what you do to the mind of the prospect."
>
> —Jack Trout, *Positioning: The Battle for Your Mind*

families of New York, is now in its 70th year, with 15 locations across the US. When the Dallas location was approaching its 10th anniversary, Al Biernat, the general manger, asked me to assist in creating an event to celebrate by "giving back" something significant to the community.

We discussed various possibilities, and Al decided he wanted to close the restaurant for one night to host an event benefiting an organization that helped families in some way.

After researching selected local nonprofit organizations, The Family Place was chosen for its exceptional work in helping victims of family violence. We created the event together with board representatives of The Family Place. They were excited and appreciative of this new opportunity and the support from The Palm restaurant.

3 Build an interested team. Al shared his enthusiasm for the event with regular, loyal customers, many of whom offered to participate, either by serving on the host committee or by buying a table.

There are many well attended weekend gala events in Dallas, Texas. So we chose a weeknight to lessen the possibility of conflicting dates with other important events.

The "Palm Night" Positioning Was A High Five!

We worked closely with the host committee, made up of community leaders from The Family Place board and from The Palm's family of customers to make the evening one of great value and lots of fun.

The fun factor is extremely important! We invited a celebrity

Important Tip!!!

Always find out what's happening on the date of your scheduled event as well as immediately prior to, and following, that date.

from the world of sports and a famous screen star to be honorary chairpersons. They accepted because of established friendships and affiliations with our "team."

The Palm's signature menu of steak and lobster with all the trimmings would be served, and the committee worked hard to get twelve one-of-a-kind, high-dollar items for a live auction (for example, a framed Dallas Cowboy football jersey signed by the team and a Dallas Stars hockey jersey).

Live music, sawdust on the floor, balloons, flowers, a professional auctioneer, a super emcee, and elegant gifts for everyone from Stanley Korshak and Saks Fifth Avenue created a tradition, from a one-time anniversary celebration, that is now in its *third* year!

4 **Walk the event from the audience's perspective.** I learned one of the most important techniques for creating truly effective special events from one of the most successful on-air personalities in the US.

Ron Chapman is the ace "morning man" and program manager of KVIL Radio 103.7 FM in Dallas. Consistently tops in ratings for more than 25 years, he is a marketing genius and an excellent emcee. In fact, Ron served as master of ceremonies for the aforementioned USA Film Festival Master Screen Artist Award and Gala. The first thing he asked me in preparation for that event was if I had "walked the space."

It is important to walk the path of the guests to make sure that everything will be right for their experience. This includes: arrival, parking, signage necessary to know how to get where they're going, the welcome, the entrance impression, tickets, check-in, coat check, seating, dining, entertainment, and the exit. In other words, walk the other side of the fence.

5 **Be creative and cost efficient.** When a charity is the beneficiary, everyone works to hold costs down however possible. Everyone involved works to get goods and services donated where appropriate, and pitches in to give what they can.

Every Penny Counts

Whether you're a public relations professional, development director, volunteer, or administrator, your success in producing special events is directly related to your ability to save money when there is a nonprofit beneficiary. With a little thought, there are always ways to cut corners without cutting creativity.

Every penny that is saved in the production goes to charity, so a delicate balance is necessary to produce an event that gives an excellent value to the guests and yet raises as much money as possible for the beneficiary.

Creative Cost Efficiency Can Be Fun

Fun was important in raising money for a little, low-profile inner city primary school that had closed its doors for lack of funds. A couple of community leaders reopened those doors.

One of them, a former county judge and very successful businessman, Judge Dave Fox, wanted to make sure the doors of St. Anthony School never closed again. He inspired others to help in "marketing" the school to the community.

In the beginning, the marketing team consisted of Judge Fox, the principal, an enthusiastic parent, and me. We decided that the best way to let people know about the need for the school in the area, the happy students getting a quality education in a safe environment, and the involved parents and dedicated teachers, was to let people see for themselves.

An Inexpensive, Creative Centerpiece

At one event, instead of flowers, we placed a theme-related toy in the center of the table on a square mirror that was provided by the hotel's catering department. We sprinkled festive, colorful mylar stars, hearts, and squiggles around the toy. Three votive candles flickered in each centerpiece, reflecting the lights, mirror and colors, creating a delightful conversation piece for the table.

At the end of the award dinner event, which included lots of grandparents, the master of ceremonies announced that the grandparents at each table with the youngest grandchildren got to take home the centerpiece toy. The idea added some surprise and chuckles to the end of the evening.

What is going to get busy community leaders, professionals, and members of the media to support a little, off-the-beaten-path, inner-city school?

An event, of course! In this case, a series of events on a shoestring budget. People want to help if they get involved, and if they get involved, they figure out how to help.

St. Anthony School's "library lunches" began with boxed lunches prepared by a restauranteur friend at cost, and tied with a ribbon to make them festive. The lunches were held in the library of the school with narrow library tables and folding chairs strategically placed in a square so that everybody could feel a part of the group. Flowers for the little tables were purchased that morning, "on special," at the grocery store. Leadership, media, and professionals, who we invited informally by phone, joined with parents, a teacher, and the principal to see what *The Dallas Morning News* came to call "St. Anthony School, The Miracle on Myrtle Street."

Be Different, Be Honest, Be Enthusiastic!

The word spread. People wanted to go to the little library for lunch, hear the story, and meet the kids. About 10 of the pre-K to ninth grade boys in their starched light blue shirts and navy pants, and girls in their plaid jumpers and crisp white blouses, were outside at the gate, at the door, and at the entrance to the library, greeting guests as they arrived.

Those smiles and personal greetings like, "Welcome to St. Anthony School, my name is Eric, I'm in the third grade," made lasting first impressions that got folks from across the city interested, involved, and helping.

St. Anthony School is a primarily African-American Catholic school with support, interest, and involvement from all ethnicities and faiths. Shortly after the luncheons began, a parent and grandparent of a student attending St. Anthony attended the luncheon and offered to cater future lunches at cost, serving homemade fried chicken, steaming candied yams, fresh salad, and hot peach cobbler. The luncheon guests multiplied immediately!

If It's Meaningful, They Will Come

We did not ask guests for money. We asked for their ideas, their interest, and their help in any way they could.

Some gave money, some in-kind goods or services, some helped spread the word. The little school's enrollment increased from a low of 40 students to more than 200.

Tuition scholarships are sponsored by foundations, individuals, and corporations. Twenty-one of the top Dallas Cowboy football players were featured in a collector's calendar to benefit the school.

The ribbon was just cut at the $630,000 gymnasium and community center built on the grounds of St. Anthony School, made possible by a grant from the 1994 Dallas Crystal Charity Ball.

Little St. Anthony School not only has the doors wide open serving lots of children, but it has even become the "in" nonprofit private school to assist.

6 **Publicity is powerful.** One of the major reasons to consider event marketing is the potential for publicity. If the event has a good reason to be produced (positioning), is orchestrated with uniqueness, flair, and focus, and the media is properly informed, the event will merit publicity.

Celebrities generate publicity. Charitable tie-ins provide reasons for publicity. Unique and new twists on tried-and-true events generate publicity.

Publicity, whether in broadcast or print media, is not available for purchase. It is not guaranteed like advertising, but it is more valuable. Editorial material is read with more credibility than advertising. When a reporter writes a story about a restaurant, for example, and reports favorably, his or her opinion is an unpaid endorsement which is *far* more credible than an ad saying the same thing.

"A special event may be any newsworthy situation—from a corporate open house or a freeway ribbon-cutting to the preview of an exhibition of rare paintings."
—Doug Newsom and Alan Scott, *This Is PR: The Realities of Public Relations*

State-Of-The-Art Event Publicity Starts In How You Position Your Event

A good example is the company from California which was launching a "new" broadcast subscription service in the Dallas/Fort Worth area.

Two other companies had already penetrated the marketplace. The challenge was to generate media interest and publicity for the product even though two others were already established. In fact, I said to the Regional VP, "Unless we do something meaningful and highly newsworthy, the media will yawn!"

Press Conferences Are Dreaded Events

The company wanted to have a press conference to announce their arrival. Well, the media doesn't like press conferences, even when there is a world-famous dignitary or celebrity making an extraordinarily newsworthy announcement, not to mention a not-so-famous person making a not-so-newsworthy announcement.

The reason is that the information goes to all the media at once. There is little, if any, opportunity for a reporter to get an exclusive, or even an individual slant on the information presented.

To create a successful press conference, we had to first have a truly important announcement with solid news value presented by the highest officer in the company.

To further increase the possibility of attendance, we recommended that the news conference be held in a place the media wanted to go, but to which they did normally not have access.

A Special Venue

I wish I could take credit for this particular idea about the place of the press conference, but it was not mine. I did, however, have sense enough to call on a respected colleague in the media, Bob Brock, who was at that time the television critic for *The Dallas Times Herald* and is one of the most highly respected newspaper columnists in the US. The brilliant idea of location, location, location in this case was his. Thank you, Bob.

We found that place on a private ranch which

was the set of the hottest television show
in the US and abroad at the time—
"Dallas." The press came, they saw,
they photographed, and they wrote.
One newspaper columnist, Jerry
Coffey, TV and radio critic for *The
Fort Worth Star Telegram*, wrote in the
following morning's edition,

> There was a media event at South
> Fork Ranch the other night that had
> nothing to do with the campaign to
> build J.R. Ewing a new image.
>
> Indeed, the real life principals
> at this elegant tent-meeting in
> the Collin County boondocks
> were about as far from the
> Dallas scalawags in character
> as could be imagined.
>
> And yet, there was a shrewdness and
> flair to the occasion that a consummate
> schemer like ol' J.R. would appreciate.
> How do you attract attention if you're
> entering the subscription TV business in
> the Metroplex and three other STV
> services have the jump on you?
>
> One way is to stage a press confer-
> ence at an irresistible location. And in
> these parts, what location could be more
> irresistible than the famous facade that
> symbolizes the most popular TV series
> in history? Sure enough, the session
> was considerably better attended than it
> would have been in a more conventional
> setting, and it's likely that On TV will
> end up with more debut publicity than
> all its competitors put together.

The column went on to mention all of the
attributes of the company, quote the chairman of
the board of the parent company and the general
manager of the Dallas/Fort Worth operation. It
was one of the most thorough, accurate, and
positive columns we have ever seen. (One more
time, thank you, Bob!)

Punch List

(Note: Here is a much abbreviated special event punch list. For a more comprehensive punch list, see the disk that accompanies this book.)

FACILITIES
☐ Walk the space
☐ Additional equipment (specify)
☐ Sound system/lighting

GRAPHICS
☐ Invitations
☐ Decor
☐ Posters, banners, tickets

SPECIAL ARRANGEMENTS
☐ Invitation lists
☐ Beverage arrangements
☐ Emcee

PERSONNEL
☐ Security
☐ Greeting committee

EVENT PRESENTATION
☐ Room arrangement
☐ Flowers
☐ Awards, prizes

MEDIA PUBLICITY (PRE EVENT)
☐ Comp invitations
☐ Press passes
☐ Media kits

PROMOTION
☐ Celebrity appearances
☐ Paid advertising

MEDIA PUBLICITY (POST EVENT)
☐ Photo distribution
☐ Follow-up releases
☐ Post interviews

P.S. Don't Forget The Special Touch

We had filled the yellow-and-white-striped tent erected for the "Dallas" press conference with yellow roses, a well known symbol of Texas.

Exactly one year later, each reporter who attended the press conference received a long stemmed yellow rose with a thank-you note for taking the time to attend on that day the year before. The appreciative response to that surprise was wonderful.

7 Make a "punch list" of details. This is a key word list of all the details you need to cover. By having it in one place, you don't overlook "minor" details that can become important if they're skipped. Until I began working with Al Biernat, General Manager of The Palm restaurant in Dallas, I always called it a "checklist."

The term "punch list" says it better. When you're in the throes of making an event come together and selling reservations, every detail not only has to be checked off the list, but has to have punch, and pizzazz, while you prevent any problems!

10 ACTION SECRETS

1 Position your event to create positive public awareness and a lasting impression with your chosen audience.

2 Choose or create an event that has meaning for your client and your audience, such as an approriate charitable benefit.

3 Have publicity in mind for everything you do. Then let the media know. One may even become a co-sponsor.

4 Walk the other side of the fence. In every step of the event-producing process, think of the Golden Rule when brainstorming and planning. In particular, look at how the event will "feel" for your audience. The results will be enhanced considerably for everyone involved. In other words, "Do unto others...".

5 Be creative and cost efficient.

6 Build a committed team who will both help with the work and to spread the word.

7 Create a checklist covering all the duties and items for each step of the planning and event (a "punch list").

8 Give it 110% effort. Pull every string to make the event succeed. If you don't show this level of commitment, no one else will either.

9 Take chances. If it's never been done before, that makes it even better, so do it!

10 Don't make impersonal appeals. Personally invite as many people as possible to help, attend, etc.

This chapter is dedicated to my inspirational family and Guardian Angels including: Elizabeth Leahy, my creative mom who had such a great sense of style and guided me in the literary direction; my dad, William H. leahy, an example of strong faith who taught me to sell by serving; my brother, Bill Leahy; my niece and nephew, Lauren and Will; and Uncle Norman and Aunt Jerri Honnet, who provide support and laughter, and keep me dancin'!

Chapter 20

SECRETS OF NETWORK MARKETERS
That Could Make You Wealthy In Any Business

David Klaybor

David Klaybor
provides companies and entrepreneurs with marketing
advice and tips that immedi-
ately increase sales. Klaybor researches both corporate and home-based
businesses, analyzes their problems, and provides innovative solutions.

Mr. Klaybor has gained his experience as an airline captain, broker,
business owner, radio talk show co-host, and personal development instructor.
He is a member of the National Speakers Association, the International Network
Association, and the Educational Committee for the Natural Foods Association.

Mr. Klaybor's teaching technologies have earned him feature and cover
story articles in major magazines. He has given thousands of wealth building
seminars worldwide to his direct sales and network marketing clients: Fuller Brush,
Rexall, Avon, Amway, Shaklee, Enrich, Quorum, Alliance, LifePlus, FreeLife, and
hundreds more. Mr. Klaybor is the author of *Books Don't Work Unless You Do.*
He has a Time Management Business Planner and several audiotapes, and has
published his own magazine.

David Klaybor, 1223 Marquette Avenue, South Milwaukee, WI 53172; voicemail
(714) 450-3123, (714) 433-2128, or (801) 288-2434.

Chapter 20

SECRETS OF NETWORK MARKETERS
That Could Make You Wealthy In Any Business

David Klaybor

"If it works, use it." —Anonymous

Despite the fact that 10 million people earn commissions on **$36 billion** in sales worldwide, it's still necessary to define network, or multilevel, marketing for many people. Shaklee, Mary Kay, Jafra Cosmetics, Herbal Life, Nu-Skin, Amway, Tupperware, etc. are all examples of network marketing companies.

WHAT IS NETWORK MARKETING?

Network marketing—also called multilevel marketing (MLM)—in its simplest form is the movement of goods and services via "person to person" marketing. It's just friends, neighbors, and family members who can be thought of as "customers" or the ultimate consumers of the product. They are individual entrepreneurs sharing information about a product or service in order to make a commission or get their personal product for free.

The big difference between a normal salesperson or distributor and a multilevel marketing representative is that additional profits are earned by multilevel distributors through commission overrides gained from managing a sales force that they build. Commission overrides are not just on the people you recruit, but on the people they recruit as well. This continues "downline" through several levels. This gives you extra commissions. Unlike the corporate world where many people are a bit afraid to help people climb up the corporate ladder, there is the incentive to help the people in your downline be successful in their businesses.

HOW YOU CAN BENEFIT

You don't have to be a network marketer—or even like the industry—in order to benefit from the sales secrets they use. I'll show you some of the MLM sales tools we use to produce record sales, and how to transfer these techniques into any kind of business. I'll show you ways to maximize your productivity to serve more people, and earn more money than you earn today.

I personally know thousands of overworked, underpaid people who have changed their lives by mastering the marketing techniques of network marketing, and are earning five-figure monthly incomes today! Although, sadly, there are scams in every walk of life, do not ignore the marketing techniques used by this sometimes misunderstood industry. If you are looking for an edge over your competitors, review the techniques I'll share with you in this chapter.

TECHNIQUE #1
PERSONAL TESTIMONIAL
SELLING

Unlike most professional salespeople, network marketers are predominantly **customers of the product** themselves. They share their personal testimonial stories about their successful use of the products they are selling.

This **personal story selling formula** is powerful because the multilevel marketer's success is grounded in the solid foundation of their unwavering BELIEF and total CONVICTION that the product works. *The untrained layperson can sometimes outperform many professional sales people.* Prospects perceive—correctly—that the person marketing the product to them is passionate about the product, not just trying to earn a commission from the sale.

Remember that most people buy things emotionally, with logical justification. Successful network marketers do not think of themselves as salespeople. All they are taught to do is *share* their personal experiences and those of others. All professional salespeople should consider the powerful concept of *sharing* vs. *selling*.

A network marketer is emotionally involved with the product. Can you get emotionally caught up in the product or service you are currently marketing? Can you see the benefit of installing this belief system into your sales environment?

Sales Require Emotions

Tom Hopkins and many other sales "gurus" define selling as the process of transferring your enthusiasm for your product or service to your prospects. If you don't feel enthusiasm, you can't sell.

TECHNIQUE #2
NETWORK MARKETERS ARE "PAID PROFESSIONAL STORYTELLERS"

Facts tell...stories sell. Most salespeople try to sell their products by brain-dumping everything they know about the product or service. The salesperson hopes that prospects will eventually discover *something* they like about the product and buy it. This sales technique is called "throwing it up against the wall and seeing what sticks."

"Would you like to hear my personal story," sounds much more inviting than "Let me tell you about my product!" Network marketing distributors get paid by how well they can communicate the company "story" and "testimonial stories" to their prospects.

Techniques Of A Good Storyteller

If you've ever been told a story by a person who kept your attention, and studied their delivery, you'll find that there are certain characteristics they use to capture your attention—and maybe even your money.

Emotion. Most network marketers sell products to which they are emotionally attached. They usually were consumers of the products or services *before* they became distributors. They operate on a belief system far different from the classic mercenary-type sales professional who would sell anything if paid the right commission. (There are mercenary sales types in the MLM industry too, but they're in the minority. Often they capture the public's attention. Ignore them—they are not career professional networkers.)

Most MLM distributors sell products that are **cause-oriented** consumable products or services in areas like: environmental, security, personal development, health and nutritional, fitness, telecommunications, etc. Perhaps you've been approached by some MLMers trying to sell you a nutritional product they claim has solved some ailment they or someone they know had.

You can learn from these people. Rediscover how to become **passionate** about the work you do, your product, and the results your clients will receive once they use your product.

If your clients or prospects feel you really care about what you're selling, they will trust you more. When they respect what you say, they become involved with your presentation, and perhaps decide that what you are offering is what they want, too!

Expressions and gestures. Every good speaker uses his or her hands on stage.

Ceremonial and ballet dancers move their bodies to create drama while telling a story. Don't be rigid...move your body when you talk.

God gave us facial expressions so that others looking at us would better understand us. The use of a simple smile can be extremely powerful in marketing our products. Practice in front of a mirror. If you can, place a mirror directly in front of you at your workplace. Watch yourself as you speak on the phone to others. You may be surprised at what you look like and do as you speak. Strive to improve in this area.

You'll Love
Vita-Gems
because

Props. Gestures interact well with charts, graphs, and the merchandise you are trying to sell. "A picture is worth a thousand words" is the rule here. Ross Perot spurred a new public interest in the use of props to make a point with his presentations on political and economic issues.

Pictures, diagrams, using color to highlight main points, 3D effects, CD-ROM interactive software, Internet displays—all help you get your point across. They all mean better communication. More information is transferred from you to your client...which ends up putting larger commission checks into your bank account. The right costume or outfit can also work like a prop in helping you communicate your story by setting a visual mood.

A word to the wise: The right prop will become the catalyst to the sale. The wrong prop will give the wrong message or kill the sale. Use it—don't over-do it.

Handling Your Product

A six-figure-per-month income earner, who was one of my first teachers in the MLM industry, taught me the importance, and the art, of holding your product correctly. Many TV spokespersons or models demonstrate my point by cradling the product in their hands with reverence and respect, like they're holding a priceless museum artifact.

Handling your product, or your marketing

materials, is an art form. Too many sales people throw their products around as if they were toys. This suggests a complete lack of respect for the items that earn them their keep. Do not let your prospect hear or see you showing disrespect for your product or service.

Timing, Pausing, and Listening

Comedians make their living knowing the exact time they should say something. Storytellers use timing in much the same way. Knowing when to say something important (or not say something) about your product or service can be a critical factor in your marketing efforts.

Never get caught up in spewing fact after fact to your clients in a fixed presentation that you know by heart. Every prospect and presentation should be customized and unique to the circumstances at hand.

Asking questions is the key to unlocking the buying impulses of your prospects. Probing for information about your client can help you neutralize objections before they become adversarial. Knowing when to initiate a trial-close and knowing when to ask your prospect for the check are critical to record-breaking sales.

Getting the listener involved. There are at least two general ways to get your listener

Set The Right Tone With Your Tone Of Voice

A beautiful TV spokesperson selling perfume was right when she said: "If you want to get someone's attention...whisper."

Dull monotone presentations may be tolerated in corporate business, scientific research, or academic classes. But the sales situation should be FUN, EXCITING, and DYNAMIC to move the prospect along the sales path. This will not work for all items (cemetery plots, life insurance, etc...). But even in somber situations, you can use EMOTION, PASSION, CAUSE, CEREMONY, etc. You can also add dynamics to the sales process by varying the tone of your voice.

Sound Effects

Kids use them all the time. Adults need to use them more often. Get out of your comfort zone and make your presentation memorable! If you have a lot of competition—take some risks, take some chances. As long as you stay professional, and do not use vulgarity or poor taste, "special effects" will help you be remembered by your prospect before your competitors.

more involved. In addition to asking questions, use examples to which the prospect can relate. For instance, if the person is a pilot, use an analogy a pilot would use or understand. If the person is from the Midwest, tell the story about a person like them from that area.

TECHNIQUE #3
THIRD-PARTY SELLING

It is critical for you to learn the power of the "third person." Men usually hate to use other people to help them make the sale. Since the caveman days, they've been programmed to "do it themselves."

Do not fall into this trap. Prospects aren't stupid. They know the salesperson is receiving a commission if they buy. Therefore, prospects are more reluctant to take immediate action in a one-on-one situation.

Prospects are more receptive to testimonial stories from people who are happy with their purchase decisions. So why not give prospects what they want instead of trying to talk them into buying?

Are you guilty of using the "pushy salesman" technique? Here are some methods you can use to introduce third parties into the sales presentation—pick those best suited for your business.

Using Audio- And Videotapes

Tapes are an economical and extremely effective method of correctly and consistently telling the story of your product or service to your prospects. We call it the "Power Play"...just put the tape in the machine, then press POWER, then the PLAY button!

From a company management standpoint, tapes also insure that the product is presented the right way. This could help prevent over-exaggerations, resulting in legal action, returns, and customer complaints.

Once the tape project is complete, depending on protected territories, a salesperson could potentially hand out tapes to everyone in his or her city, county, state, or region! Can you see the advantages of making hundreds or thousands of taped presentations every month in your prospects' cars or homes via your tape? And the best part was, you didn't have to say the same thing over and over doing these presentations in person!

Follow up on the prospects who listened to or viewed the tapes. Answer their questions, neutralize objections, and then take orders. This is how you maximize your potential and earn huge commission checks.

Every business needs to use tapes to market their products. Creating a "tape" is not going to necessarily make you rich...but making a GREAT TAPE *will*! If you make the right audio or video presentation, your prospects will be very interested in finding out more about your products. They might even buy them.

Extra Benefits Of Testimonials

Testimonials do more than help you sell to prospects. The act of giving a testimonial story solidifies the beliefs of the person giving it! Psychological research shows that recording a person's testimonial usually makes that person a stronger advocate for you.

> Best vitamins we ever used. -- Mandy Sheridan

TECHNIQUE #4
THREE-WAY CALLING TECHNOLOGIES

"The bigger your phone bill, the bigger your commission check!" It only costs pennies a month for you to gain the ability to add another person to your phone conversations with your prospects.

Why bring another person into the conversation? Because it's FUN (party lines are always successful) and because you'll make more commissions if you do! This is one very good way of implementing the third-person success formula.

Adding a third-party testimonial. Who should you add to your conversation? Anyone who

How To Gather Testimonials

If someone compliments your product or service, always ask them to write their comments down for you on their stationery. (Many times you can offer to type it up for them to sign.) Let them know you want to display their comments in a brochure, company newsletter, etc. (This will make them write an even better one.) Next, get a tape-recorded testimonial (to use on the audio tape you need to make about your product). And finally, start to involve your *customers*—on phone sales calls and at in-person presentations—by telling their story to others. Each step will make them more committed to you.

has a testimonial story to tell...anyone who adds excitement... anyone who is fun to talk with...anyone who is a celebrity in your industry...any satisfied client...maybe even your boss to help you close the deal.

When invited to participate on a three-way call, third parties should quickly tell why the product or service has positively changed their lives, and then the third party should hang up. You should then attempt to "close" the prospect or add *another* third party! It only takes seconds to add someone to your conversation. And the three-way event need not take more than a few minutes of the other person's time. If you had to, you could easily introduce five different experts in a 15-minute phone conversation.

Most clients are impressed at any salesperson's ability to use technology. They also feel comfortable directly asking other unbiased third parties about their particular needs. *Let other people neutralize objections, promote your product, tell your prospects how good you are, and answer all their question and concerns. The best part is, it's easier than doing it yourself, it's more effective, and it's free!*

If I were trying to sell you a Chrysler automobile, would you really mind if I connected Lee Iacocca on the phone with us? You get the idea. Develop a network of people you can count on to join in on your presentations. It is okay for you to coach people on how to behave on a three-way call. Don't tell them what to say. Just suggest ways for them to state what's truly in their hearts, quickly and effectively.

TECHNIQUE #5
CONFERENCE CALL STRATEGIES

This is a more powerful version of the three-way call above. Conference calls are generally more professional in nature. Collectively, company owners, administration staff, researchers, doctors, people who have had good success with your products, and many invited prospects all join together on one phone line. This party-line-style product presentation event uses the power of group dynamics to create an interactive sales environment.

In order for you and your firm to maintain control of the event, ask the *conference call company* to make it so that everybody on the call can hear everything...while only specially designated experts can talk and be heard by the "group." Find out all your options from the conference call company so you can customize your call to fulfill your special needs.

Tape calls. Most conference call companies have the ability to tape your call. These taped conference call events can be edited and then reused by any company salesperson hundreds of more times in the future. Check with the legal department of your firm to be sure it is okay, but I've never heard of any negative legal action regarding this issue. Additionally, each individual salesperson can add this tape to any phone conversation via three-way call technology in the future as they talk to their respective prospects.

You can also dedicate a voice mail box or special phone number and have prospects call on their own and listen to the event as it happened. If you have clients in remote areas, if your clients do not like coming to see you, if traffic is bad in your area, or if your clients do not mind calling in to listen to your company presentation via the phone, conference call technology may be right for you.

Using Satellite Dishes, Cable Networks, And Teleconferencing

If you have lots of distributors like Avon or General Motors, if you have many locations like Wal-Mart or Holiday Inn, or if you happen to have lots of clients with satellite dishes, marketing and training via this method can quickly triple your revenues. There are several ways to use the new smaller satellite dishes, Kinko's teleconferencing centers, and the newer cable services.

• **Market to your employees.** If it's possible, make it

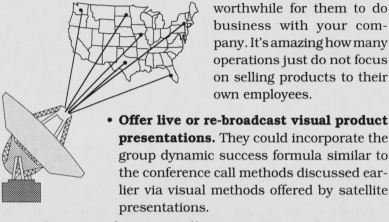

worthwhile for them to do business with your company. It's amazing how many operations just do not focus on selling products to their own employees.

- **Offer live or re-broadcast visual product presentations.** They could incorporate the group dynamic success formula similar to the conference call methods discussed earlier via visual methods offered by satellite presentations.

- **Arrange to have your clients meet your sales team at a local Kinko's teleconference facility.** Your team can pick up your clients or prospects and drive them to the live interactive sales meeting. One day, all businesses and every home in America will be able to participate in remote meetings. Stay on the cutting edge of technology. Call to arrange one of these events this quarter and start gaining experience in this telecommunications area... before your competitor does it first.

TECHNIQUE #6
FAX-ON-DEMAND AND INTERNET "PAPERLESS SYSTEMS"

Fax-on-demand systems allow you to make a call from any touch-tone phone and have documents faxed to any fax machine.

All companies have sales aids or marketing materials. These include sales kits, brochures, and many other promotional items. Fax-on-demand means that you can get important data into the hands of your prospects in minutes, even while talking to them on the phone. You'll spend less time faxing documents and have more time to prospect. Just give your prospects the fax-on-demand number with an index that enables them to choose and obtain whatever information they need 24 hours a day. It's just like downloading information from the Internet!

The same thing can be done with your Web site on the Internet where people can download the information they want any time.

These *paperless systems* let you avoid keeping large quantities of documentation in inventory or having to throw away thousands of brochures just because the company changed something. Changes can be made and available for use by the sales force in the field the *same day*.

TECHNIQUE #7
TODAY'S TECHNOLOGIES—YOUR PERSONAL SECRETARY

Basic beepers and answering machines are great, but a bit old hat these days. Today's professional salespeople must be able to be contacted at all times. You also want to be able to do from the field what you can do in the office.

Today's interactive communication technologies enable a salesperson to fax documents using a car phone. Technology can track you down no matter where you are, and can translate documents into verbal messages. It can do virtually everything your private secretary does for you. Find out about companies like "Wildfire" that perform all these functions for you for $2–3 a day max, before your competition does. (See the disk for details.)

If you plan on earning a great income or winning sales awards, you must learn how to use a computer. If you are not connected to the Web, if you are not interested in learning more about using telecommunications technologies, you will be left behind as the world accelerates into the next century. Promise yourself right now that you're going to call this week to upgrade your telecom services and start *stumbling forward* with the rest of us.

TECHNIQUE #8
EVENTS, EVENTS, EVENTS

Smart aggressive companies use grand openings, seasonal kickoffs, wine tastings, celebrity appearances, book signings, and many other reasons to hold events.

Besides office Christmas parties or employee birthdays,

Sponsored by
MLM Company
and
The Community Chest

there should be only one real reason for having an event—creating sales. The network business *IS* the "events industry." It's hard to "network" without them. Inviting someone to listen to a conference-call presentation is an event. It is easy to turn a routine two-way conversation into an "event" using three-way calling technologies.

Networkers also use many other events to market their products: home office tours, hotel briefings, home parties, training seminars, etc. Musicians, politicians, and even preachers/rabbis use events as the staples of their business. (See Chapter 19 for much more on event marketing.)

How to run events. At events, you need a method to *collect the names* of everyone who attends. (Having a drawing, sign-up sheets, or collecting tickets are easy ways to do this.)

If you're a local business, *send out a press release* to get lots of free media exposure. One way to get more publicity is by linking your event to another bigger local event! If there's already a large group coming to an event, perhaps many of them will want to visit yours as well. Maybe you could even be one of the sponsors of the other event and negotiate to use their logos and theme? If you sold sports products internationally, you could have held an event in Atlanta during the Olympics.

You could host a 5K run, a beauty pageant, or some type of contest. Give away prizes and make sure the press is invited. An event must be fun in order for it to attract lots of press and people.

A more conservative approach might be for you to *put on a seminar workshop* with industry experts. You'll get a chance to share the stage with some of the greatest minds in your industry or area. This is one way to look bigger than you are.

Making your event an annual occurrence can lead to city parades, industry recognition, and expert status among your clients, prospects, and peers. What kind of event could you host this quarter? Any reason will do.

Make sure you design a professional *follow-up system* to use after the event has ended so you can keep promoting the connection to the event months after it is over. This is also where most sales will be made. Contact me if you need help.

TECHNIQUE #9
CAUSE-DRIVEN MARKETING

A special way to do events is in partnership with worthy causes. By pooling your efforts, you both benefit. Sometimes you'll do all the work, just to benefit from using a charity's name.

This is one of the most powerful tools in the network marketer's bag. The MLM industry is known for its concern for the environment, its concern for health issues, its focus on making people look and feel younger, and for donating to worthy causes.

What worthy cause is your company sponsoring? All your company literature should state your company's position regarding the causes it supports. If your company is only paying *lip service* to the cause, never bring it up to your prospects because it might backfire if your prospect finds out your firm is not *really* serious about it.

Cause-driven marketing works in the networker's world because most people really believe in the cause.

Be sure to tie company activities to events put on by the nonprofit organization to whom your company is donating money. Do not be afraid to ask your boss for supporting materials that justify your company's claims to helping some needy operation.

Samples

If you can give out samples, do it. But never give out samples indiscriminately. If you do not have a *follow-up system* in place and designed properly, you'll be wasting a lot of money.

Huge corporations get suckered into giving away millions of dollars worth of products to unqualified people. You need the name, address, and phone number of each person who "tests" your product or service so you can learn why the prospect bought or didn't buy your product. The *puppy-dog close* is a form of temporary sampling (see disk).

TECHNIQUE #10
REWARD REFERRALS

Part of a network marketers presentation is showing clients how they can get their products for free by giving referrals. This may not be possible under the rules of your industry, but maybe *this* method will work for you.

Offer to give your prospects a finder's fee or commission for every referral they give you that results in a sale. If they were reluctant to purchase your product initially, they might be lured back if they thought they could earn enough money to purchase your product with the commissions they earn and, in effect, get the product for free. Maybe they could earn some free upgrades or features if they give you referrals.

Get your customers involved with helping you make sales in this fashion. These people would also be great to use on a three-way call.

TECHNIQUE #11
AUTOMATIC MONTHLY PRODUCT ORDERS

If you have a consumable product or service...you would be wise to understand this network marketing virtue. All your company has to do is:

(1) Secure the services of a financial operation that automatically debits your clients' accounts a fixed amount each month. (Your firm must have excellent credit.)

(2) Create a legal form for your customers to authorize.

(3) Train the sales force how to offer this fantastic option to their clients and prospects.

Now, instead of worrying about whether your customer is going to remember to buy your product or service each month or quarter, your operation can count on much more regular sales.

Commission checks will stabilize and steadily grow. Note: Automatic debits can come from *checking* or *savings accounts* as well as from credit cards!

TECHNIQUE #12
HOME OFFICE TOURS

I was born in Milwaukee, Wisconsin, and I grew up with brewery tours. I remember tours through the local Harley Davidson factory, the Mercury Outboard Marine company, and the American Motors factory. I went on tours through the Johnson & Johnson headquarters, the Case Tractor operation, Allen Bradley, and the Excalibur Motorcar factory.

Factory tours made sense to me. We bought many of the products from the companies I just listed because we took these tours. (Now you know why my mom rides a Harley!)

Could your company benefit from this form of marketing? Even a simple "open-house" two or three times a year might really help sales people get up close and personal with some of their prospects. Do not be afraid to pick up your prospects and drag them to your office if you have to! (See the disk for more on this.)

TECHNIQUE #13
DUPLICATING YOURSELF

Profit By Teaching, Too

Don't forget that people are paid for training others. Your teaching may become a profit center all its own. For instance, you can give public classes at local colleges which pay you AND market your services.

Our industry focuses on duplication, therefore it is mandatory that we teach people how to teach. Many businesses sell a lot of products or services because they focus part of their business on educating the public. Some intelligent computer companies teach students how to "use computers" and then sell them the software and hardware!

Some businesses offer classes on interior design, pottery, or wine making...

and then sell the students their wares. Health food stores often offer clinics on health-related issues and offer many alternatives to their customers to solve individual health concerns. If you sell automobiles and have a sports car line, why not offer race car driving lessons? If you market nutritional products, why wouldn't your firm co-sponsor a health fair? What can your company *teach* that would support company sales?

Never forget that the teacher often learns more than the students. It's a lot of hard work and money to pull this type of marketing program together and make it work. But the process of teaching the classes will establish you as an *expert in your field* and guarantee you a much larger income.

I love being a paid professional speaker, and you will, too. Make a commitment to launch a seminar or schedule a school-type program within the next year.

SUMMARY

Network marketing may or may not be for you. But one thing is certain. Many of the methods used in it are *valuable to all salespeople.*

If you want to increase your succes and productivity, and decrease stress, you need to be professional in your approach.

Congratulations on buying this book as one step in your education. I suggest that anyone who wants to sell things for a living, should take professional training classes or buy in-home (in-car) learning systems. I invite you to try out some of the techniques I've shared with you in this chapter and write me with your successes.

10 ACTION SECRETS

1   Prepare yourself to give a personal testimonial for your product or service. Explain in natural terms why you like your product, etc. If you can't use your product personally (e.g., industrial equipment), use stories from others who do. But you can still say why you like working for a company that deals fairly with customers, etc.

2 Start collecting testimonials both for your product or service, and for you as a salesperson looking out for your customers. Trade these company testimonials with other salespeople in your organization.

3 Start a binder collecting stories from users of your product or service. This goes beyond testimonials and explains ways to use the product that will produce the results your new prospect desires.

4 Practice the techniques of good storytelling: Using emotion, gestures, props, phonics, timing, and listener involvement.

5 Involve users in your sales process. Start with audio or video recordings of happy users.

6 Learn to set up and perform three-way calls with your prospects and happy users. Then move on to performing larger conference calls.

7 Set up a fax-on-demand "paperless" system and/or Web site to make your sales material available 24 hours a day at less expense to you.

8 Investigate an advanced voice mail system that follows you wherever you go, etc. (See disk for sample details.)

9 Create events to market with. Involve industry events, local events, or charities.

10 Offer classes to educate users, sell prospects, and create new profit centers.

Part Five

SECRETS OF ACTION

Are You Ready to Launch? How To Plan A
Successful Product Launch
Cynthia J. DeForge

How to Get Going:
10 Secrets For Accomplishment
Rick Crandall

Chapter 21

ARE YOU READY TO LAUNCH?
How To Plan A Successful Product Launch

Cynthia J. DeForge

Cynthia J. DeForge is president of Ready 2 Launch, a marketing consulting firm specializing in helping software companies launch their products through direct, online, channel, and distributor marketing.

Ms. DeForge started Ready 2 Launch in 1992, after having worked with many software companies in a marketing management capacity. She found that both the thrill and heartbreak of a software product could be found in the launch process, so she started a company dedicated to helping software companies launch their new product lines.

Since then, Ready 2 Launch has helped US and international companies successfully launch products in the mass market, specialized areas, and development tool fields by providing market research, competitive analysis, target market definition, channel and direct marketing, and public relations.

Ms. DeForge has published articles in industry magazines on marketing and packaging. She has spoken at many industry conferences, including the Software Publishers Association and SoftExpo International.

Cynthia DeForge, Ready 2 Launch, 60 Lincoln Avenue, San Anselmo, CA 94960; Phone 415-455-9687, fax 415-455-9682; e-mail deforge@ready2launch.com; Web site www.ready2launch.com.

Chapter 21

ARE YOU READY TO LAUNCH?
How To Plan A Successful Product Launch

Cynthia J. DeForge

"A journey of a thousand miles starts with the first step."

—Chinese proverb

"Oh, please, please, please can I have another week?"

As a marketing consultant, I'm often asked to write articles, give speeches, or in this case, write a chapter in the book you're holding now. And often you can hear me utter the words above. I have the irritating (at least to editors) habit of waiting until the last minute to submit any work, because clients' work comes first.

Launching a new product is similar to writing a book. I'll use new software as an example in this chapter, because that's what I work with.

Most developers have a set process for developing their product, and follow that plan to fruition. Unfortunately, many product developers literally have a blank page for their launch plan.

AN OVERVIEW OF COMPLEXITY

This chapter will give you an idea of what elements your launch should consist, and will help you get over that "Where do I start?" feeling. By the end of this chapter, you'll know what to do when you have a product to market. And, hopefully, once you know that, actually doing it will be a matter of following the process.

One overriding theme in this chapter is the need for consistency in your marketing program. You must position yourself clearly, target your audience, and consistently communicate who you are.

I must also provide a warning, however. Every subject in this chapter could have a book written on it alone. This is definitely a condensed, speed-course on the basics of product launch. It's up to you to explore further. Go for it!

KNOW YOUR MARKET

There's a story about a man on a deserted island who built an amazing invention that allowed voice communication, even when the parties involved were not in the same area. This invention was so far and beyond anything he'd ever seen, he knew that once people saw it, he would be a millionaire in a matter of weeks.

The man spent his last clamshells to ride to the mainland, with thoughts of great wealth accompanying him...Unfortunately, the rest of the story is not a happy one. After spending a day in the city, the man swam back to his island, penniless, never to be heard from again. You see, he

> ## A Proven Fallacy:
> ## If you build it, they will come...
> Ralph Waldo Emerson was not the only person to believe that if you write a better sonnet, build a better mousetrap, etc., the world will beat a path to your door. He was wrong then. Don't make the same mistake today!

never would have imagined that the telephone had been invented many decades before. How was he to know? He had never explored off his island.

THE BIG PICTURE

It's the same with the launch of any product. If you don't see the whole picture, what you think is exciting and state-of-the-art may fall short of that claim.

Most companies think their new product is the best in the world. (At least some "champion" in your company better think so if you hope to be successful!)

But the best marketing in the world will fail if you have a bad product. It is your task as a developer to give your customers a superior product and one that addresses their needs. Don't think that you can fool the public into buying an inferior product if the packaging looks good. Our customers are (luckily) smarter than that.

In fact, your new product may be great—but without the necessary market research to back up that claim, your "world's best" product will fail to become a bestseller.

WHAT TO ASK ABOUT YOUR PRODUCT

The following questions should be asked and answered by the time your product comes out of beta testing (by "real" users). Too often, market research begins only when the product is ready to ship. If you make this mistake, you will be adding costly months to the ship date, and will lose momentum, market share, and money.

What are my product's strengths and weaknesses? Even the most optimistic developer knows that his or her product has flaws as well as shining features.

It's imperative to look objectively at your product and chart what you think are its best selling points, and what you think needs improvement and revision in version 2.0. Since this chart should be kept from product inception, it will be a living document as the product evolves.

COMPETITIVE ANALYSIS

First, you've looked at your product in a vacuum. Even more important is to compare it to competitive products already in the market, as well as announced products.

What are your competitors' strengths and weaknesses? What features do they have that you don't? What are their selling points that you don't have? Are they addressing a specific market? Do they have an angle that you don't?

Don't just look at their product. Look at the total "package" of how they sell their product. Call their pre–sales staff and ask questions. Call their technical support department and see how you're treated.

Try to find their products in stores. Check their price points. See if their packaging would convince you to buy their product. And see what type of money-back guarantee they have. In other words, put yourself in your potential customer's position, and see how your competition rates. And then, (of course!) try to exceed those parameters.

Product Check-Up Sheet

STRENGTHS

1. USP (Unique Sales Proposition)
   _____

2. Competitive advantages
   _____
   _____
   _____

3. Main features
   _____
   _____
   _____

4. User benefits
   _____
   _____
   _____

WEAKNESSES

1. Competitive disadvantages
   _____
   _____
   _____

2. User needs expressed
   _____
   _____
   _____

3. Speed/cost ratio
   _____

4. Unknown positioning
   _____
   _____

FOCUS GROUP TESTING

It's a rare cook who will serve a dinner for 25 VIPs before testing the recipes. It's also a rare developer who would think of putting out a piece

of software without beta testing it.

The same holds true for marketing strategies. If you want to position your product correctly, and entice people to buy it over others, you have to have real-life feedback on those issues.

With the luxury of a large budget, you could hire focus group coordinators in various cities throughout the country. They would test a cross-section of the community, administer preference tests, and solicit visual opinions.

They would then give you a report that would package the conclusions together, along with their recommendations on the issues your product should address. It's then up to you to implement these changes or additions to your product and marketing materials to garner as much market share as possible.

Creative "Focus Groups"

Even without a huge marketing budget, you can do your own focus group testing. Be creative! For example, if you have a new game you've developed, perhaps a middle school computer course teacher would love to have you come in for a week and explain your product, set it up on the student's machines, and have them go at it.

To the teacher, it's value-added to his or her course. To the students, it's a blast. And to you, it's invaluable feedback on a product into which you've put a lot of money and effort.

Don't just solicit answers to questions you've come up with. Talk to them about what appeals to them, what they think is great, what they think stinks, what they would change, etc.

Ask what colors they like, what graphics they think best describe the product, and how much money they'd be willing to part with to buy it. Then try another school. Or the mall. Or the local babysitter's club. Focus groups are all around us!

Don't use a shotgun approach. Find and keep your eye on a narrow target.

PROPER POSITIONING IS KEY

Now that you've gotten internal and external feedback on your product and your competition, you have to decide how you're going to position yourself. Your product should be positioned in a way that you can explain in a simple sentence, because this message has to be very clear.

For example, if you can fill in the blanks in the following statement, you've come to a point where you know your product position and can market with that in mind:

"My customers are _____ who have a need to _____, and my product can do this better than _____ because _____, and it benefits my customers more by _____."

IS IT IN THE BUDGET?

You should start your marketing planning when you've just started development work on your product. Come up with your launch plans. Then do some research to see how much those plans will cost.

The time to start planning your marketing budget is early. If you have your monies allocated, great. If you need venture capital money, start looking. If this chapter shows you that you don't have enough money to launch the way you'd like, either look for more or adjust your marketing plans. Just don't get yourself into the position

---

Guerrilla Marketing

There are other ways to make a big splash in a product launch than just spending money. For instance, the founder of Hayes modem originally bartered his skills for three full-page color ads in the biggest computer magazine. He looked big to start with and quickly dominated the market.

---

where you have a product, have started to market, and then can't afford to build or sell your product properly.

If you can't do all the programs you want, pick the most effective ways you think you can grab customers. You can always boost your marketing efforts if you have an influx of money from sales or elsewhere. But if you don't have the current funds for a comprehensive retail sales effort (for example), maybe you should start with direct and Internet marketing to test the water or get the sales to boost your marketing efforts.

IS YOUR BOX COOL?

The software industry has recently realized what book publishers have known for a long time: While it's true that you can't judge a book by its cover, what's on the cover can certainly spur sales.

As of this writing, there were no packaging standards in place for software. However, the Software Publishers Association has issued guidelines for packaging size, etc. and many retail stores have strong preferences as to size, shape, and weight of product boxes.

Designing The Package

When you get to the design phase of your packaging, there are many things to consider. Remember, this should be happening in tandem with your product development, not after

First, you should get the "certainties" out of the way. You'll need to license any operating system logo from the proper company. You'll need to license any other logos from included software, as well as any other third–party artwork. This can be done early in the process; just don't forget to check that you have the most current versions before you go to print.

Test, Test, Test

Then you can get to the fun part. In packaging, as with so many other elements of software marketing, the key word is testing.

It may turn out that if your graphics professional designs ten different packages, you'll end up picking the first one. But you can't know that it's the best unless you have something to compare it to. So come up with at least a few designs, and head for the proverbial mall again.

That's right; ask anyone who could be your potential client what they like. The main thrust here should be what they want on a front panel.

- What catches their eyes?
- What colors do they associate with your type of product?
- What graphic stands out most?

And, by the way, how do they like the competition's packaging?

If you have a corporate look or corporate colors that you need to work with, do so. Branding is ever-important in this industry. If you have a family of products that are well received, make sure you carry over that good feeling to your new product by making it look like part of the family.

The Rest Of The Box

After you capture people's interest with the front cover, turn your attention to the back of the

Marketing Checklist For Package

☐ Front Of Box
☐ Testimonials
☐ Spines
☐ Logo
☐ Color Scheme
☐ Related Products
☐ Screen Shots
☐ Registration Card

box. This is where you get to show potential customers why they should buy your product.

Use exciting text, graphics that grab, and real-life screen shots to show the benefits of this product over others. If this is a version 1.0 product, you may not have press quotes yet, but you probably have people already using your product. If you have great quotes from users (and you should), use them.

And don't forget the spines of your box. A lot of retailers are beginning to display software like books, so your side spines are important to graphically capture attention, tell the operating system, and give system requirements. There may also be room for a descriptive tag line. On the top and bottom spines, you'll probably have to include product and store codes.

Beyond The Box...Collateral Materials That Sell

After you've designed your box, you're only halfway through the design process. All your pre-sales work, advertising and upsell pieces should include a consistent look to help sell your product.

If you have a tag line, use it consistently. If you have a product logo, use it consistently. Same with colors. Make sure that all your collateral pieces, whether they're in your box or used elsewhere, have a family feel and are complementary to each other. Become recognizable by consistent presence.

And think about the media you're going to use. Your fact sheets should be checked in black and white to look good via faxing. Your Web-site graphics should be compressed and doctored to look like the originals, but load very quickly.

SO MANY CHANNELS... SO LITTLE TIME

Wouldn't it be wonderful if you could just announce that you have a product people want, and that they could get it in the way that's easiest for them?

They could pick up the phone and call you, go to the nearest store and make a purchase, order from a mail order house, or log on and download the software.

There are many avenues in which to sell your product. Study your options carefully and make decisions about the best ways to make your product available.

CHANNEL SELECTION

A channel mix is beneficial to any product. The more people see your product, the more faith they'll have that it's stable and successful. You should make sure, however, that any channel efforts can be supported by your company, and not just be a source of expense.

Direct Marketing

Direct marketing consists of telemarketing, direct response advertising, and direct mail. These approaches garner a bigger gross margin, but costs can be high too. It can be targeted at a precise audience. Your chal-

---

Give It Away?

In retail, product sampling is common in places like grocery stores. Netscape and other Internet software companies are best known for giving away their software, but "shareware" and "freeware" have been around as long as computers.

This strategy allowed Netscape to dominate their market quickly. Some users later register (perhaps 10%). And big businesses often buy expensive upgrades or site licenses. You can also program your shareware to stop working after a few uses, etc.

Why Direct Mail?

As a channel supplement:
- It reaches another segment
- It provides the second hit in a "hit 'em three times" strategy
- But watch for channel conflict

As a channel alternative:
- It's a cheaper alternative
- It gives a higher ROI
- It focuses efforts on your target market
- It is more easily outsourced and financed

lenge is to find the correct lists, come up with an enticing offer, and hit these people at the correct time.

Retail Sales

Being in the retail channel takes a two-pronged effort. You have to speak to your end-users through packaging, advertising, and public relations. You also have to sell to your resellers.

Getting in the door to big resellers is a daunting task. They have plenty of product and little shelf space. Some even charge for placement (slotting fees). Getting in the door to local stores may be easier. But without major distribution, you may not achieve an acceptable return on investment (ROI).

Most important: Your retail channel is like any other "customer"—they need to be supported. Just getting corporate headquarters to accept your product does not guarantee it will be stocked on shelves. It may just be on "special order" status.

To have your product sell through, you need to train the retail salespeople, reward them, set aside marketing development funds (MDF), create point-of-sale (POS) pieces, and develop the relationships so that retailers get excited about your product. If they're excited, they'll sell it.

Co-op Money

Many retailers will want matching dollars for local advertising featuring your product. If you're already doing business with them, kicking back 5% for co-op is easy. But if you're starting up, this can involve an expensive flat fee, because you have no sales base.

Mail Order

Mail order houses typically carry more products than retail stores. They spread their costs over a large catalog with many products. They have supporting warehouses and/or next-day distributor delivery. In addition to direct sales, this may be the quickest way to get your product into customers hands.

The rules of retail sales still apply here. Keep your mail order house people informed on product news, set up a training day, set up incentive programs (SPIFFs), and fight for proper placement in the catalog. Track your sales on a monthly basis and work with your product rep to see how sales can be enhanced by special promotions, bundling, etc.

Distributors

Distributors sell your product to wholesalers and retailers. They have already created the sales channels you need. But obtaining a distributor is getting increasingly difficult. Literally thousands of products are coming in the door for review, while distributors are looking to cut their SKU numbers.

You may find that a distribution agreement is a matter of timing for you and your product; timing for you because of the up-front monies involved in marketing in the distribution channel; timing for the distributor in terms of gaps in their product line; timing for your product based on demand.

If you have a product that's a proven seller in either the direct channel or retail channel, the chances of a distributor picking your product is a lot higher than if you come in with an unproven product. Like any company, distributors cannot afford to bet on unknown factors. Get your packaging, collateral, marketing, and sales strategies in place; get some proven sales; and then decide which distributor is right to affiliate with.

SKUs

Stock keeping units refer to each version of a product in a retail store. The more SKUs, the more to keep track of, the more to inventory, etc.

Co-marketing And Bundling

Everybody loves a deal—you do, and so do your customers.

- Solicit upsell products for your marketing
- Position your product to be a sales incentive for another product
- Form a "suite solution" by bundling with products that provide equal benefit to your users
- Co-market and bundle only with products that enhance your product
- Watch out for cannibalization

Online Marketing

Last, but certainly not least, keep your eye on the Internet as a way to capture direct sales in the future.

No software company should be without a Web site. But right now that site is mostly a marketing expense that helps capture indirect sales and is a proven way to decrease tech support calls and improve customer service.

In the future, as the world becomes more comfortable with electronic commerce and bandwidth increases, more and more people will be turning to the Web for instant-gratification sales. There is no excuse for not having a Web site that, at the very least, provides marketing materials, tech support, files of answers to frequently asked questions (FAQs), and directs readers on how to order products directly or from various resellers.

Accepting Orders

The best marketing in the world will fail if the customer can't get the product. Fulfillment issues are critical in the success of a product. You have to deliver your product in a timely manner, and in excellent condition.

It is extremely important that once someone wants to order your product, they can do so without hassle.

Your telesales people must be helpful, knowledgeable about the product, and be able to quickly take address information and calculate tax. You have to be able to take credit card orders. Don't make it difficult for someone to order from you!

And don't forget that with an influx of sales, you may have an influx of tech support calls as well. Have your people ready.

MAKE YOURSELF KNOWN!

Having your product in as many places as possible is one thing. But you also have to gain mindshare by drawing attention to your product via publicity, advertising, trade show presence, and other techniques discussed in this book.

Again, the key is in keeping your eye on the target of product position and being in the places where your potential customers are.

Public Relations (PR)

Good editorial coverage and reviews are worth more than any advertising you can design.

Best-in-category product awards are worth far more than the metal statues that come with them. And recommendations of user groups make them your virtual sales staff.

All of these goals should be in the mind of your PR agent. Have a great press list, and let the press know all the news about your product. Be generous with review copies. Be extra generous with your support in walking the press through the product once they are interested!

Appoint a VIP tech support person to handle all press product questions. Time your press tours to coincide with new prod-

---

Work With Your Target Market In Mind

Target your press lists
- Industry magazines
- Audience magazines
- Product magazines
- Vertical market magazines
- Complementary lifestyle magazines
- User groups and newsletters

Beef up your PR
- Network at industry events
- Run contests and giveaways
- Seek out speaking engagements

User Groups

In non-computer product sales, there are few equivalents to computer user groups who band together to share information. Demonstrations at user groups can be very potent marketing. They like to see the newest products. They will do beta tests for you and give you other feedback. And they are opinion leaders whom other computer users look to for advice.

How To Save Money On Advertising

- Never, ever, ever settle for the initial rate
- More advertising = more discount
- Test "black plus one" ads versus four color
- Ask for right-hand position in the first 25 pages
- Follow up on bingo card leads
- Position ads during and after related editorial coverage
- Try direct response advertising
- Tracking response is the only definitive way to trace the success of an ad. If sales aren't generated, try something else.

uct releases (be aware of magazine lead times).

Get speaking engagements at conferences having to do with your product's market category. Make yourself, your company, and your product what people think of when they think of your product category.

Advertising

Those magic words again: consistency and product position. Keep them in mind when you're looking at advertising opportunities.

Never, never, never make the mistake of splashing big full-page ads in ten magazines on the month you ship, and then disappearing for the next six months because you've blown your whole advertising budget. It is much better to have smaller, consistently placed ads in targeted magazines than to use the shotgun approach.

Here are some questions to ask when you choose ad media:

- Does the magazine have the same market you have?
- What's the focus of the issue?
- Have they given you or your category editorial coverage?

Similar questions should be asked about online advertising.

Trade Shows

By this time, the message of consistency and targeting must be drilled into your head. But it's true that the same rules apply for shows.

If you're going to exhibit at trade shows, make sure your potential customers will be there. Use consistent graphics and messages to be recognizable. Capture all leads for sales follow-up.

If you're advertising, it's most likely that the magazines are having bonus distribution at the show, so you can hit thousands more people with the same ad. And have your PR agent send out pre-show press releases and set up press conferences and/or meetings at the show.

WHAT TO DO WHEN YOU CAN'T DO IT ALL

If you don't have the time or the expertise to take on all the tasks of a product launch, don't worry. If you have the vision and the passion, there is usually a way.

For instance, there are many excellent sources of marketing expertise available. Take your time in contracting with a person or company who has expertise in your product area, who works well with you, and who can work with the available resources. Don't be shy about asking for a full plan of action. And make sure you're both clear as to the tasks the consultant has to accomplish. Also ask for a timetable for delivery and a quote on the whole project before you sign on the dotted line.

SUPPORT WHAT YOU SELL

The best marketing in the world will fail if your product and support don't perform. There is not one software product on the market that does not need post-sale tech support. No one should be on hold interminably for tech support. No one should have to wait for a tech support person to get back to them. Your people must be friendly, and must know your product (and often other products) inside and out.

You can help your tech support staff by providing excellent online help within your product, have a comprehensive manual, a quick-start guide, and provide answers to frequently-asked tech support questions on your Web site. But this is no substitute for a real-life person to help in an emergency situation.

I wish you all the best in launching your new products, and hope that the blueprint you've been given here will help relieve some of the stress from this exciting adventure upon which you're embarking.

FULL SPEED AHEAD

10 ACTION SECRETS

1   *Before* bringing out a new product, develop a specific plan for what marketing channels you'll use.

2   Be clear about your positioning in the marketplace vs. your competitors.

3   Talk to your projected market *before* you develop the product, not after.

4   Use natural "focus groups" to get input from prospects.

5   Make sure to beta test your product with testing labs and real users.

6   Collect testimonials from beta testers.

7   Develop a chart of product strengths and weaknesses. Evolve it with the product.

8   There's more to selling a product than just the product. Work on your sales, distribution, and tech support.

9 Packaging is important in retailing. Test, test, test.

10 There are many specific ways to market. You may not be able to do them all, but you should test the effective mix for your product.

Chapter 22

HOW TO GET GOING
10 Secrets For Accomplishment

Rick Crandall

Rick Crandall, PhD, is a speaker, writer, and consultant, specializing in talks and workshops on marketing and sales, creativity, and change. He has spoken for *Inc.* magazine, the American Marketing Association, Autodesk, and Chambers of Commerce. Crandall has presented well over 1000 seminars on applied business, marketing, entrepreneurship, etc., and given many keynote presentations.

Crandall is the author of *Marketing Your Services: For People Who HATE to Sell* (1996), and editor of *Marketing Magic: Proven Pathways to Success*. In addition, he serves as editor and marketing columnist for *Executive Edge* newsletter (a popular middle management newsletter).

He is the founder and executive director of the Community Entrepreneurs Organization (since 1982). He is the recipient of an SBA Small Business Award, and is listed in various *Who's Who*s. With a PhD in Group Dynamics, Crandall taught business, research, or psychology full time at the University of Michigan, University of Illinois, and Texas Christian University in the 1970s.

Rick Crandall; Agent: Select Press, PO Box 37, Corte Madera, CA 94976-0037; phone (415) 924-1612; fax (415) 924-7179; e-mail SelectPr@aol.com.

Chapter 22

HOW TO GET GOING
10 Secrets For Accomplishment

Rick Crandall

"The best time to plant a tree was 20 years ago. The second best time is today."
—Chinese Proverb

The most important secret of better marketing is to do *something*, and do it regularly.

Getting things done is an art and a science in itself. This chapter will show you how to put new marketing ideas into practice. These techniques are also applicable to every area of your life, from spending time with your family to getting ahead in business!

This book is full of ideas you can use to improve your marketing and sales efforts. In the 10 Action Secrets at the end of each chapter alone, there are more than 200 ideas you could apply. In the unlikely case that only 10% applied to you, that would still give you 20 ideas to start on today.

FOUR STEPS TO IMPLEMENTING NEW MARKETING

There are four specific steps you can take that will help you implement a new behavior. These steps are necessary to make new marketing happen.

1 **Have A Vision.** Putting this into down-to-earth terms, you need to know what you want to do. You need to be inspired by an idea, or the profits it can bring you. You'll get ideas in this book that show you how to go forward. You need a strong desire to accomplish something.

The stronger your commitment to a goal or vision, the easier it will be to attain. Even if you're not inspired, there are ways to set a goal. I'll cover some of these issues in the next point.

"That's the third time this week his pilot light has gone out."

2 **Break It Down.** In order to start taking action, you have to break a larger vision down into smaller, specific steps. Here's a mini-course in project management. Set a completion date for your big goal. For example, your goal is to implement three new marketing methods within three months.

In order to achieve your big goal, you have to determine what the first step is. In a sense, you divide the time you have by the steps you need to take. Then you work backwards from the completion date to schedule each of the steps.

These short-term goal-directed steps should be very clear and simple—for instance, to address 100 envelopes today; call 10 past customers and ask for referrals; etc. (See the chart for an example.)

MAKE A LIST
Write your goals down. Later when you're not sure what to do, refer to your list and take action!

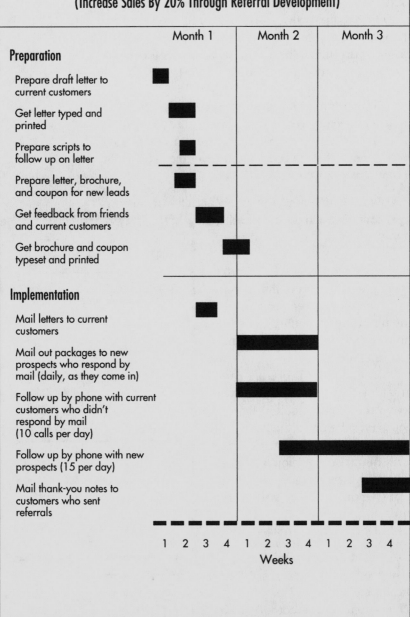

Tracking Chart For Marketing Project
(Increase Sales By 20% Through Referral Development)

	Month 1	Month 2	Month 3

Preparation

Prepare draft letter to current customers

Get letter typed and printed

Prepare scripts to follow up on letter

Prepare letter, brochure, and coupon for new leads

Get feedback from friends and current customers

Get brochure and coupon typeset and printed

Implementation

Mail letters to current customers

Mail out packages to new prospects who respond by mail (daily, as they come in)

Follow up by phone with current customers who didn't respond by mail (10 calls per day)

Follow up by phone with new prospects (15 per day)

Mail thank-you notes to customers who sent referrals

1 2 3 4   1 2 3 4   1 2 3 4
Weeks

You'll find that some of the steps have to be done in a specific order, while others are more flexible. For instance, before you can cold call 1,000 new prospects, you have to first determine who makes a good prospect and obtain a list with phone numbers. Then you have to decide what you're going to say to people or their answering machines.

Other details like what time of day you'll call, or how many calls you'll make each day, are more flexible. For example, if you have to call 1,000 people in two months, that requires an average of 17 calls a day plus return calls.

3 Schedule It. Put your new activity in specific time slots on your calendar. If you don't schedule it, it won't get done.

I believe that you'll find it easiest to pick a consistent time slot each day or week to focus on the new activity. Using the same time every day makes it a simple-to-remember habit.

Since you're probably busy most of the time already, you may find it best to schedule new behaviors before or after your normal workday. Putting in a half hour before normal work hours avoids phone interruptions. Or quiet time in your study after dinner instead of TV can add to your total productivity.

JUNE

16 MONDAY
8:30 am--Call past customers

17 TUESDAY
8:30 am--Call new prospects

18 WEDNESDAY
8:30 am--Call past customers

4 Build A New Habit. Some people say it takes 21 days to form a new habit. You may find it takes much longer. If you have a particular activity that "wastes" a lot of time, like watching TV, replacing it with your new marketing habit will make it easier to change the old habit, too. You'll kill two birds with one stone.

The secret to building a habit is that repetition leads to comfort. By sticking with the new habit, change will become easier and easier. Usually, the new habit also becomes enjoyable as it leads you to develop new skills and experience successes. For example, you may even find that you'll miss cold calling if you do it for a month or two and then take time off!

BENEFITS OF NEW MARKETING

When you systematically develop new marketing behaviors, you will get more business, make more money, and be more successful.

Two subtle aspects of getting more business provide additional benefits. First, you will be able to select the type of business you like, and cut back on the less enjoyable and less profitable parts. "Firing" a difficult customer can be both satisfying and can clear the way for better customers.

Second, if you're building relationships with clients and acquiring new high-quality customers, you will be stimulated intellectually and meet more interesting people. You're not selling "at" people, you're making more friends.

Once the new behavior is developed, it will become easier. When you've finalized the letter to send out, researched the lists of prospects to contact, or found the groups with whom you'd like to network, your behavior is no longer new. It becomes routine. It can even become a pleasure.

"The world is moving so fast these days that the man who says it can't be done is generally interrupted by someone doing it."
—Harry Emerson Fosdick

A NEW "LAW" OF MOMENTUM

I believe that there is a little-known "law" of momentum that works against disorganized attempts to change. By turning it to your advantage, you can be much more successful.

Inertia works against us in a nonlinear fashion. If you take action quickly after your resolution to act, your action will be far more effective than if it is delayed.

The power of inaction to work against us is subtly recognized. For instance, I believe that the negative power of "paralysis by analysis" occurs because delays allow goals to weaken, and motivation to decrease, more than we would expect.

> ## Crandall's Inverse Square Law of Inertia
>
> As the time increases from a new decision to the first action, the motivation to act decreases by a squared factor. Or, as time increases between setting a goal and the behavior taken to achieve it, the difficulty in acting increases by a squared factor.

Action tends to reinforce further action AND better action. If the first action is wrong, the correct course becomes clearer and more compelling. If the first action is right, it encourages further successes. When you don't act, the learning process is delayed.

When you *plan* action, only you are affected. When you *take* action, others can get involved to help you, and bring you new information. Tom Peters sees a bias for action as a sign of success. He prefers "Ready, Fire, Aim" to "Ready, Aim, Aim, Aim." I agree.

REASONS NOT TO GET STARTED

Most of us hesitate to start on new things. Why is that?

Perhaps we don't want to fail. If we never commit to new activities, we can't fail.

We are emotionally conditioned to avoid failure. Failure causes psychological pain. We were probably conditioned by our parents or in school when we were young and unaware. Hearing "NO" was painful because it was often associated with actual pain—spankings if we disobeyed, classmates' laughter for failure in class, etc.

What we now know intellectually is that without failure, there is little success. Remember the old story of the beginner who asks the old pro, "How did you get so successful, smart, etc.?" The pro responds, "Through experience." "Well then, how did you get the necessary experience?" The answer, of course, is "By failing!"

Action Leads To Better Decisions

Similarly, many models of decision making have a series of steps like generating choices, analyzing them based on a set of criteria, and taking action.

But the key step that many people forget is gathering *new* feedback based on the action. You then use the new information to make a more informed decision. In most circumstances, you can test decisions through action this way.

"Failure" is seldom failure, unless you're dead! Most successful entrepreneurs report having had multiple failures before their big success. These "failures" might be more accurately called test marketing. It only becomes failure if you don't learn from the experience.

Emotionally, we hate failure. But intellectually, we know that we should test things and learn in a continuous process. It's a long-known paradox. Only through action can we learn what action we should take. *Either* the chicken or the egg can come first if we apply a learning system.

AFTER 9,000 LIGHT BULB FAILURES... "Results! Why, man, I have gotten a lot of results. I know several thousand things that won't work."
—Thomas A. Edison

If You Hate Pushy Marketing

Because I wrote a book called *Marketing Your Services: For People Who HATE to Sell*, I give a lot of talks about why marketing not only doesn't have to be pushy, but shouldn't be.

Selling, and by association, *all marketing of products and services*, has a bad image in our culture. Few children plan to grow up and go into sales or marketing. So there are a lot of poorly trained amateurs bringing down the standards of marketing.

When I looked up "pushy" in my children's dictionary, the sample phrase was "A pushy sales-man." When I looked up "sell," the sample sentences were "Sell your soul to the Devil" and "Sell out your cause." Not the best images of professionalism for marketing and sales!

The really good models and research in mar-keting and selling, like Mack Hanan's Consultative Selling™ and Neil Rackham's Spin Selling™, prove that you should NOT be pushy. Instead, you should act in the best interests of your prospects, as a consultant who makes money for them within their businesses. You should not try to "sell" things to people. You should ask specific types of questions to find out how you can help them better. (See the references for more details on these approaches.)

> "99% of failures come from people who have the habit of making excuses."
> —George Washington Carver

If you're not in a high-pressure sales mode, prospects are less defensive. This provides you with an opportunity to build a relationship with them for the future. So don't even try to be pushy. Use your knowledge to see if you can help pros-pects. If they're too defensive to let you help them, invest what you can afford in building a relation-ship so that you may be able to help them later.

No Time, No Money, No Focus

These are all excuses. We all have some extra time. Many of the ideas provided in this book don't take any money. The bigger problem is lack of focus, which probably comes from low motivation. It's up to you to decide to act.

PASSION IS NEEDED

When you passionately care about some-thing, getting started is not a problem. For more routine tasks, I'll give you a structure to apply that will make you more efficient.

But what about when you "don't feel like it?"

When you're tired or depressed, the last thing you feel like doing is something that will bring you out of your "funk." When you're not passionate about anything in your life, it is a slow cancer that eats away at you. It's depressing just thinking about it!

Fortunately, there are a number of theories or practical bits of folk wisdom that deal with this issue. They are ideas like, "The motion brings on the emotion" and "Fake it till you make it." Only in action can you overcome inertia, mental or otherwise!

If you "don't feel like it," do it anyway. That's one reason that the "Swiss Cheese" method of overcoming procrastination works. When a task looks intimidatingly big, you nibble away at the edges. You poke holes in it by doing little pieces. You commit to working for ten minutes, which gives you energy and feedback to work a bit more after all.

WHAT IS MOTIVATION ANYWAY?

Another way of explaining why things don't get done is motivation. We all know what motivation means in general, but how does that help us in specific?

If you're motivated, you do something. If you don't do something, you weren't motivated. That tells us nothing we can use. Supposedly motivation can't come from outside you. You need to be internally motivated. Baloney! A pay-check or a gun can motivate you.

Most people's ideas about motivation are like the idea of true love. If it doesn't happen spontaneously and easily, it can't be true love or motivation. Not likely!

The argument is that internal motivation really means continuing motivation without external force. But how do we internalize things? We're "brainwashed" when we're too young to defend ourselves. Or we "pro-

"We used to call Ferguson 'lazy'—but now it's 'motivationally impaired.'"

gram" ourselves by repeating a message over time. Or we rationally make a decision and make changes (e.g., Rational Emotive Therapy, see Ellis in references).

For adult decisions, we have to work at motivation. It doesn't always happen naturally. When you find yourself really fighting a job, it's usually just because you don't want to do the work required. Of course, therapists would be happy for you to pay them to look into deeper causes of lack of motivation!

In other words, to be motivated, act motivated. It may sound simple and contradictory, but it works.

To get started, you have to get started.

10 TECHNIQUES TO ACCOMPLISH YOUR GOALS

As promised in the chapter title, here are ten ideas that can help you get new marketing projects done. Some of them are like memory techniques. They are proven technologies that most of us don't bother to learn or use. But success takes a little effort. We should be willing to learn and use any proven techniques.

Some of the ideas feel artificial. They can sound or feel silly. Some of them are "tricks." But they can all work if you'll use them. Many have been proven over the ages.

1 The ancient Greeks talked about **support or Master Mind groups**. Einstein used a variation of them with other physicists. Napoleon Hill, author of *Think and Grow Rich*, advocated them. They often include a brainstorming rule of no criticism. That rule has been proven to be effective in many formats.

Find at least one person and encourage each other. Such a group can provide a sounding board, sympathy, brainstorming, encouragement, role models, mentors, and more. This requires a regular commitment of time to meet at a regular place. But it works. Make the effort and you'll get ahead, while having your friends thank you besides. A variation of this is to set up a buddy system where two of you report in to each other without having to meet.

2 Make **a public commitment** to your goal. This will make it more real. And it

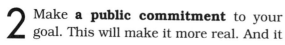

will motivate you to avoid the embarrassment of public failure. Hey, life is tough if you want to succeed!

3 Make a bet with someone about your performance. A good way to do this is to each bet on your own performance. If you both achieve your goals, you both win. A variation of this approach is to pay someone and earn it back with your performance. For example, a commitment of $50 makes a significant difference in people losing weight. It seems minor, but it works.

4 Give yourself a specific reward for accomplishments. Again, the reward doesn't have to be major. An extra dessert every day, or 30 minutes reading your favorite book may do it.

5 Develop proper files. One activity can be done in a rush based on your memory. Ongoing organization requires an infrastructure of paper. Today, there are many computer programs to keep track of paper, phone calls, contacts, etc. But old fashioned file cards can work wonders, too, if they're used properly.

6 Clean off your desk at the end of every day. It creates a sense of organization. A variation of this is to lay out the material for tomorrow's work so that you can get a fast start.

7 Start each day with a quick success. This gives you positive reinforcement to keep going. One way to do this is to leave a simple task unfinished at the end of each day. Your natural desire for closure will motivate you to zip through it and give you momentum. Another way is to schedule a call or meeting for the morning that will give you a quick success. Many salespeople do this to get off to a quick start.

8 Act—even when you don't feel like it. This is a tougher one. When planning something

> A way to get help, and make a public commitment, is to do a comarketing project with another business. Commit to doing a newsletter, a seminar, etc. together. You'll create mutual focus and support.

new, too many people wait to start until everything feels right. The right combination of your good mood, the weather, enough free time, etc., may never come. Be prepared to plod along for a time. Often this gives you momentum and you become more effective.

9 Have a month-at-a-glance calendar available at all times. Again, this is a simple technique that is proven. It gives you a place to make notes. And it keeps your goals in sight so you are constantly reminded.

DECEMBER

SUNDAY	MONDAY	TUESDAY	WEDNESDAY	THURSDAY	FRIDAY	SATURDAY
1	2	3	4	5	6	7
8	9	10	11	12	13	14
15	16	17	18	19	20	21
22	23	24	25	26	27	28
29	30	31				

10 When you're bored, take a walk. If you're unable to concentrate, walk briskly for at least 15 minutes. This will improve circulation and your mood. It provides a boost of oxygen to your brain. A variation of this is to work standing up or pacing. This also increases blood oxygen to the brain, giving you a mental lift. (Walking also works to avoid overeating. Walk, and your appetite will go down.)

That Was Good, What's Next?

When you got a good idea while reading a chapter in this book, you probably thought, "That was good, I wonder what will be next?"

Too many people read a book or go to a seminar, and then *wait* for the next good thing. It only takes one new habit or method to make the difference for you. It won't be as dramatic as waving a magic wand. It's more like compound interest. If you can continually improve your effectiveness 10%—or even 1%—you can reap big dividends.

THE KEY SECRET

The real secret to success in marketing is to take action. It doesn't matter how many good ideas you have. If you don't take action, nothing happens. You never get any "lucky breaks" because your "preparation doesn't have a chance to meet your opportunity."

Once you accept responsibility for the outcomes of your action (or inaction), you will want to apply what you know. Please apply the ideas you like from this book and let any of us know about your successes.

Good luck and great marketing!

Benefits Of Taking Action

- You get feedback.
- People pitch in to help you.
- You learn from your mistakes.
- You become more effective.
- You meet people.

FULL SPEED AHEAD

10 ACTION SECRETS

1 Pick a specific marketing idea to implement. Choose one that will fit into your normal behavior patterns and personal style. If you don't already have lots of ideas, review the Action Secrets at the ends of the chapters in this book as a first step.

2 On a single piece of paper, write down the steps you'll take to implement the marketing idea you've chosen.

3 Schedule a consistent time on your calendar to get started on the first task. Remember Crandall's law of momentum. Act as soon as possible after you make the commitment for stronger results.

4 Experiment with some new techniques that can help you achieve new marketing goals. Consider some of the following first.

5 Find a "buddy" or develop a small group to help all of you focus on your new goals.

6 Put yourself on the line publicly for your goals. Tell others, make a bet with someone about your performance, or promise your spouse a reward if you make your goal. (That will encourage your spouse to put up with any extra time you spend, or may even get them prodding you on!)

7 Develop a separate file drawer or computer file for the new commitment. Always note everything right there so you'll never have to hunt for material.

8 Set up your day so that you can start off with a quick success. For instance, save an easy call for first thing in the morning.

9 Be a fanatic. Act when you're scheduled to act, even if you don't feel like it. This will give you momentum to keep your commitment.

10 Have a bias for action. Act soon and act often. Sins of omission are far worse than sins of commission. Make your motto, "It's better to ask for forgiveness later than permission now."

INDEX

References and Recommended Readings

Albrecht, K. (1992). *The Only Thing That Matters: Bringing the Power of the Customer into the Center of Your Business.* New York: Harper Business.

Barlow, J., & Møller, C. (1996). *A Complaint Is a Gift.* San Francisco: Berrett-Koehler Publishers, Inc.

Bennis, W., & Nanus, B. (1997). *Leaders: The Strategies for Taking Charge.* New York: Harper Business.

Berry, L.L. (1995). *On Great Service: A Framework for Action.* New York: Free Press.

Blanchard, K., & Johnson, S. (1981). *The One Minute Manager.* New York: William Morrow & Company.

Blanchard, K., & Bowles, S. (1993). *Raving Fans* New York: William Morrow & Company.

Byham, , W.C. (1990). *Zapp! The Lightning of Empowerment.* New York: Harmony Books.

Carlzon, Jan. (1987). *Moments of Truth.* Cambridge, MA: Ballinger Publishing Co., 1987.

Covey, S. (1989). *The Seven Habits of Highly Effective People.* New York: Simon & Schuster.

Crandall, R. (1996). *Marketing Your Services: For People Who Hate to Sell.* Chicago: Contemporary Books.

Cross, R., & Smith, J. (1996). *Customer Bonding: Pathway to Lasting Customer Loyalty.* NTC Publishing Group.

Ellis, A., & Whitely, J.M. (1979). *Theoretical and Empirical Foundations of Rational Emotive Therapy.* Monterey, CA: Brooks/Cole.

Glass, S. (1976). *Life Control: How to Assert Leadership in Any Situation.* Publisher: M. Evans.

Hanan, M. (1995). *Consultative Selling (5th Ed.).* New York: AMACOM.

Kriegel, R.J., & Patler, L. *If It Ain't Broke...Break It!: And Other Unconventional Wisdom for a Changing Business World.* New York: Warner Books.

Levinson, Jay. (1985). *Guerrilla Marketing.* Boston: Houghton-Mifflin.

Mackay, H. (1989) *Swim with the Sharks Without Being Eaten Alive.* New York: William Morrow & Company.

Mandino, Og. (1989). *The Greatest Salesman in the World.* New York: Bantam.

McCormack, M.H. (1985). *What They Don't Teach You at Harvard Business School.* New York: Bantam.

Ogilvy, D. (1985). *Ogilvy on Advertising.* New York: Vintage.

Peppers, D., & Rogers, M. (1993). *The One to One Future: Building Relationships One Customer at a Time.* New York: Doubleday.

Phillips, M., & Raspberry, S. (1986). *Marketing Without Advertising.* Berkeley, CA: Nolo Press.

Peters, T. (1995). *The Tom Peters Seminar: Crazy Times Call for Crazy Organizations.* New York: Vintage.

Rackham, N. (1988). *SPIN Selling.* New York: McGraw-Hill.

Rapp, S. (1993). *Beyond MaxiMarketing: The New Power of Caring and Daring.* New York: McGraw-Hill.

Reichheld, F.F. (with T. Teal). (1996). *The Loyalty Effect.* Boston: Harvard Business School Press.

Ries, A., & Trout, J. (1981). *Positioning: The Battle for Your Mind.* New York: McGraw-Hill.

Stanley, T.J. (1993). *Networking with the Affluent and their Advisors.* Homewood, IL: Business One Irwin.

Stone, M., Davies, D., & Bond, A. (1996). *Direct Hits: Direct Marketing with a Winning Edge.* Landham, MD: Pitman Publications.

Trout, J. (with S. Rivkin). (1995). *The New Positioning.* New York: McGraw-Hill.

Whitely, R., & Hessan, D. (1996). *Customer-Centered Growth.* Reading, MA: Addison-Wesley.

A Note About The Disk On The Inside Back Cover

The attached disk contains more marketing material for your use. It contains material that supplements the content of the chapters.

The files are saved as text-only files (ASCII), so that they can be opened by any word processing software on IBM-compatible or Macintosh systems.

Unless you have a software conversion program like MacLink, you won't be able to open the files by clicking on them directly.

To open the files: Open your word processing software. From your word processing software's menus or commands, choose "Open." Specify the drive that contains the disk, and then choose the file you wish to open.

Storing the disk: You may find it convenient to store the disk in it's envelope with the book. In that case, simply cut the top of the envelope open with scissors, and you'll be able to slide the disk in and out.

If you need a Mac-formatted disk: Since the majority of computers out there are IBM-compatible, and the newer Macintoshes read DOS-formatted disks, the attached disk is DOS-formatted. If you have a Macintosh computer that won't read a DOS-formatted disk, return the disk with a self-addressed stamped envelope (55¢) to Select Press, P.O. Box 37, Corte Madera, CA 94976, and we'll send you a Mac-formatted disk.